OXFORD IB COURSE PRE

PSYCHOLOGY

FOR IB DIPLOMA COURSE PREPARATION

Darren Seath and Lee Parker

OXFORD
UNIVERSITY PRESS

OXFORD
UNIVERSITY PRESS

Great Clarendon Street, Oxford, OX2 6DP, United Kingdom

Oxford University Press is a department of the University of Oxford. It furthers the University's objective of excellence in research, scholarship, and education by publishing worldwide. Oxford is a registered trademark of Oxford University Press in the UK and in certain other countries

First published in 2019

British Library Cataloguing in Publication Data
Data available

978-1-38-200494-7

10 9 8 7 6 5 4 3 2 1

Paper used in the production of this book is a natural, recyclable product made from wood grown in sustainable forests. The manufacturing process conforms to the environmental regulations of the country of origin.

Printed in India by Multivista Global Pvt. Ltd

Acknowledgements
The authors and publisher are grateful for permission to reprint the following copyright material:

Bartlett, F: excerpt from *Remembering: A Study in Experimental and Social Psychology* by Frederic Bartlett, 1932, Cambridge University Press.

David M Buss, Todd K Shackelford, Lee A Kirkpatrick, and Randy J Larsen: excerpt from *A Half Century of Mate Preferences: The Cultural Evolution of Values from Journal of Marriage and Family*, volume 63, issue 2, pages: 283-597, May 2001, John Wiley & Sons Ltd.

Center for Science in the Public Interest (CSPI): excerpts from report *Carbonating the World: The Marketing and Health Impact of Sugar Drinks in Low- and Middle-income Countries* by Allyn L Taylor, JD, LLM, JSD, and Michael F Jacobson, Ph.D., reprinted by permission.

Dittrich, Luke: excerpt from *Patient H.M.: A Story of Memory, Madness and Family Secrets* by Luke Dittrich, published by Vintage, reprinted in English by permission of The Random House Group Ltd. © 2017, and by permission of Random House, an imprint and division of Penguin Random House LLC, all rights reserved, copyright © by Luke Dittrich, and in other languages by permission of ICM Partners.

Ritchhart, R, Church, M, and Morrison, K: short extracts and exercises adapted from Ritchhart, R, Church, M and Morrison, K (2011) *Making Thinking Visible: How to Promote Engagement, Understanding, and Independence for All Learners*, © 2011 by Ron Ritchhart, Mark Church, Karin Morrison, all rights reserved, Jossey-Bass, San Francisco. CA, USA, reprinted by permission of John Wiley & Sons Ltd.

Sapolsky, RM: quotation by Robert M Sapolsky published on www.wgbh.org, WGBH's Innovation Hub, reprinted by permission of WGBH and Robert M Sapolsky.

Cover illustrations: vectoriart/iStockphoto

Although we have made every effort to trace and contact all copyright holders before publication this has not been possible in all cases. If notified, the publisher will rectify any errors or omissions at the earliest opportunity.

Links to third party websites are provided by Oxford in good faith and for information only. Oxford disclaims any responsibility for the materials contained in any third party website referenced in this work.

Contents

Introduction to IB psychology

In this introduction, you will learn:

- why this book was written
  - a handbook for your mind
  - the biopsychosocial model—approaches to behaviour and concepts
- about the IB Programme
  - mission and purpose—the IB mission
  - the learner profile
  - approaches to learning (ATL)
  - practising ATL skills
  - theory of knowledge (TOK)
- how to use the features in this book
  - Key studies, Psychology in real life, Reflection activities, Links to IB psychology topics, the IB psychology syllabus, Exam-style questions, Big ideas
- about the IB psychology syllabus

Why this book?

A handbook for your mind

If you are reading this book, you have a brain. Congratulations! You are the proud owner of most complex known object in the universe. There is nothing more worthy of study than the lump of tissue in your skull responsible for every thought you think, every breath you take, every friend you make (or not), and every decision you have ever made.

You are a learning machine. In fact, it is impossible for you not to learn. You were born intuitively interpreting everything you see, hear, feel, smell, taste and touch. You automatically activate prior learning, compare, contrast, evaluate and seek answers to questions incessantly. In short, your brain is fascinating, to say the least. You may think you know how to use your brain, after all, you have been using it your whole life, haven't you?

You might be surprised to learn that there is much to know below the surface of perception. Your thinking is full of biases and predictable errors, automatically triggered actions and behaviours that you would probably prefer to avoid. This book is an introduction to your brain and your mind. Think of it both as a "heads up" and a "how to" manual for your brain.

This book is organized conceptually and aligned with the IB psychology syllabus. Each chapter is organized into concepts and big ideas. There is a focus on ideas explaining human behaviour; examples of research and evidence for ideas are given but they are deliberately not a focus of this book. Research is central to knowing things in psychology, but first you have to understand the concepts and ideas they claim to support.

The biopsychosocial model—approaches to behaviour and concepts

IB psychology is organized around a core made up of biopsychosocial approaches to understanding mental health and human behaviour. This means that human behaviours are explored through three lenses or approaches. These approaches make up the biological, cognitive and sociocultural chapters of this book. The IB psychology curriculum follows these approaches when exploring human behaviour. The table below shows the IB psychology outline.

General	Approaches	Options
Research methodology Ethics in research	Biological Cognitive Sociocultural	Abnormal psychology Health psychology Developmental psychology Psychology of human relationships

In addition to the core, IB psychology contains four options. Each option explores concepts in applied psychology. Applied psychology is an umbrella term that describes the use of the biopsychosocial lenses when studying one specific area.

Like other IB courses, psychology is broken into higher level and standard level. Students at standard level study one option. Students at higher level study two options and place a stronger emphasis on research methods.

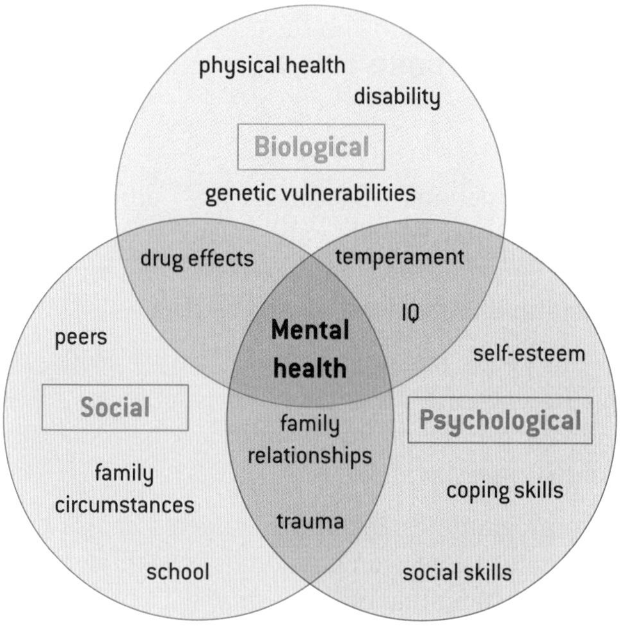

▲ **Figure 1.1** The biopsychosocial model applied to health

The table below summarizes the content of chapters 1–6 in this book.

Chapter title	Content
1 Concepts in psychological research	Explores how psychologists learn new things about behaviour
2 Concepts in biological psychology	Explores how the structure and chemistry of your brain and body determine your behaviour
3 Concepts in cognitive psychology	Explores how you think, speak, pay attention, remember (and forget), solve problems and show creativity
4 Concepts in sociocultural psychology	Explores how other people impact all of your cognitive processes listed above
5 Concepts in applied psychology	Briefly introduces you to the options in IB psychology (abnormal psychology, developmental psychology, health psychology and the psychology of human relationships)
6 Assessments—how to show your understanding	Explores the best practices in writing responses to assessment prompts in psychology

It is not enough to know the concepts of the course, it is also necessary to show that you have understood them. IB psychology requires learners to write clearly and concisely on complicated concepts. This book provides guidance on communicating those complicated concepts in a way that is designed to set you up for success on IB psychology assessments.

The IB Programme

This book is meant as an introduction to the IB psychology course at both standard and higher levels. It is designed to be accessible for people whose only experience with their brain and mind is having one. If this is your first time studying psychology, welcome to a fantastic journey!

Mission and purpose

The IB mission

> "The International Baccalaureate® aims to develop inquiring, knowledgeable and caring young people who help to create a better and more peaceful world through intercultural understanding and respect.
>
> To this end the organization works with schools, governments and international organizations to develop challenging programmes of international education and rigorous assessment.
>
> These programmes encourage students across the world to become active, compassionate and lifelong learners who understand that other people, with their differences, can also be right."

The learner profile

The purpose of an IB education is to foster the growth of "internationally minded people who, recognizing their common humanity and shared guardianship of the planet, help to create a better and more peaceful world" (www.ibo.org). Responsible local and global citizens have to think about their place in the world in a particular way. The IB learner profile is a starting place for fostering responsible globally-minded and locally-minded people.

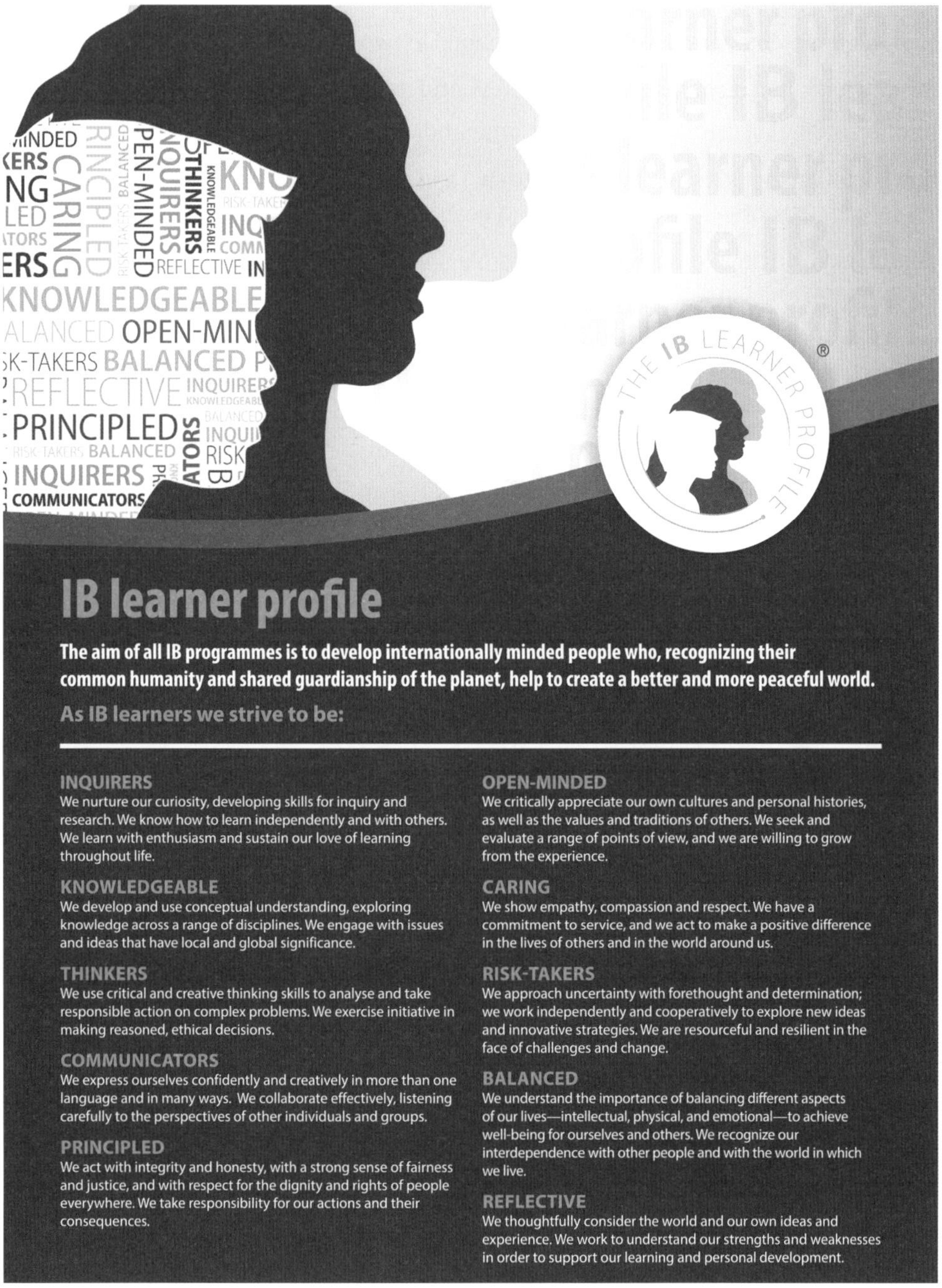
THE IB LEARNER PROFILE
IB learner profile
The aim of all IB programmes is to develop internationally minded people who, recognizing their common humanity and shared guardianship of the planet, help to create a better and more peaceful world.
As IB learners we strive to be:
INQUIRERS
We nurture our curiosity, developing skills for inquiry and research. We know how to learn independently and with others. We learn with enthusiasm and sustain our love of learning throughout life.
KNOWLEDGEABLE
We develop and use conceptual understanding, exploring knowledge across a range of disciplines. We engage with issues and ideas that have local and global significance.
THINKERS
We use critical and creative thinking skills to analyse and take responsible action on complex problems. We exercise initiative in making reasoned, ethical decisions.
COMMUNICATORS
We express ourselves confidently and creatively in more than one language and in many ways. We collaborate effectively, listening carefully to the perspectives of other individuals and groups.
PRINCIPLED
We act with integrity and honesty, with a strong sense of fairness and justice, and with respect for the dignity and rights of people everywhere. We take responsibility for our actions and their consequences.
OPEN-MINDED
We critically appreciate our own cultures and personal histories, as well as the values and traditions of others. We seek and evaluate a range of points of view, and we are willing to grow from the experience.
CARING
We show empathy, compassion and respect. We have a commitment to service, and we act to make a positive difference in the lives of others and in the world around us.
RISK-TAKERS
We approach uncertainty with forethought and determination; we work independently and cooperatively to explore new ideas and innovative strategies. We are resourceful and resilient in the face of challenges and change.
BALANCED
We understand the importance of balancing different aspects of our lives—intellectual, physical, and emotional—to achieve well-being for ourselves and others. We recognize our interdependence with other people and with the world in which we live.
REFLECTIVE
We thoughtfully consider the world and our own ideas and experience. We work to understand our strengths and weaknesses in order to support our learning and personal development.

Activity

Read through the IB learner profile. Decide which of the characteristics you think is the most important to be an effective learner and rank this characteristic as 1. Explain why you made that choice. Now rank the rest of the characteristics from 2 to 10. Reflect on why you put each one where it is on your list. Show your list to other students and discuss the similarities and differences between lists.

Approaches to learning (ATL)

The ATL categories are a group of strategies, attitudes and skills that help to build successful and engaged learners. They include thinking, self-management, communication, research and social skills.

ATL skill	Meaning
Thinking	Emphasis is placed on skills such as metacognition, reflection and critical thinking. You will be given the chance to practise these skills throughout this book.
Self-management	Self-management covers a wide variety of skills in two categories: • affective skills: resilience, self-motivation and mindfulness • organizational skills: managing your time and your tasks and goal-setting.
Communication	Communication includes the ability to listen, read and understand as well as to write, formulate arguments and communicate in a variety of forms.
Research	Research skills include practising responsible and ethical research and information literacy during independent, self-managed, inquiry learning.
Social	Social skills involve practising self-management of emotions and behaviours while working collaboratively with others towards a common goal, focusing on the ability to understand the perspective of others.

This book is written with the ATL in mind. Throughout this book there are tasks that provide ATL skills practice. Completing these tasks will improve learning and encourage thoughtfulness, action and collaboration.

Practising ATL skills

ATL skills boxes are designed to give you a chance to practise the skills of a learner. These boxes are often accompanied by a task that is designed to improve your understanding of the concepts being presented. An example of a Thinking skills box is shown opposite.

Thinking: these tasks encourage you to take it to the next level. You may be asked to make a metaphor or to challenge an idea or theory. ATL thinking skills will often be paired with research or communication skills.

Self-management: self-management tasks ask you to reflect on how you think about things and how you behave. These reflections can be uncomfortable at times. You may be asked to think about and record how often you check your phone, or to reflect on what makes you frustrated. The aim is that you apply psychological concepts to your daily life.

Communication: these tasks vary widely. You may be asked to write a paragraph, or create a chart or table, poster or mind map. The aim is to start you thinking about how you can show your learning. This does not always have to be in writing; in fact, it can be very helpful to explore various ways to show understanding.

Research: these tasks are designed to take your learning beyond the pages of this book. Responsible researching can be done online but requires that you consider your sources. Despite

DP ready | ATL Thinking skills

The visual cortex

If a person is born blind, what happens to the visual cortex (the part of the cortex responsible for interpreting information from the person's eyes)?

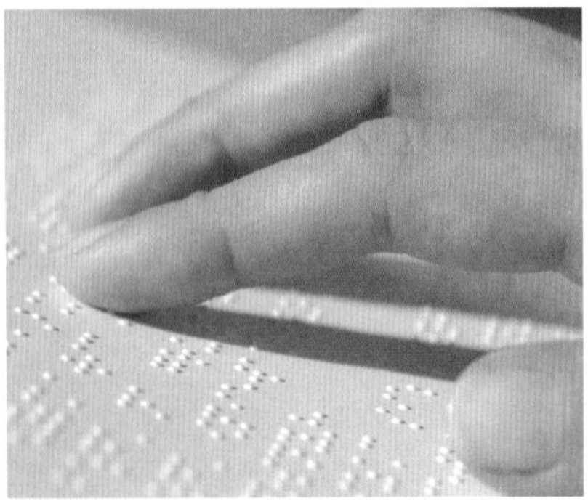

its flaws, Wikipedia can be a great first step in your research. Considering your sources means asking yourself several questions. Is this information recent? Is this information consistent with other sources? Who is the author? Who is the publisher? Is the information referenced?

Social: these are tasks that encourage you to share your ideas and discuss with others. They normally require you to talk and listen with others to understand how others might think differently from you.

Theory of knowledge (TOK)

TOK encourages students to reflect on what they think they know and how they know it. In essence, TOK encourages questioning—that is, it is where curiosity is fostered so learners can begin to question their own assumptions about the nature of knowledge and learning. TOK asks you to slow down and think carefully about some important questions.

TOK questions

What is the difference between scientific and unscientific knowledge? Which is better and why?

Is psychology a science?

What is the difference between a "hard" and "soft" science?

How do you know you have free will?

Can two opposing ideas be true at the same time?

What is truth?

What is knowledge?

TOK is a part of all IB subjects. Psychology is a unique field of study: it has one foot in the natural sciences and one in the social sciences. This raises some very interesting questions about the value and accuracy of knowledge gained from reasoning and experimentation in psychology.

You will find TOK sections throughout this book, asking compelling questions about the nature of "knowing" and "knowledge" in the field of psychology, with some including linked TOK activities. Here is an example.

TOK

What determines whether a discipline is a science? Many would argue that the more certain you can be of an answer, the more scientific the discipline is. For example, many would argue that physics is a science because it has discovered many fundamental and unchanging truths about the universe.

- Rank the following disciplines in order of how much you trust their findings: mathematics, psychology, physics, English literature, chemistry, biology.
- Why did you rank them link that order?

How to use the features in this book

In addition to the TOK and ATL features (explained above), the following features are included to help you understand and engage with the concepts in this book. These features are designed to improve understanding and support learning new concepts.

Key studies

Key Study KS

Summaries of key studies are included to draw your attention to an important piece of research that helps to explain and support one of the key concepts. The summary oftens include the aim, procedure, results and conclusion of the key study.

Psychology in real life

Psychology in real life PRL

This feature shows you how the ideas you are studying connect to everyday life or issues in the news. You will find these features where theories can be used to explain something you see in your world, perhaps every day.

Reflection activities

Reflection Activity

These are activities designed to encourage you to think deeply about a series of ideas after a unit of learning. You will find these at the end of concepts sections and at the end of chapters. The following example gives ideas for reflection activities.

Reflection Activities

This list gives examples of possible reflection activities.

1. "I used to think … ." "Now I think … ."
2. Reflection and sharing a concept
3. Create your own concept map, to help you briefly explain one of the concepts in this section.
4. The Four Cs: connections, challenge, concepts, changes
5. Claim, support and question
6. Step inside: step into the mind of a person or animal impacted by the concepts discussed
7. Sentence—phrase—word—share

These activities were inspired by some great work by Harvard University's Project Zero.

Adapted from: Ritchhart, Church and Morrison (2011)

Links to IB psychology topics

Internal link

Chapters 2, 3, 4 and 5 include a flowchart to show you how the concepts covered in the chapter are organized into the syllabus for the IB psychology course. A flowchart showing the whole syllabus is given on page 9.

In addition, in some chapters, Internal link boxes point you to other places in this book where a particular topic is discussed.

Exam-style questions

In IB psychology you will be asked some very challenging questions. To give you an idea of the types of question you may be asked in your exams, sample questions appear at the end of each chapter.

Exam-style questions

Big ideas

At the end of each chapter the "big ideas" that have been covered are summarized. You can use these sections as a review to make sure that you have read and understood all the ideas in the chapter.

Big ideas

The IB psychology syllabus

Biological approach to understanding behaviour

The brain and behaviour
- Techniques to study the brain
- Localization

Hormones and pheromones and behaviour
- Hormones and behaviour
- Pheromones and behaviour

Genetics and behaviour
- Genes and behaviour
- Genetic similarity
- Evolutionary explanations of behaviour

HL extension: The role of animal research in understanding human behaviour

Cognitive approach to understanding behaviour

Cognitive processes
- Models of memory
- Schema thinking
- Thinking and decision-making

Reliability of cognitive processes
- Reconstructive memory
- Biases in thinking and decision-making

Emotion and cognition
- Cognition and emotion
- The influence of emotion on cognitive processes

HL extension: Cognitive processing in the digital world

Sociocultural approach to understanding behaviour

The individual and the group
- Social identity theory
- Social cognitive theory
- Stereotypes

Cultural origins of behaviour and cognition
- Culture and its influence on behaviour and cognition
- Cultural dimensions

Cultural influences on Individual attitudes, identity and behaviour
- Enculturation
- Acculturation

HL extension: The influence of globalization on individuals' attitudes, identity and beliefs

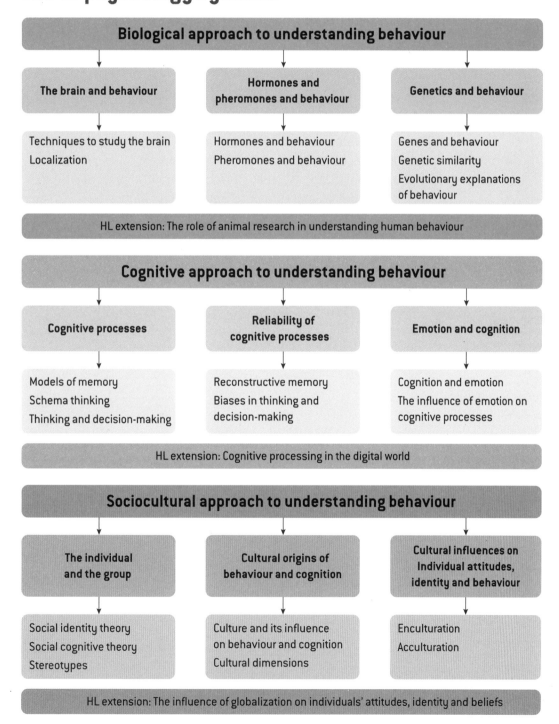

Chapter conclusion

We sincerely hope you enjoy reading this book and that it inspires fun and curiosity. Today's researchers are a long way from having a full understanding of the brain or the mind; there is a lot of work ahead. Psychology as a field of research is a lot like physics was 300 years ago or biology was 200 years ago. We know some things definitely, some things probably, and some things not at all.

With dedicated researchers and scientists like you preparing to shine a light into the dark areas of the brain and the mind, we will eventually pry more and more secrets from ourselves.
Stay curious and open-minded as you read this book. What follows this introduction is an explanation of psychology as it is understood today. No doubt, future researchers will discover truths not yet learned and theories not yet proposed. Maybe one of those researchers will be you.

1 Concepts in psychological research

In this chapter, you will learn four key concepts in psychological research.

- Concept One: Using the scientific method
  - the scientific method
  - forming hypotheses
- Concept Two: Ethical research—how should psychologists determine right from wrong in research?
  - ethical considerations of research using humans
  - ethical considerations of animal research
  - why we use animals in psychological research
  - ethical decision-making in research
- Concept Three: Research methods—what methods do researchers use to study behaviour?
  - using quantitative methods: studying behaviour "by the numbers":
    - laboratory experiments
    - field experiments
  - using qualitative research methods—the search for meaning:
    - case studies
    - semi-structured interviews
    - observations
- Concept Four: Research quality—is research in psychology trustworthy?
  - validity
  - sampling
  - credibility, bias and generalizability

Introduction

This chapter explains four key concepts in psychological research.

- Research using the scientific method—is psychology a science?
- Ethical research—how should researchers determine right from wrong in research?
- Research methods—what methods do researchers use to study behaviour?
- Research quality—is research in psychology trustworthy?

Research methods are the "how" of psychology—including how psychologists conduct research, and how psychologists test and develop their theories. A psychologist's choice of method will be influenced by whether the psychologist is studying human behaviour from a biological, cognitive or social perspective, and by the topic or nature of the research. Each research method brings with it a specific set of strengths and limitations that will influence the extent to which researchers can trust the findings.

You should always use your critical thinking skills and search for alternative explanations for findings. You may even be able to suggest better ways of conducting research. Psychology uses both human and animal participants. Both of these are living beings with feelings and rights that need to be protected. As a result, psychologists need to consider the ethics of research in order to protect the safety of participants. You will learn how all these factors interact as you read through this chapter.

What: psychologists study human behaviour and mental processes.

How: they use objective, scientific research methods.

Why: their aim is to better understand why humans act the way they do.

Concept One: Using the scientific method

This section focuses on three main ideas.

- Psychology can be studied using the scientific method.
- Researchers form hypotheses.
- A psychological hypothesis must be testable.

What does it mean?

Empirical: based on, or verified by, observation or personal experience rather than on logic or reason alone; empirical evidence is testable

Theory: a system of ideas that intends to explain or give reasons for something

Cause and effect: a relationship where one thing (a cause) is the reason why a second thing (effect) occurs

The scientific method

Psychology can be defined as "the scientific study of human behaviour and mental processes". It is considered a social science, which is the study of people and their relationships. People have free will; they are alive and unpredictable. This makes studying them a complex and often difficult process. When possible, psychologists employ the scientific method in studying human behaviour.

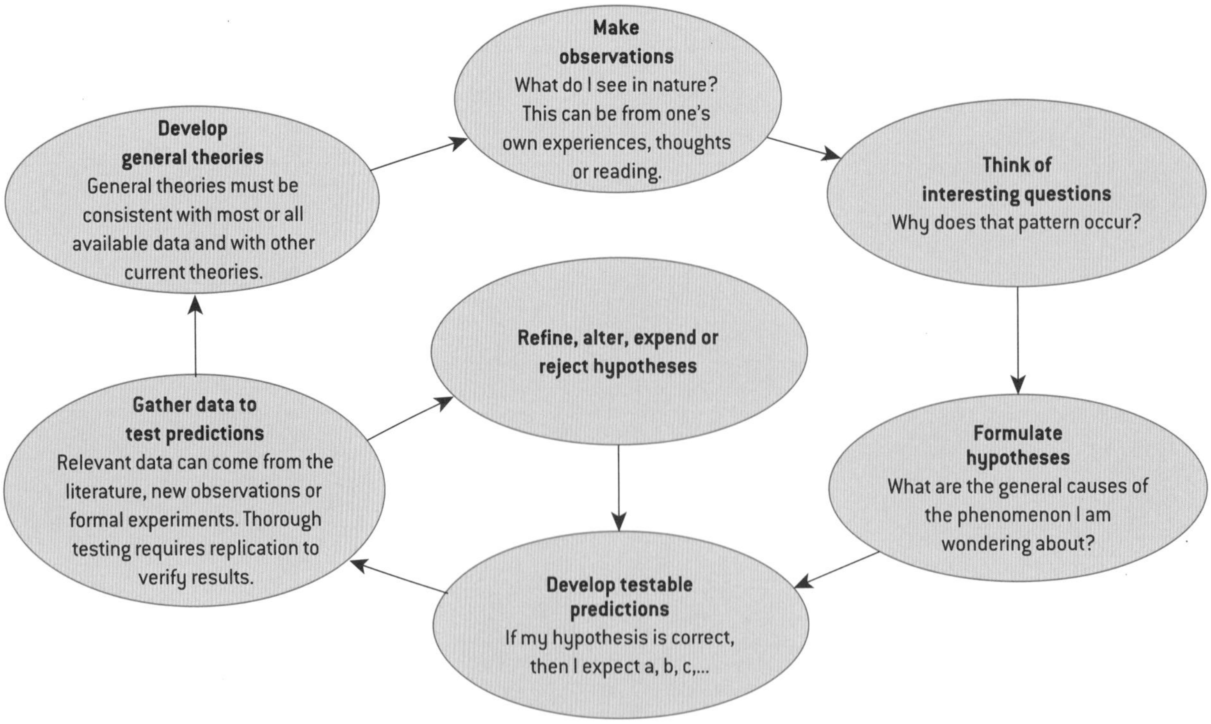

▲ Figure 1.1 The scientific method as an ongoing process

This process has some key implications.

- Psychological theories should be able to be tested and possibly proven false.
- Psychological research should be supported by **empirical** research.
- Psychological research should be as objective as possible.

It is important to be able to test a **theory** as this allows researchers to develop the theory further and build on the body of knowledge related to human behaviour. Without the ability to test a theory, there is no possibility of generating any supporting evidence. Testing a theory allows for a relationship to be examined and possibly strengthen the validity of a hypothesis.

DP ready ATL Thinking skills

Human behaviours

Let's conduct a quick thought experiment. Make a list of human behaviours that you find interesting. For example, sleep, addiction or stress. Pick one and work through these steps.

1. Develop a general theory about the behaviour.
2. Make some general observations and questions in relation to the behaviour.
3. Make some predictions relating to the behaviour, based on your observations and questions.
4. Outline how you would test your predictions.

You have just been through the scientific research process. Creating the experiments and procedures that would make this possible in real life is a lot of hard work. You will explore each stage of this process as you progress through this chapter.

TOK link

Can human behaviour be studied objectively?

Watch this

www.youtube.com/watch?v=ZohkzdOMYil

Search terms

"Is psychology a science? SciShow Psych"

Do you think that we can study human behaviour without our personal values influencing the process? What makes you say that?

Forming hypotheses

In order to be able to test a psychological theory, researchers form well-constructed predictive statements about a behaviour. These statements demonstrate what is known as a **cause and effect** relationship between the behaviour and something else—known as a *variable*. For example, a researcher may believe that there is a relationship between the hours spent studying and academic test performance. In this example, the hours of study can easily be manipulated by researchers in test conditions so that they can observe variations in performance. A variable manipulated by the researcher is called the **Independent Variable**. Academic performance could simply be measured by using a test score. The variable that is measured by the researcher is called the **Dependent Variable**. A simple hypothesis statement makes clear the influence of the Independent Variable on the Dependent Variable. Table 1.1 shows a simple way of constructing hypotheses.

Levels of hypothesis formation			
Basic structure	Independent Variable	will affect	Dependent Variable
Non-operational statement	Hours of study	will affect	academic performance
Operational hypothesis statement (two-tailed)	The number of hours (0, 2, 4 or 6) spent studying for a maths test	will affect	the final test score on a written maths test
Operational hypothesis statement (one-tailed)	The number of hours (0, 2, 4 or 6) spent studying for a maths test	will have a positive effect on	the final test score on a written maths test

▲ Table 1.1 Constructing hypotheses

This first example in the table is rather vague as it does not tell you how the researcher is controlling the Independent Variable or how the researcher is measuring academic performance. These factors need to be made explicit so that another researcher can test the theory if needed. This process of making the variables clearly defined and measurable is called **operationalization**. For a variable to be considered operational you should be able to see how the researcher is changing the Independent Variable. In this case, an experiment may involve allowing a student no time for study, and other students between two and six hours.

Finally, hypotheses can vary in the level of detail of their predictions. Some may claim that there will be a relationship between two variables but show no indication of the direction of this relationship. This is called a **two-tailed hypothesis**. If the hypothesis states the direction of the relationship, such as better academic performance, it is known as a **one-tailed hypothesis**. In the Internal Assessment in IB psychology, you will be required to write a one-tailed hypothesis. For an easy way to remember this, try to imagine a one-tailed fish swimming downstream. This fish has a clear direction and knows which way to go. A two-tailed fish may find it harder to swim straight and may be unsure about which direction to travel.

What does it mean?

Independent Variable: the variable that is manipulated by an experimenter; this variable affects the Dependent Variable

Dependent Variable: the variable that is measured by an experimenter; this variable is affected by the Independent Variable

Operationalization: the process of strictly defining variables in a measurable way; this enables concepts to be measured and quantifiable

Two-tailed hypothesis: a hypothesis that explores both sides of the relationship that you are looking at

One-tailed hypothesis: a hypothesis that explores one side of the relationship that you are looking at, by predicting an outcome in a specific direction

DP ready ATL **Thinking skills**

Hypothesis formation

Write your own one-tailed hypothesis statements for:

- the effect of the number of people witnessing an accident on helping behaviour
- the effect of rote rehearsal (learning by repetition) on memory

A clear one-tailed hypothesis will always:

- contain clear Independent and Dependent Variables
- be testable
- identify how the variables will be measured
- be clear and easy to understand
- explain what you expect will happen.

TOK link

To what extent can we test theories of our unconscious mind?

Examine Sigmund Freud's interpretation theory of the Oedipus Complex. Is it a good theory? What makes you say that?

Explore the idea of an unconscious mind by watching this video.

Watch this

www.youtube.com/watch?v=DAPq2GUUhiY

Search terms

"great courses—Do you have an unconscious mind? scishow"

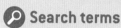

▲ **Figure 1.2** Sigmund Freud

Psychology is a fascinating, yet complicated discipline that aims to answer questions about human behaviour. These questions may arise from observations of specific everyday human behaviours, genuine wonderings about why we do the things we do, and sometimes in response to real-life events such as high school shootings, terrorist attacks and natural disasters. Some of these behaviours are controlled by our biology, some by our thinking and some by other people and the environment.

Table 1.2 shows sample research questions in psychology.

Psychological approach	Possible research questions
Biological	How does brain damage influence behaviour? To what extent do our genes influence our intelligence?
Cognitive	Is our memory reliable? How does our attention influence our decision-making?
Social	How does belonging to a group influence violent behaviour? What factors influence stereotype formation?
Human relationships	How does communication influence the success of a relationship? What factors influence helping behaviour?
Health	How does stress affect your health? How can we encourage positive healthy behaviours in children?
Developmental	How does the development of healthy attachments to a parent influence the behaviour of children? What is the impact of childhood trauma on child development?
Abnormal	How does culture influence the diagnosis of depression? What causes schizophrenia?

▲ **Table 1.2** Sample questions in psychological research

Concept One

Concept Two

Watch this

For a short overview of the research methods covered in this chapter watch this video: www.youtube.com/watch?v=hFV71QPvX2I

Search terms

"Psychological research Crash Course Psychology #2"

Conclusion: Concept One

The job of psychologists is to ask and test questions about human behaviour. The method they choose to conduct their research will depend on the nature of the behaviour. Sometimes researchers will want to control the environment. At other times they will want to observe a natural situation. Natural experiments can result in a less scientific approach to research and data collection because researchers cannot control all variables. This leads to questions surrounding truthfulness and bias in research.

A thorough understanding of research methods used by psychologists will not only strengthen your understanding of psychological research, but also allow you to understand the decisions made by researchers when conducting research. This will make you a better psychologist.

What does it mean?

Practical decision: a decision based on the factors involved in getting the job done

Ethical decision: a decision based on moral principles

The Belmont Report: a psychological report that proposed ethical guidelines that would protect research participants

Concept Two: Ethical research

How should psychologists determine right from wrong in research?

Studying human behaviour and mental processing is a complicated process. It requires you to make **practical** and **ethical decisions** when designing and conducting research in order to protect the participants you are studying. Human beings and non-human animals have rights, feelings and opinions, therefore they must be treated with respect. Much research in psychology is performed on animals and a robust set of guidelines exist for their treatment.

In the 1970s the **Belmont Report** was written to help ensure that human participants will be protected, and today psychological associations around the world maintain human safety by ensuring all researchers abide by this code of ethics.

Ethical considerations of research using humans

Ethics is a branch of knowledge that is concerned with what it means to "to the right thing". Acting morally and ensuring that you do the right thing is important all the time. Ethics in psychological research is important because it is essential that psychologists do not harm their participants and do not damage the reputation of the field, or of the researchers themselves. The main ethical considerations used when conducting research on human participants are as follows.

- Informed consent: participants in research must volunteer to participate and be aware of the aims of the study. This is made possible by providing as much information about the research as possible before participants begin the study. When studying children (usually below the age of 18 years), parents or guardians will be required to give consent on their children's behalf.

- Protection from harm: all participants should enter and leave the experiment in the same mental and physical health. Researchers should follow-up and support participants if they think there may be longer-lasting effects from participating in the study.
- Deception: some studies will not work if participants are fully aware of the aims of the study. This is because the participants may act differently, thus influencing the results (an issue known as demand characteristics). Psychologists must ensure that deception is kept to a minimum when it is needed, and that participants are made aware of the true nature of the experiment after the study is complete.
- Debriefing: after participating in the study, participants must be given all the details surrounding the experiment. This includes explaining the need for any necessary deception. Researchers must explain what theory they were testing, their predictions, and how the participants' data will be used.
- Right to withdraw: participants are volunteers and can therefore leave the experiment at any time. The right to withdraw from the research must be made clear to participants. Researchers must allow participants to withdraw from the research at any time.
- Anonymity and confidentiality: When participants agree to take part in psychological research they do so knowing that their personal information is confidential. This means researchers will not share their details with anyone outside the study. Sometimes, not even the researcher is aware of a participant's identity and, in this case, the participant would be considered anonymous.

DP ready ATL **Research skills**

Ethics across cultures

Create a Venn diagram like the one below.

Now select three countries such as Japan, the UK and the Netherlands.

Go online and look for the ethical guidelines for psychological research for each country. For the UK this would be the British Psychology Society (BPS).

Identify any differences between the ethical guidelines for each of the three countries you have chosen. Place similar information in the centre of your Venn diagram and any information unique to each country in that country's own section.

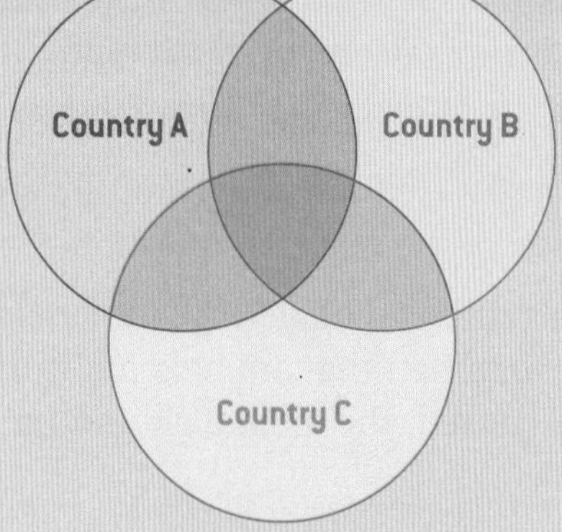

Are there differences in the way psychologists conduct their research across cultures? What makes you say that?

Ethical considerations of animal research

As a psychologist your aim is to understand human behaviour. Animal models have often been used to help achieve this aim. Animals and humans share similar biology, which means that, to some extent, we can generalize the findings of animal research to humans. Psychologists debate the extent to which this generalization is possible, and ask this question: even if we can generalize to humans, should we be using animals in psychological research?

Internal link

The main reasons why psychologists use animals to study human behaviour are discussed in detail in Chapter 2 on concepts in biological psychology: "Concept Three: Animal research".

Why do we use animals in psychological research?

Animals are often used to study certain areas of behaviour where it would not be possible to study humans. These areas include, but are not limited to, stress, cognitive processes, disease and addiction. Animals are used in research for a variety of reasons.

- Humans and animals share similar physiology and genetics.
- Animals often live shorter lives and so it is possible to study animals over the course of their entire lifespan. This is useful when looking at developmental and genetic psychology.
- **Invasive procedures** are more easily administered, allowing psychologists to study the effects, such as brain damage and substance abuse.
- Animals are easy to find and cheaper than humans to study.

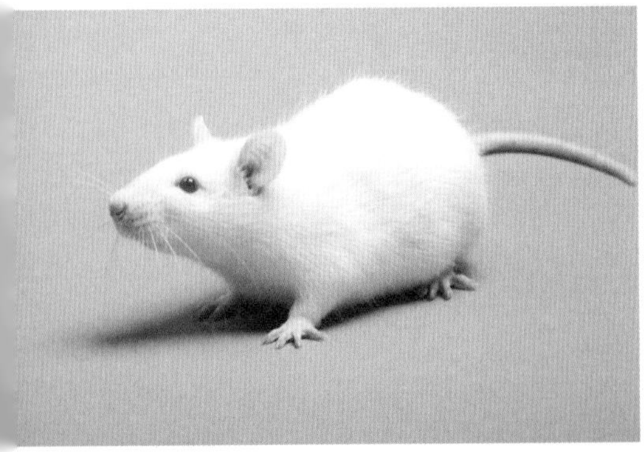

One example of animal research is Weaver *et al* (2004) who studied stress and rats. The study investigated how the ways in which a mother nurtured (licked or groomed) her young influenced the way the young rats responded to stressful situations as adults. The researchers found that the rats who received less nurturing in their early years were more likely to suffer the consequences of stress in adult life due to the increase in production of stress hormones. This was due to the suppression of a particular gene. By understanding the influence of a harmful environment or neglect on health, it is believed that we may be able to discover ways to reverse these negative effects.

What does it mean?

Invasive procedures: procedures that involve entering or inserting instruments such as needles, into the body

Hindsight: understanding a situation and its implications, after it has happened

There are specific guidelines for the use of animals in psychological research. The American Psychological Association (APA) states the following.

- Using animal subjects must be justified by increasing the scientific knowledge of behaviour.
- The results should add value to both human and animal life.
- The animal used must be carefully chosen so that it best fits the demands of the research question.
- Animals must be treated as humanely as possible and it should not be forgotten that animals feel pain. In cases where chronic pain is caused, the animal should be euthanised.

Ethical decision-making in research

It is very easy to look back on a situation with **hindsight** and label it as good or bad. The same is true for psychological research, and many of the most famous psychological studies owe their reputation to poor ethical decision-making. This may be due to the nature of the topic under study, such as violence or obedience, or a lack of judgment on the part of the researcher. Whether using human or animal participants, often the ethical issues surrounding psychological research can be minimized if the researchers ask themselves the following questions.

- Can this research be conducted without breaking any ethical guidelines?
- What is the benefit to society and the field of psychology from this research?
- Do the benefits of breaking or relaxing the ethical guidelines outweigh the costs? In other words, will the ends justify the means?

DP ready ATL **Research skills**

Studies you could not do now

Watch this video on psychological studies that you could not do nowadays.

Watch this

www.youtube.com/watch?v=zZ3I1jgmYrY

Search terms

"5 psychology experiments SciShow Psych"

Watch the video then conduct your own research on one of the five studies described. Choose the study you find most interesting and answer the questions below.

- What are the ethical considerations associated with the study?
- Could the research have been conducted without breaking any ethical guidelines? What makes you say that?
- How did the research benefit society and the scientific community?

Consider the study you have chosen, or select a different one featured in the video, and imagine you are the researcher responding to criticism of your study. Write a short article for a newspaper, explaining why you believe that the aim and the findings of your research justify the methods you used.

Conclusion: Concept Two

Psychologists have an obligation to protect both human and animal participants in their research. Conducting a cost–benefit analysis (a way of assessing the strengths and weaknesses of different approaches) prior to the study may reduce ethical issues associated with research. Psychological research aims to increase scientific knowledge and benefit society. All ethical decisions should therefore be considered with the aim in mind.

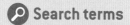

What does it mean?

Qualitative research: research that involves small sample sizes and collects data that is rich in subjective detail about an individual's experience of the world

Quantitative research: research that involves the collection of numerical data, such as surveys and laboratory experiments

Causal relationships: when there is a correlation between two variables; the first variable is manipulated and this has an effect on the other

Operational definition: a clearly defined explanation of the variables under study

Concept Three: Research methods

What methods do researchers use to study behaviour?

Two main types of research are used when studying psychology. **Qualitative research** is a process that seeks an in-depth understanding of a behaviour or event in a natural setting. This type of research normally uses small sample sizes and collects data that is rich in subjective detail about an individual's experience of the world. Researchers analyse this descriptive data to develop new explanations and theories.

Another type of research is **quantitative research**. This is an empirical investigation of observable behaviour or events that results in statistical or mathematical findings. This is very different from qualitative research and normally focuses on large samples sizes. This data is measurable (numbers) and strives to generalize the findings to a larger population of people, rather than limiting itself to understanding the subjective truth of a few individuals.

Quantitative research:	Qualitative research:
• focuses on behaviour outcomes in controlled conditions • collects numbers • is standardized and objective • includes experiments and field experiments	• focuses on human experiences and their meaning • collects words and voice • has more bias due to the nature of data collection • includes interviews, case studies and observations

▲ **Table 1.3** Comparing quantitative and qualitative research methods

Using quantitative methods: studying behaviour "by the numbers"

Quantitative research refers to a way of collecting data in the form of numbers. Collecting large amounts of data allows theories to be tested and then generalized to large groups of people. This is because the method used to collect the data often allows large groups of people to be tested. One such method is the laboratory experiment.

DP ready ATL **Thinking and research skills**

Media violence

1. "Violent video games make the people playing them more aggressive in real life."

   If this is true, it means that these games are bad for you and society and should be restricted or even banned. It is not surprising, therefore, that psychologists have been fascinated by this topic and conducted much research in this area.

Without looking online or anywhere else, consider the problem and how you would choose to research it.

Create a mind map of your ideas. Make sure you consider the questions below.

- How do you research the topic of violence in video games on behaviour?
- What practical and ethical issues do you need to consider?

2. Design an experiment so that you can test the hypothesis:

"Violence in video games can be learned and applied by those who watch it."

Your experimental design should include:

- a clear and testable hypothesis
- Independent and Dependent Variables
- specific reference to your chosen participants
- an account of your proposed procedure to explain how you will test your hypothesis
- an explanation of any ethical considerations related to the study
- a consideration of any possible practical or ethical issues.

It is important that you go through this process now as you will return to your experimental design at the end of this chapter.

Hint: it may help you to bullet point the events so that you can make sense of your procedure more easily.

Laboratory experiments

Earlier in this chapter you learned that psychologists aim to study human behaviour in an objective and scientific way. The laboratory experiment is often used for this purpose as it allows psychologists to infer **causal relationships** between the Independent Variable and the Dependent Variable. No other research method can do this. The key characteristics of a laboratory experiment include the following.

- It is conducted in a laboratory or artificial setting.
- It uses a standardized procedure that manipulates the Independent Variables and controls other variables.
- Participants are randomly allocated to a condition.

In order for an experiment to infer a cause and effect relationship it is essential that the psychologist create an **operational definition** of the phenomena being studied. This definition should make very clear how the phenomena being studied are measured and manipulated.

Think back to your experimental design on violence and video games. How did you define violence? Did you distinguish between verbal and non-verbal violence? In order to conduct a successful controlled experiment you would need to define clearly what you mean by violence. This will allow you to make sure that you are measuring and testing violence accurately.

What does it mean?

Confounding variable: a variable that was not controlled or eliminated by the experimenters which will, in turn, damage the internal validity of the experiment

Construct validity: the degree to which an experiment correctly measures what it is claiming to measure

Demand characteristics: the process where participants may change their behaviour due to the factors of the experimental design, the actions of the experimenter or the belief that they should act in a particular way

Ecological validity: the extent to which research can be generalized and applied to conditions outside the experimental setting

Reliability: the extent to which research findings are consistent if repeated under similar conditions

Researcher bias: the process where the experimenter may influence the outcome of an experiment

Failure to operationalize your variables (make them measurable) and control your laboratory environment may mean that you cannot infer a cause and effect relationship for the following reasons.

- **Confounding variables**—these are outside variables that may influence one or both of the variables you are studying. For example, if you are studying sleep and academic performance you may need to control the number of sleeping hours and restrict stimulants such as caffeine so that all participants receive a standard number of hours of sleeping time.
- **Construct validity**—if you have clearly operationalized your variables you will have high construct validity allowing you to claim that the Independent Variable was responsible for the effect on the Dependent Variable. If the variables are not clearly defined and made measurable, you cannot claim that you have found a causal relationship as the Dependent Variable may be responding to a confounding variable, such as caffeine.
- **Demand characteristics**—participants may respond differently from the way they would normally behave because they may have guessed the nature of the experiment, or the design of the experiment may have affected the behaviour it is trying to examine, thus becoming its own confounding variable.

DP ready | ATL Thinking skills

Reflection and review

Look at your video game experiment. Do you think you have operationalized your variables?

Strengths of a laboratory experiment	Limitations of a laboratory experiment
It can determine a cause and effect relationship between the Independent Variable and the Dependent Variable. This is because all variables except the Independent Variable are controlled.	It often has low **ecological validity** due to being conducted in an artificial setting. This means the findings may not always be generalized to a real-life setting.
The control of the variables and the standardized procedure allows for replication. This means that this method has high levels of **reliability**.	Results may be influenced by **demand characteristics** and **researcher bias**.

▲ Table 1.4 Laboratory experiments—strengths and limitations

In order to test his social learning theory, Bandura proposed that behaviour is learned from observing other people. He studied aggression, and was interested to see if children would copy aggressive behaviour when performed by adult role models. In order to do this, he first needed to create a strong operational definition of aggression and operationalize his hypotheses. Read the summaries provided in the links on page 23 before attempting to answer the questions.

DP ready ATL **Thinking and research skills**

Learning through observation

A classic study in psychology conducted by Bandura and colleagues in the 1960s aimed to answer the question "Can children learn aggressive behaviour from observing other people?" Read the summaries of the study at:

http://psychyogi.org/bandura-1961/

www.simplypsychology.org/bobo-doll.html

Search terms

"Bandura et al Psych Yogi" and "simply psychology bobo doll social learning"

To check your understanding, identify and explain:

- the experimental hypothesis in the study
- the Independent and Dependent Variables
- how the variables are being operationalized
- the **control variables**
- two strengths of the method used to study this particular form of human behaviour
- two limitations of the method used to study this particular form of human behaviour.

Suggest an alternative or additional research method that may improve the quality of the findings.

Field experiments

Social psychologists often wish to observe behaviour in a real-life (or natural) setting. Field experiments allow this, but they lack the control of a laboratory experiment and so may be subject to many confounding or extraneous variables. The following are key characteristics of field experiments.

- The research takes place in a real-life (or natural setting), increasing ecological validity.
- As events are allowed to evolve naturally in a field experiment, researchers have less control than when using other research methods.
- The researcher manipulates the Independent Variable (or Variables).

Hofling's (1966) famous hospital experiment is an example of a field experiment. Nurses were asked to administer an unauthorised medication to patients after receiving a phone call request from an unknown doctor. Following this request would mean that the nurse broke three hospital rules. The results demonstrated that 95% of the nurses were willing to administer the dose at the doctor's request. The researchers concluded that people are unlikely to question people in authority even when they may have good reason to do so.

Strengths of a field experiment	Limitations of a field experiment
It has increased ecological validity because it has taken place in a natural environment.	Replication is difficult as the procedure is not standardized due to less control of the variables in the study.
Less control of the variables increases ecological validity but can also reduce demand characteristics and bias. The natural setting reduces the experimenters' hold over the order of events.	One practical issue is an increased difficulty in recording the data. Events may occur unexpectedly or quickly, making data difficult to notice or record.

▲ Table 1.5 Field experiments—strengths and limitations

DP ready ATL Thinking and research skills

Field studies and ethics

Find out about the Robbers Cave experiment at

www.age-of-the-sage.org/psychology/social/sherif_robbers_cave_experiment.html

Search terms

"Robbers Cave experiment Muzafer Sherif social psychology"

Read the summaries of this field experiment and the brief summary of ethical guidelines for psychological research.

- Describe the ethical considerations that the researchers applied in the study.
- Do you think further ethical considerations should have been applied? What makes you say that?
- Describe the ethical considerations that the researchers would face when reporting these results. For example, what would have been the ethical considerations after they have collected all the data and wanted to publish their findings?
- What factors would you take into account if you wanted to apply the findings of the study to another setting?

Using qualitative research methods—the search for meaning

Qualitative research methods are more exploratory in nature than quantitative methods and they focus on gaining an understanding of a specific behaviour by examining the meaning behind participants' actions. Qualitative research methods include case studies, interviews and observations.

Case studies

A case study can be defined as an in-depth study of one person or group of people. A case study can be considered a technique rather than a research method as a case study may contain a variety of research methods, such as an interview, observations and even a laboratory experiment. This is known as **method triangulation.** All of these individual components can be combined to provide a detailed understanding of an individual or group behaviour. The following are key characteristics of case studies.

- A case study is longitudinal and requires the researcher to study the participant or group of participants for an extended period of time, sometimes months or years.

What does it mean?

Method triangulation: the process of using multiple research methods to increase the quality of the research

Credibility: the extent to which research can be trusted

- A case study focuses on one person or group of people and therefore there is no concern over sampling methods or even generalizing to a wider population. The researcher is only interested in that person or group of people.

Strengths of a case study	Limitations of a case study
It allows researchers to employ a range of research methods in combination in order to increase credibility of the findings. This is called method triangulation.	The imposition effect: researcher bias can influence the choice of research question, the data collected and the interpretation of this data. This is because people will respond to the mere presence of another person in the group and act differently. The researcher may also act in a way that influences the study.
It provides the researcher the opportunity to see events that may not be observable in a laboratory setting.	It is not always possible to generalize the findings of a case study as it is an isolated case.

▲ Table 1.6 Case studies—strengths and limitations

Thigpen and Cleckley (1954) conducted a case study on a woman called Eve who had been suffering from severe headaches and blackouts. During the course of the consultations with her doctors Eve began to display strange behaviour that indicated that the doctor may in fact be talking to another person. The researchers conducted interviews, observations, intelligence tests and even the famous Rorschach inkblot test to investigate her behaviour. During the course of their research, Thigpen and Cleckley attributed the strange behaviour to the existence of multiple personalities. This combination of research methods or method triangulation allowed them to be thorough in their investigation and establish as much **credibility** as they could in their research. Multiple personality disorder was a much debated topic in psychology and it was important for the researchers to gain as much information as possible to support their claims. To learn more, work through the Key study box below.

KS

Key Study: Thigpen and Cleckley (1954)

Case study: multiple personality disorder

Read the account in the link below for more details of this famous case study.

www.holah.karoo.net/thigpenstudy.htm

Search terms

"holah Thigpen study"

- What was the original aim of the study?
- What research methods did the researchers use in this case study?
- Do you think the findings of this study can be generalized? What makes you say that?
- Do you think the results of this study are credible? What makes you say that?

▲ Figure 1.3 The Three Faces of Eve

Semi-structured interviews

Various types of interview can be used in psychological research. The semi-structured interview is the most common type of interview that is used.

Interviews allow researchers to collect in-depth and personal information from interviewees, which is often not achievable through other methods. This is because interviews rely on human relationships. An interviewer must develop trust and **rapport** with a participant if the interview is to be successful. Participants may not be willing to talk about sensitive issues such as bullying or parental divorce to a person they did not trust.

The goal of any interview is to collect as much information as possible from the interviewee and find meaning in the person's responses. As interviewees only give their perspective on the subject, their responses cannot be generalized to a wider population but they allow researchers to attach meaning to the experiences and create new theories for research.

What does it mean?

Rapport: a bond or close relationship between two people

Structured interview: an interview carried out using a standardized procedure where the interviewer has a prepared list of questions

Narrative interview: an unstructured interview that places the interviewee at the heart of the process and lets the interviewee tell his or her story

Semi-structured interview: an interview that follows the topic of the conversation and allows the interviewer to deviate from prepared questions if necessary

Interviews vary in their structure. In contrast to semi-structured interviews, some interviews are very structured and consist of a set list of questions that must be followed. These are appropriately called **structured interviews**. Other interviews, called **narrative interviews**, are more free-flowing and allow participants to tell their stories in their own words. You are probably most familiar with **semi-structured interviews** as you will have seen many of these on television. This type of interview involves the researcher creating a list of questions and a script, but unlike a structured interview the researcher can follow the natural flow of the conversation and ask questions that are not on the original list. It is much more like a structured conversation than an interview. The following are key characteristics of a semi-structured interview.

- The researcher has an interview guide or list of questions and themes to explore during the interview.
- The interviews are mostly conducted in face-to-face situations.
- The interviews are often informal due to the nature of the interview structure.

Strengths of a semi-structured interview	Limitations of a semi-structured interview
The interview structure allows researchers to explore areas of interest in more detail by focusing on one particular response or topic.	One practical issue is that a lot of time is needed to prepare and conduct the interview and also to analyse the data.
It allows the researcher to use social skills in order to develop trust and rapport. This can allow sensitive topics such as domestic violence to be discussed in a manner that considers the needs of the interviewee.	There is a possibility that the participant gives socially desirable answers. This will influence the credibility and validity of the findings.

▲ Table 1.7 Semi-structured interviews—strengths and limitations

DP ready | ATL Research skills

Focus groups and narrative interviews

Conduct some research into the use of focus groups and narrative interviews. Create a list of key characteristics and a table of strengths and limitations for each method.

Consider which method(s) you would use to research:

- bullying in schools
- healthy eating and food choice in the workplace
- life as a professional musician.

Justify your choice, making reference to the key characteristics, strengths and limitations you have identified.

Observations

Observations allow researchers to study behaviour in a natural setting. A researcher can observe behaviour as a member of the group being studied (**participant observation**) or from the outside looking in (**non-participant observation**) in order to gain meaningful insight into the interactions and behaviours displayed by the person or group being studied. A researcher can also make a choice between revealing that he or she is a researcher (**overt observation**) when observing the behaviour of a person or group, or remaining anonymous or hidden from view (**covert observation**). All of these choices will have an impact on how the observation is structured and on the expected outcomes.

For example, you may want to investigate the online behaviour in a class of middle-school students. If you decide to observe behaviour, it is likely that you will not pretend to be part of the group if you are an older student. However, by being in the room you are going to change the actions of the group whether you mean to or not, and so you must be aware of your own influence on the behaviour of others. This awareness is known as **reflexivity**. The following are key characteristics of observations.

- The researchers aim to study human behaviour in a natural setting.
- The researchers experience the events in real time and so they are collecting data based on their own observations. This means that researchers need to be aware of their own **selective attention** and bias.

What does it mean?

Participant observation: an observation that involves the researcher becoming an active member of the group under study

Non-participant observation: an observation that does not involve the researcher becoming an active member of the group under study

Overt observation: an observation where the researcher's identity is made known to the group under study

Covert observation: an observation where the researcher's identity is concealed from the group under study

Reflexivity: an approach to research that involves the researcher being mindful of the effect that he or she could be having on the research and adjusting his or her behaviour accordingly

Selective attention: the process of focusing on one piece of information or stimuli when there are many occurring at once

Response bias: the tendency for participants to respond to questions or experimental conditions in a way that is untruthful or misleading

Strengths of an observation	Limitations of an observation
The researcher is able to observe natural behaviour and so ecological validity is high.	The presence of the researcher may influence the behaviour of participants, causing a **response bias**.
It provides the researcher with opportunities to see rare behaviours or those that occur infrequently.	Creating suitable categories can be difficult. This can result in very time-consuming coding and data analysis.

▲ Table 1.8 Observations—strengths and limitations

DP ready | ATL Research skills

Observations

Conduct some research into the use of participant observations and naturalistic observations. Create a list of key characteristics and a table of strengths and limitations for each method.

Consider which method or methods you would use when researching:

- brainwashing in religious cults
- the influence of praise on academic performance in a classroom

Justify your choice making reference to the key characteristics, strengths and limitations you have identified.

Conclusion: Concept Three

There are many research methods for a psychologist to choose from. The research question, target population and the beliefs of the researcher will interact and influence the researcher's choice of method. All methods have their relative strengths and weaknesses and it is the researcher's job to be aware of these and design the study accordingly.

Concept Four: Research quality

Is research in psychology trustworthy?

You probably don't believe everything you are told. If someone told you that they had read 20 novels in a day, you might ask the person to tell you the stories to check the facts. Or, if friends claim to have climbed Mount Fuji and you had not seen them do it you might ask for proof. When you do not have all the information, you exercise caution in belief and check the facts. Psychologists do the same thing. When a new piece of research is published claiming to have discovered the cause of a behaviour, psychologists also reserve judgment while they examine the quality of the research. Psychologists refer to various concepts to determine the quality of research studies.

In this section you will learn about:

- validity
- sampling
- credibility, bias and generalizability.

What does it mean?

Construct validity: the extent to which a test measures what it claims to measure

Internal validity: the extent to which the variables have been controlled and the procedure standardized, ensuring an objective and scientific study

Population validity: the extent to which findings from a study can be generalized from a research experiment to a wider population

Ecological validity: the extent to which research can be generalized and applied to conditions outside the experimental setting

External validity: the extent to which research findings can be applied outside the study

Validity

A quantitative research study is said to be valid if the study successfully tested what it was designed to measure. There are four main types of validity that psychologists use when discussing validity.

- **Construct validity** refers to the extent to which researchers successfully operationalized their variables. This requires researchers to make clear what each variable is, how the variables are being controlled or manipulated and how they are being measured. Failure to operationalize variables makes it difficult to infer cause and effect relationships, as it is unclear as to what is being tested and how. This may be because other factors could have easily accounted for behaviour changes.

- **Internal validity** refers to the extent to which researchers controlled the variables and standardized the procedure, ensuring an objective and scientific study. Reducing any confounding variables allows researchers to infer a cause and effect relationship resulting from high internal validity.
- **Population validity** refers to the extent to which findings from a study can be generalized from a research experiment to a wider population. For example, if researchers studied the effects of exam stress in teenagers at your school, the issue would be whether they could apply those findings to explain stress of students elsewhere.
- **Ecological validity** refers to the extent to which researchers can generalize their research findings to real-life situations. Experiments conducted in controlled laboratory conditions are often said to have low ecological validity because the situation is not typical of everyday life.

Population validity and ecological validity are both forms of **external validity** as they seek to generalize to situations or people outside the experiment.

PRL

Psychology in real life

A crisis of replication

Psychology has been suffering from what is being called a crisis of replication. An ever-increasing number of classic research studies have failed to have their findings replicated over the last few years.

Read the article about the replication crisis in psychology at

www.theatlantic.com/science/archive/2018/11/psychologys-replication-crisis-real/576223/

Search terms

"Atlantic Magazine psychology's replication crisis is real"

Conduct some of your own online research on this topic. Apply your understanding of *validity* to help you answer these questions.

- Why is being able to replicate research so important in psychology?
- What are some of the explanations given by psychologists for the replication crisis? It may help you to review some of the concepts discussed earlier in this chapter.
- What do you think will be the impact of the replication crisis on the field of psychology?

Concept Four

Validity in quantitative research

Internal	External		Construct
To what extent is the change in Dependent Variable caused by the Independent Variable?	Population	Ecological	To what extent do the operationalizations reflect the construct?
Credibility	To what extent can the findings be generalized to the wider population?	To what extent can the findings be generalized to real-life settings?	Generalizability (to theory)
	Generalizability (to other people)	Generalizability (to other situations)	

▲ Figure 1.4 Validity in quantitative research

Credibility (trustworthiness) in qualitative research

Triangulation				Rapport	Iterative questioning	Reflexivity		Credibility checks	Thick descriptions
method	data	researcher	theory			personal	methodological		

▲ Figure 1.5 Trustworthiness in qualitative research

Sampling

A **sample** refers to the people or animals that took part in an experiment. Psychologists consider who they study and how they select participants very carefully. This is because their selection may impact the outcome of the research and the extent to which the findings can be applied to the **target population**. The target population refers to the group of people that researchers would like to generalize their findings to.

Quantitative and qualitative researchers employ different sampling methods. Quantitative research needs to use a **representative sample** in order to be able to generalize the findings to a wider population. This means that the sample used in the research contains people that reflect the demographics of those in the target population. On the other hand, researchers using qualitative research aim to extract specific meaning from the research about individuals and groups and will often be less objective in the choice of participants.

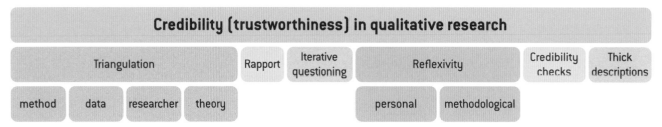

While the participants in psychological research are carefully considered, it has been argued that the people that volunteer to participate are all very similar. Often participants are volunteers from universities, and therefore possess the same characteristics. Norenzayan *et al* (2010) claim that psychologists use WEIRD participants—that is, participants who are from Western, Educated, Industrialized, Rich and Democratic societies. They therefore argue that psychologists should exercise caution when generalizing their assumptions across whole populations. As you progress through this book, keep notes on the studies that you think use WEIRD participants.

Complete the ATL Thinking task below to gain a more detailed understanding of why using WEIRD participants may be an issue. This is an important topic because you will be required to explain and justify your choice of sample and sampling method in your internal assessment.

DP ready | ATL Thinking skills

WEIRD research

Watch this

www.youtube.com/watch?v=Ho60lPrD7sA

Search terms

"hidden biases WEIRD research SciShow Psych"

Watch the video on WEIRD research then consider these questions.

- To what extent are the credibility of the findings in each study influenced by the choice of participants? What makes you say that?
- Why is selecting a representative sample important when conducting quantitative research?
- Do you think the replication crisis in psychology can be explained by the use of WEIRD participants in past research studies?

Credibility, bias and generalizability

In psychological research, **credibility** refers to the extent to which the research is true to life and trustworthy. When psychologists conduct research it is important that the study captures the participants at their most natural. This is important if the research findings are to present an accurate representation of a specific behaviour. If the findings do not represent the reality of the situation, we should not trust the research as it lacks credibility.

DP ready | ATL Thinking and social skills

Over-simplification

Read this article from The British Psychology Society Research Digest.

https://tinyurl.com/yywfavpn

Search terms

"bps many undergrad psych textbooks do a poor job"

- To what extent do you think your school textbooks, including this one, offer an over-simplistic view of the subject they aim to teach?
- If you think a textbook offers an over-simplistic view, does this affect its credibility? What makes you say that?
- In a small group of peers, discuss ideas and prepare a bullet list of key points that everyone in the group agrees with.

What does it mean?

Triangulation: a research technique that involves looking at data or theories from a variety of perspectives in order to increase the quality of the study and reduce bias

Sample: the people who are being studied in psychological research

Target population: the group of people researchers would like to generalize their findings to

Representative sample: a sample of people who are reflective of the larger population from which they are drawn

Credibility: the extent to which research can be trusted

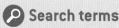

Ensuring high credibility includes:

- eliminating confounding variables
- using a process of **triangulation**
- ensuring that researchers are reflexive and aware of their own impact on the study.

DP ready | ATL Thinking skills

Evaluating credibility

Review the Thigpen and Cleckley case study. Do you think this is an example of credible research? What makes you say that?

What does it mean?

Bias: a prejudiced or a one-sided view of a topic or argument

Social desirability bias: a bias that involves the participants responding in a way that they perceive to be socially acceptable

Researcher bias: the process where the researcher may influence the outcome of an experiment

Generalizability: the ability to apply the findings of a study to a wider population

Theoretical generalization: the extent to which a theory or findings unique to an individual can be generalized and applied to situations outside the research

Bias in psychological research is inevitable. The researcher is responsible for choosing the research topic, the hypothesis and for making the major decisions about how the research is conducted. Researchers therefore need to reflect on the impact that they are having on the direction of the research throughout the entire process.

In quantitative research, bias may appear in the form of demand characteristics. Participants may become aware of the aim of the research and act in a way they think is desired by the researcher. This is known as **social desirability bias**. Similarly, **researcher bias** may occur whereby the researcher treats participants differently from each other. This may result in different participants experiencing a different form of procedure influencing the quality of the experiment.

DP ready | ATL Research skills

Researcher bias

There are multiple forms of researcher bias. Conduct some of your own research into:

- confirmation bias
- biased reporting of results.

Do you think any of the studies discussed in this chapter could have displayed bias? What makes you say that?

Generalizability refers to the extent that the research findings can be applied to populations and situations outside the experiment. As discussed earlier, high construct validity and high ecological validity allow generalization to situations outside the controlled environment of an experiment.

Psychologists using qualitative methods may seek to gain as much information as they can about one person, but may develop a theory of behaviour as the research progresses. While the research findings are unique to the one individual, the theory may be more widely applied. This is known as **theoretical generalization**.

Conclusion: Concept Four

Psychological research is never perfect—but researchers take great care to ensure that their research can be trusted. It is essential, therefore, that variables are clearly operationalized and the experiment's procedure is standardized and controlled. This will allow the researchers to ensure that their study is valid, and they are studying what they intend to study.

When choosing participants, psychologists should consider the extent to which they would like to generalize the findings of their research. Picking a sample that contains unique or very specific characteristics may limit the ability to generalize findings to a wider population. Psychologists should also be aware of their own biases and those of their participants as these can influence the credibility of their research. It is essential, therefore, that researchers reflect upon the impact of their own behaviours during the research process.

Reflection activities

1. Create your own concept map to help you briefly explain one of the research methods in this chapter.

   Generate a list of ideas or concepts related to the method you have chosen. Sort the ideas by placing the most important ideas in the middle, and least important on the outside. Connect linked ideas with lines and describe the connections on the connecting lines. Use the remaining space around the outside of the page to elaborate on any new ideas that extend your thinking.

2. Revisit the experimental design that you proposed to test "Media violence can be learned and applied by those that watch it". In light of what you have learned, redesign the experiment so that you clearly explain:
   - the hypothesis that you will be testing
   - the Independent and Dependent Variables
   - how you will be manipulating and measuring the variables.
   - the procedure—this must allow for replication
   - the data that you will be collecting.

3. Consider the concepts discussed in this chapter: the scientific method, ethics, reliability, validity, bias, credibility and generalization. How do each of these apply to your proposed experiment?

Chapter conclusion

Psychological research aims to develop our understanding of human behaviour using objective and scientific methods. The scientific method allows for theories to be developed, tested and then improved. A psychologist's choice of method will depend on the nature of the research and the hypothesis. All hypotheses should be written in a way that defines the variables clearly and explains how they are being measured. Before conducting any research, a psychologist needs to consider the welfare of the participants. Ethical guidelines have been developed to support researchers in this process.

There are many research methods for psychologists to choose from. Quantitative methods allow for empirical data to be gathered and for findings to be generalized across populations. Qualitative methods are usually conducted on one person or a small group of people, restricting the ability to generalize the findings outside the research sample, but offering great insight into the meaning of the behaviour under study. Many factors can influence the quality of an experiment, such as the sample population and bias. As a result, psychologists need to exercise caution and be reflexive in their approach to research.

Exam-style questions

Q

1. **Outline** one research method used by psychologists to investigate the relationship between the brain and behaviour.
2. **Evaluate** research methods used by psychologists when investigating the relationship between the individual and the group.
3. **Outline** one ethical consideration with research in the cognitive approach.

Big ideas

Concept One: Using the scientific method

- Psychology can be studied scientifically. This is often done using laboratory experiments as this research method allows psychologists to control variables and determine causal relationships.
- A psychological hypothesis must be clear and testable.

Concept Two: Ethical research

- There are ethical guidelines that psychologists must follow which are designed to protect participants from physical and mental harm.
- There are specific ethical guidelines for research involving animal participants.
- Psychologists must protect the safety and wellbeing of their participants. Participants are therefore given the opportunity to withdraw from research and should be fully debriefed when the experiment is over.

Concept Three: Research methods

- Psychologists conduct quantitative research (collection of numerical data) in order to be able to generalize findings to a wider population.
- Psychologists conduct qualitative research in order to understand the behaviour of a single person or a group of people.
- All research methods have strengths and limitations that will influence the credibility of the study.

Concept Four: Research quality

- Research is only valid if it tests and measures what it claims to. It is essential to define variables clearly and explain how they are being tested.
- The choice of sample can influence the ability to generalize the research findings.
- The quality of research is influenced by bias and choice of research method.

2 Concepts in biological psychology

In this chapter, you will learn the key concepts in biological psychology.

- → Concept One: There are biological reasons for behaviour
  - neurons
  - brain structures
  - neurochemicals
  - brain imaging technologies
- → Concept Two: Behaviour can be inherited
  - exploring whether your genes determine your potential
  - inherited characteristics
  - epigenetics—how your environment can influence your genes
  - genetic inheritance and behaviour
- → Concept Three: Animal research
  - three reasons for using animal research to teach us about human behaviour:
    - ethics
    - anatomy
    - biochemistry

In this chapter you will also learn:

- → about important research studies in biological psychology
- → about ideas and theories related to:
  - localization of function
  - the role of neurotransmission in human behaviour
  - the role of hormones in human behaviour
  - plasticity
  - heritability of behaviour
  - animal models of human behaviour

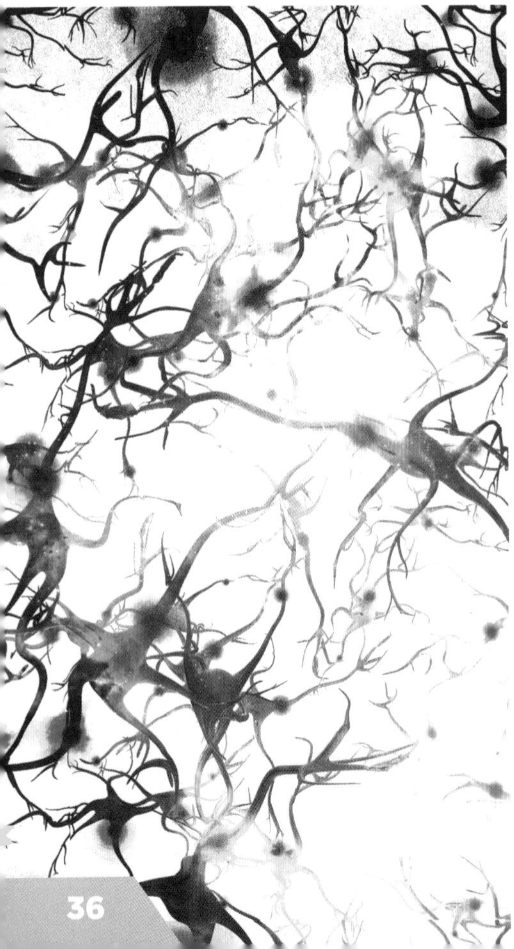

Introduction

This chapter explains three concepts behind biology and behaviour.

- There are biological reasons for your behaviour.
- Behaviour can be inherited.
- Animal research can teach us about human behaviour.

This chapter explores how psychologists study biology to learn about behaviour. Some people believe that your behaviour is entirely determined by your biology. Others believe that your environment and how you think and make decisions is most important. This is the essence of the great debate over nature and nurture. What determines your attitudes, behaviours and beliefs? Is it nature (biology) or nurture (your environment)? This chapter is about the nature side of this great debate in psychology.

Concept One: There are biological reasons for behaviour

Are you a prisoner of your biology?

This section can be broken down into two main ideas.

- Different brain structures can influence your behaviour in different ways.
- Different chemicals can influence your behaviour in different ways.

Your brain contains many different parts and each part plays an important role in making you who you are. Similarly, there are many different neurochemicals that are released by your body and these influence your behaviour. This section begins with some basic brain and body anatomy, then explains what happens in your brain when you are learning new things. In fact, all of the incredible things you will be examining in this chapter will be happening in your head in real time as you read and learn.

Your neurons—the building blocks of your brain

There are about 100 billion nerve cells called **neurons** in your brain. Each of them is connected to many other neurons to reach somewhere near 100 trillion connections, that's 100,000,000,000,000 connections! The number of connections grows as we learn and remember new things. There are two basic ways in which the number of connections between neurons can grow:

- **neurogenesis:** the birth of new neurons
- **dendritic branching:** the growth of more **dendrites** in existing neurons.

Research has taught us that your brain will actually get thicker and heavier the more you learn and experience. Can you feel your brain getting heavier yet?

DP ready | ATL Research skills

Environment and brain density

Rosenzweig, Bennet and Diamond (1972) conducted a very famous experiment to investigate if a link exists between your environment and brain density.

- Do some research into this study to find out what the researchers discovered.
- Do you think using animals in this research was ethical?

DP ready | ATL Research skills

Structural changes in the brain

London taxi drivers have different brains from most other people—specifically they have a thicker, heavier hippocampi. Do some research into how studying for the London taxi exam—called "the Knowledge"—can give you a bigger brain.

What does it mean?

Neuron: a specialized cell transmitting nerve signals; a nerve cell

Neurogenesis: the growth and development of nervous tissue

Dendritic branching: the growth of new dendrites increasing the number of connections between neurons

Dendrites: part of a neuron that branch out from the cell body of a neuron and receive incoming electrochemical signals from neighbouring neurons

What does it mean?

Action potential: the electrochemical impulse that passes down the axon

Synapse: the gap between neurons

Neurotransmitters: chemical messengers in your nervous system that allow neurons to communicate with each other

Lesion: damaging or scarring to the neurons in a particular part of the brain

Hint: Eleanor Maguire has published several studies looking at this topic. The following video will also help you.

Watch this

www.youtube.com/watch?v=sfy9j0h9_08

Search terms

"London taxi drivers develop a different part of the brain YouTube"

Neurons are special cells that send messages throughout your brain and body. This is how your brain controls your whole body. Your brain has an "autopilot mode" so some tasks are automatic (your heart beating or your breathing) while other tasks are not (working on a mathematics problem or planning what you will wear today). When you learn something new, neurons grow in number and connections. This is how learning can give you a thicker, heavier brain.

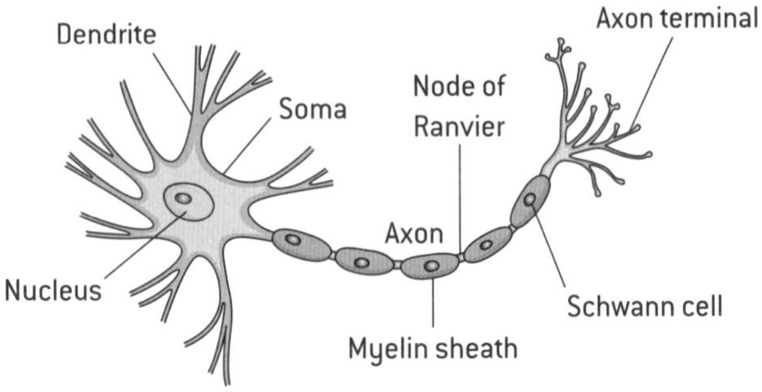

▲ Figure 2.1 A neuron

Electrical signals in neurons pass information in messages throughout your body. The messages are electrical signals (**action potentials**) that move from the dendrites through the neuron to the axon terminal where they need to jump across a gap called a **synapse**. Electrical signals cannot travel across this gap so chemicals called **neurotransmitters** are released at the axon terminal to carry the message to the dendrites of the next neuron. Each neurotransmitter sends a different message to the next neuron. When the neurotransmitter reaches the receptor of the next neuron, it creates another electrical signal and the cycle repeats itself.

Activity

It could be said that neurons are like an electric spider web.

Think of your own metaphor or simile for how your neurons work.

Brain structures—getting to know your brain

How can we possibly come to understand the universe's most complex object? Luckily, we each have one to help us understand it. The first question is: what do we know already? We have learned a lot about the brain and how each of its various parts plays a role in behaviour.

Simply put, the closer you get to the spinal cord, the older that section of the brain is and the simpler the function. For example, the brainstem is responsible for the simple, yet crucial job of keeping you breathing, keeping your heart beating and digesting food.

Your brain is divided into left and right **hemispheres**, a cortex, cerebellum, limbic system and brainstem.

What does it mean?

Hemispheres: the roughly symmetrical two halves of your brain (left and right)

Psychology in real life

PRL

Living with extensive brain damage

You might be surprised to learn that you can live with very considerable damage to your brain. Here are some examples of people surviving some radical brain changes.

- Cameron Mott had half of her brain removed in order to end dangerous seizures.
  - How do you think losing half of your brain might affect your behaviour?
  - Read about Cameron Mott at https://helpkids.kennedykrieger.org/making-a-difference/camerons-story

Search terms

"kennedy krieger making a difference camerons story"

- Phineas Gage was a railway worker who, in 1848, had a 1.1 metre-long iron bar blast a hole clean through his head. The iron bar eventually landed 25 metres away. Phineas talked with others on the way to the hospital, he recovered and lived years after the incident. Watch the following video then answer the questions below.

Watch this

www.youtube.com/watch?v=vb8Jg1PAL90

Search terms

"Why scientists are still fascinated by Phineas Gage YouTube"

  - How did this extraordinary event affect Phineas's behaviour?
  - Did his behaviour ever return to his pre-accident "normal"?
  - What does this case study tell us about the role of the left frontal lobe?

You may have heard of your left and right brain. Your brain looks symmetrical—that is, the same structures exist in both hemispheres. Functions, however, are often localized to one side or the other. For example, the right side is associated with recognizing faces and emotions, imagination, intuition and creativity. The left side is associated with language, logic, critical thinking and mathematics.

Brain lateralization

Left

- Analytical thought
- Detail-oriented perception
- Ordered sequencing
- Rational thought
- Verbal
- Cautions
- Planning
- Math/Science
- Logic
- Right field vision
- Right-side motor skills

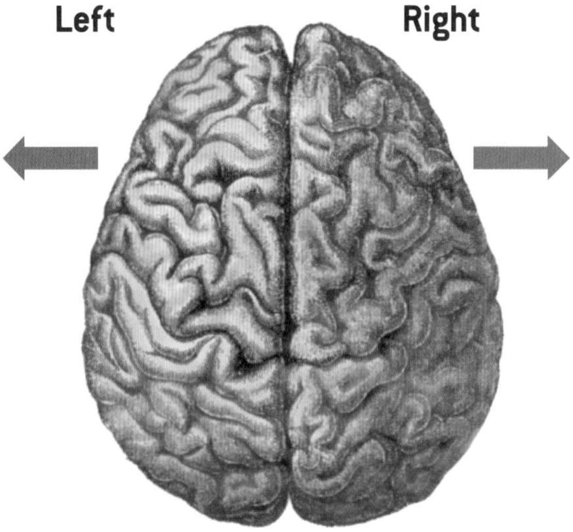

Right

- Intuitive thought
- Holistic perception
- Random sequencing
- Emotional thought
- Non-verbal
- Adventurous
- Impulse
- Creative writing/art
- Imagination
- Left field vision
- Left-side motor skills

▲ Figure 2.2 Brain lateralization

DP ready | ATL **Research skills**

Corpus callosum

The corpus callosum is the brain structure that enables your right brain to talk to your left brain. Some people are born without this structure. It is also possible to cut this structure, which was sometimes done to treat epilepsy. After this procedure, patients have two separate brains that cannot communicate with each other. These people are often called "split-brain patients".

What happens to behaviour when your two brains cannot communicate? Watch the following video to find out.

Watch this

www.youtube.com/watch?v=wfYbgdo8e-8&t=9s

Search terms

"You are two YouTube"

What does it mean?

Localization of function: the idea that particular areas of the brain have particular functions

Episodic or **declarative memories**: a type of declarative (explicit) memory, episodic memory is a memory of events; the who, what, when, where of memory

One important idea about how your brain works is the theory of **localization of function**. It would be very neat and easy if each section of the brain were responsible for a specific function. Although this is true to some extent, it is not as simple as that. For example, the hippocampus is an area of your brain associated with memory formation but it does a lot more.

Psychologists use the phrase "associated with" to describe how parts of the brain are linked to some behaviour. Let's look at memories to explore this. Memories are an example of distributed function. Unfortunately, memories are not like computer files.

A doctor cannot find a bad memory in your brain and then cut it out. Your memories are distributed throughout your brain in a network of connected neurons. For this reason, we say the hippocampus is *associated with* memory because it helps to organize networks for specific kinds of memories called **episodic** or **declarative memories**. Some additional examples of localization of function can be found in Table 2.1.

Cerebral cortex	Limbic system	Cerebellum	Brain stem
Its associated functions are: emotional control, sensation, vision, language, hearing.	Its associated functions are: sorting sensory information, controlling circadian rhythm, memory, emotion, arousal.	Its associated functions are: body control, motion memory, motor memory, balance, coordination.	Its associated functions are: breathing, circulation, digestion, swallowing.

▲ Table 2.1 Brain regions and associated functions

In the next sections, you will examine the cerebral cortex and the limbic system more closely as you will be reading about them throughout this book, and they are very important in the study of many subjects in psychology.

The cortex

The cortex is the part of the brain that looks like a big piece of wrinkled grey jelly. It is the first part you would see if you opened someone's skull and looked inside. The cortex is the newest (evolutionarily speaking) part of the brain and is the outermost layer. It is very important because this part of the brain is related to all of the functions that make us human. The cortex has four lobes.

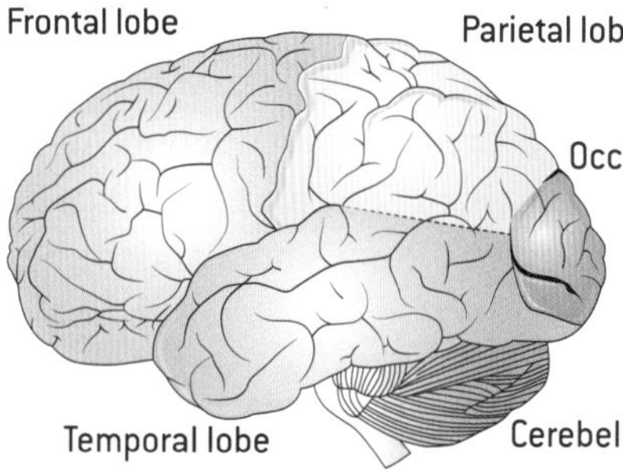

▲ Figure 2.3 Sections of the cortex

Lobe	Examples of sub-structures	Associated functions
Frontal lobe	prefrontal cortex, motor cortex, Broca's area	reasoning, planning and decision-making, voluntary action, emotional regulation, speech
Parietal lobe	somatosensory cortex	movement, perception, recognition
Occipital lobe	—	vision, perception of movement and colour
Temporal lobes	Wernicke's area	hearing, memory, speech

▲ Table 2.2 The four lobes of the cortex

Psychologists have learned much of what we know about behaviour not from people with healthy, undamaged brains, but from people who have suffered injuries to different brain regions. In looking at the behaviour of people with damaged brains, we can learn about the relationship between biology and behaviour. Dittrich (2017) explains it simply: "The broken illuminate the unbroken".

KS

Key Study: Broca (1861)

Case study: the brain and speech production

A patient named Louis Leborgne (who became known as Tan) lost the ability to speak and could only pronounce the word "tan". He usually repeated it twice "tan-tan" and did not have any problem with his speech before this happened to him. He became the subject of the following important research.

Aim: to identify the reason for this patient's unusual speech impediment.

Procedure: Broca studied Tan and observed his behaviour for many years along with other similarly affected patients. As this was well before brain imaging technologies, Broca had to wait until Tan's death at age 51 to inspect Tan's brain.

Results: when inspecting Tan's brain, Broca noticed there was a **lesion** on the left frontal lobe, as seen in Figure 2.5.

Conclusion: Broca concluded that this area of the brain must be responsible for speech production. An individual with damage to this area would not be able to produce fluent speech. The area is now known as Broca's area and the disorder is called Broca's aphasia.

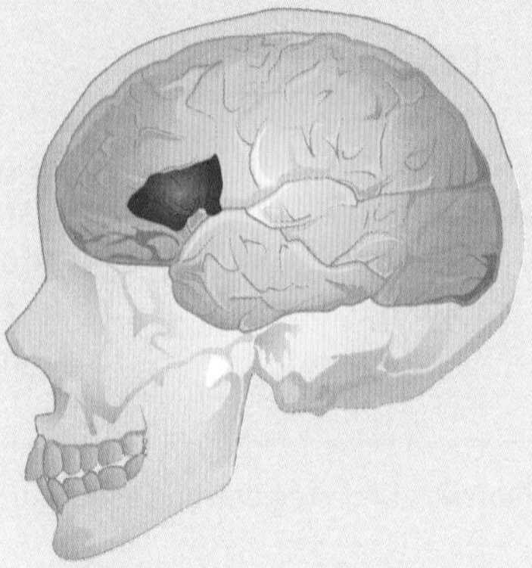

▲ **Figure 2.4** Broca's area

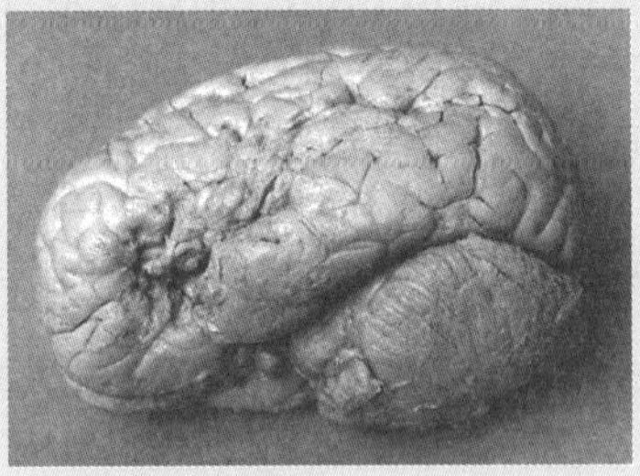

▲ **Figure 2.5** Tan's brain

The limbic system

The **limbic system** is a complicated group of brain structures located above the brainstem and within the cerebrum. The limbic system is tucked away under the cortex so you would not see it if you were just looking straight at someone's brain. The limbic system connects the cortex with the brainstem and is responsible for many important behaviours. Damage to the limbic system can result in very obvious changes in behaviour. This is the perfect region to study in order to understand how biology can affect behaviour.

What does it mean?

Limbic system: a set of brain structures located on top of the brain stem and under the cerebral cortex; responsible for emotions, motivation and memory, among other survival functions

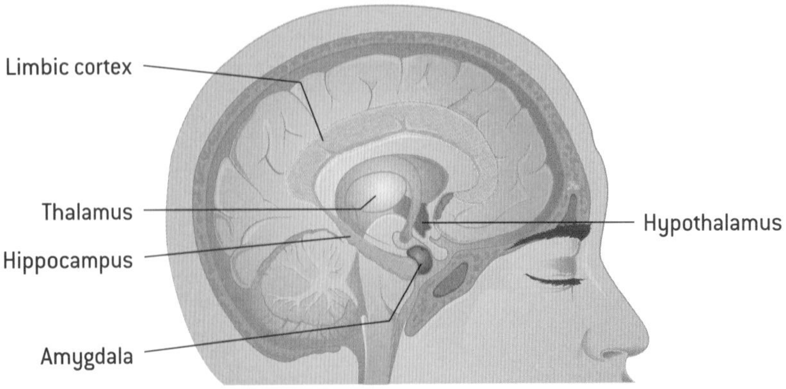

▲ **Figure 2.6** The limbic system

Table 2.3 shows the structures of the limbic system.

Structure	Associated functions
Hippocampus	Its associated functions are: learning; memory, including transferring memory from short-term to long-term storage; spatial orientation.
Amygdala	Its associated functions are: memory, emotion, fear response.
Thalamus	This acts as a hub for all sensory information. The thalamus routes information from the sense organs to the cortex for interpretation (perception). Your eyes see but your occipital lobe perceives—the thalamus links these two together.
Hypothalamus	This controls: the release of hormones, appetite, sexual behaviour, regulating circadian rhythms.
Pituitary gland	This is the master gland. It tells many other glands in the endocrine system when and how much of a hormone they should be releasing.

▲ **Table 2.3** The structures of the limbic system

The hippocampus

The **hippocampus** is a very important structure within the limbic system. The hippocampus plays an important role in processing learning between short-term and long-term memory. People with heavier, thicker hippocampi have better memories for things such as dates, names and spaces. The hippocampus helps process episodic memories but not **procedural memories**—procedural memories are processed in other brain structures such as the basal ganglia and the cerebellum.

One famous study in psychology involved a man called Henry Molaison. Henry's brain has been called the most studied brain in the history of psychology. From studies conducted over decades, psychologists were able to develop and test some of the most important theories about memory.

Damage to the hippocampus prevents someone from transferring short-term episodic ("what", "when", "who") memories to long-term memories. In other words, these patients can learn new skills but they cannot learn new facts such as details of people, places and things.

What does it mean?

Hippocampus: a structure that plays an important role in processing learning between short-term and long-term memory

Procedural memories: implicit memories about how to perform a task or procedure

Internal link

This links to models of memory, which are discussed in Chapter 3 on concepts in cognitive psychology: "Concept One: Mental representations guide behaviour".

Key Study: Scoville and Milner (1957)

KS

Case study: Henry Molaison (HM)

Henry Molaison (HM) was hit by a cyclist and cracked his skull when he was just a boy. This accident lead to increasingly worse epileptic seizures. On 1 September 1953, a neurosurgeon named Dr William Scoville removed all of HM's hippocampi (you have two—one in each **hemisphere**) to stop HM's seizures.

Researchers in this key study were interested in studying what effect removing the hippocampus would have on behaviour.

Aim: to investigate the role of the hippocampus in memory processing.

Procedure: this is a longitudinal case study so researchers were able to perform many different tests and observe HM in many different conditions over the years of his study. Methods included experiments such as the star test and countless other memory experiments.

Results: it was found that HM could hold memories in his short-term memory but he could not transfer episodic memories to long-term memory. However, he could improve performance of a task if he practised, meaning he was still able to learn new skills. This showed that procedural memories must be processed by another structure in the brain.

Conclusion: the hippocampus plays an important role in processing episodic memories from short-term to long-term memory. People who lack a working hippocampus cannot remember places, dates, people or events for longer than a few seconds.

DP ready | ATL **Research skills**

Case study

Watch the videos on the case of Henry Molaison (HM) then answer the questions below.

Watch this

www.youtube.com/watch?v=WOTTQroCjoQ
www.youtube.com/watch?v=KkaXNvzE4pk

Search terms

"Amnesiac A historia de Henry Molaison" and "hippocampus Sam Kean YouTube".

- What was the star tracing test and how did Henry do on these tests? What does this tell us about the hippocampus?
- What was the number test and how did Henry do on these tests? What does this tell us about the hippocampus?

The amygdala

The **amygdala** is another structure in the limbic system and performs a kind of watchdog function. The amygdala sits next to the hippocampus in the limbic system. The amygdala has evolved in your brain to detect fear or danger and to signal your body to enter a survival mode by activating what is sometimes called your "**fight or flight response**". The amygdala also plays a role in memory because remembering scary or dangerous events or situations can help you to survive if you meet those dangers again.

The amygdala can trigger fear for physical threats such as a barking dog or a psychological threat such as an upcoming exam at school. Your body will react the same way to both threats.

What does it mean?

Amygdala: an area of the brain that has been called the emotional centre. It is part of the limbic system, along with the hippocampus and hypothalamus

Fight or flight response: a biological reaction that happens in response to a perceived harmful event or threat

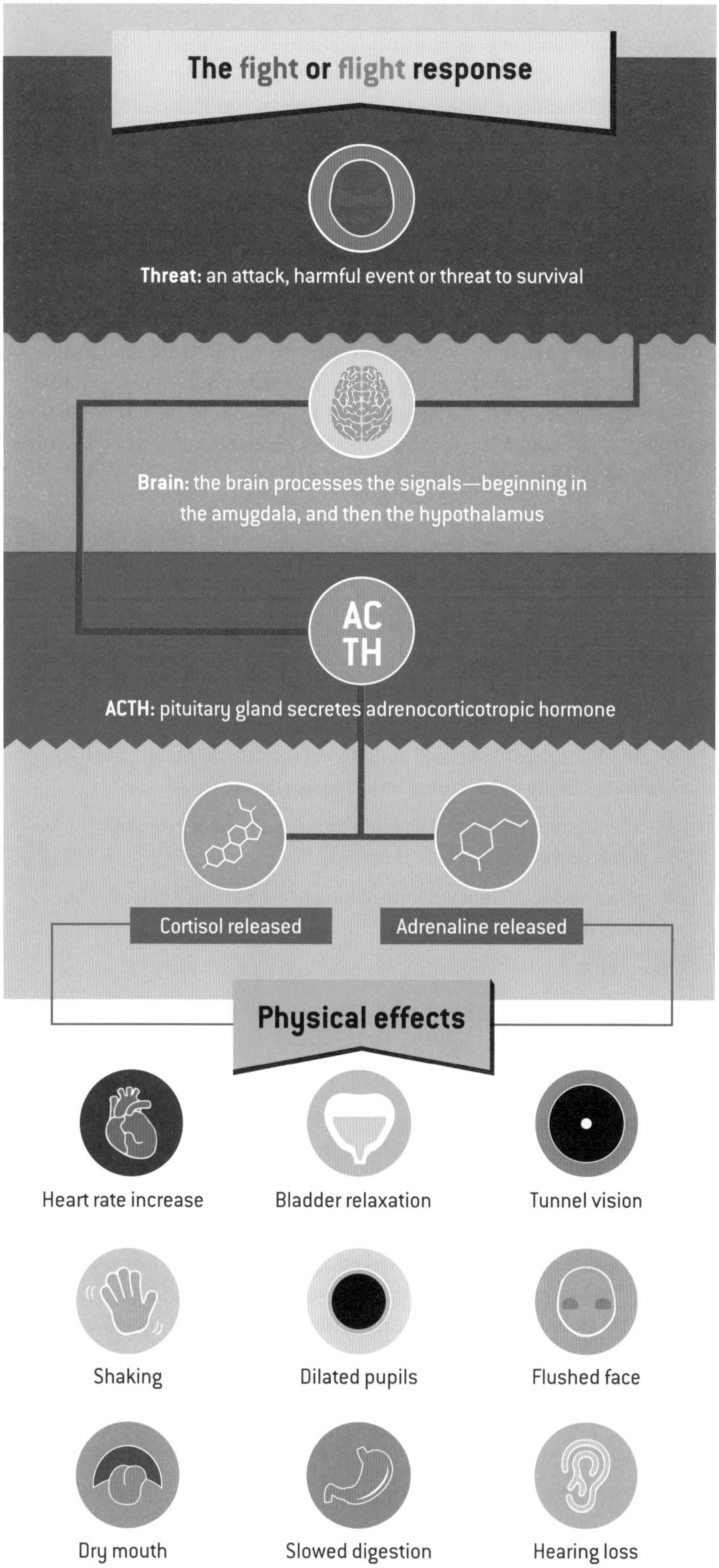

The fight or flight response
Threat: an attack, harmful event or threat to survival
Brain: the brain processes the signals—beginning in the amygdala, and then the hypothalamus
AC TH
ACTH: pituitary gland secretes adrenocorticotropic hormone
Cortisol released
Adrenaline released
Physical effects
Heart rate increase
Bladder relaxation
Tunnel vision
Shaking
Dilated pupils
Flushed face
Dry mouth
Slowed digestion
Hearing loss

▲ Figure 2.7 Fight or flight

Your fight or flight response happens so quickly that your cortex might not even have time to understand why you are frightened. It will take a little more time for your more complex brain regions to think about a possible threat and determine if something really is dangerous or not. This is why, for example, a small playful child can terrify you by jumping out from behind a door. Your amygdala does not see the child, it only registers that something dangerous might be happening. Your analytical thinking (in your cortex) will take a little longer to do its job and tell you there is no danger—"It's just a small child, no need to fight or flee". Once you realize the child is not a threat, then the whole system works in reverse and your body begins to return to normal. Unless, that is, you decide to chase the child in revenge for scaring you so badly! In other words, your amygdala does not take the time to "think" too much, it reacts to save your life; evaluating a threat takes more time and is associated with the cortex.

Psychology in real life

PRL

Patient SM-046

SM is a woman first described in 1994 who does not feel fear due to damage to her brain when she was a child. She is only known by her initials SM in order to protect her privacy. In a number of experiments, SM showed the following behaviours.

- She handled snakes and spiders with no fear, although she had feared these before the damage to her brain.
- She was not frightened walking through a haunted house attraction at a local fair.
- She showed no fear when watching scary movies such as "The Blair Witch Project" and "The Shining".

Ask yourself:

- What part of her brain do you think is damaged?
- Do you think this might be a danger or a good thing for SM?

DP ready ATL **Thinking skills**

Distribution of function

We have looked at several examples of localization of function but this idea may be too simple. We know that memories are not localized in any specific place but are networked throughout the brain. In several studies, researcher Karl Lashley (1890–1928) made two important observations about memories.

- Removing parts of a rat's cortex did not destroy memories but it did make learning new things more difficult. The less cortex there is, the slower the learning will be.
- If one part of the cortex is damaged, another part of the cortex can take over that function. This is called **neuroplasticity**.

What does it mean?

Neuroplasticity: the ability of the brain to form and reorganize synaptic connections, especially in response to learning or experience or following injury

DP ready | ATL Research skills

The visual cortex

If a person is born blind, what happens to the visual cortex (the part of the cortex responsible for interpreting information from the person's eyes)?

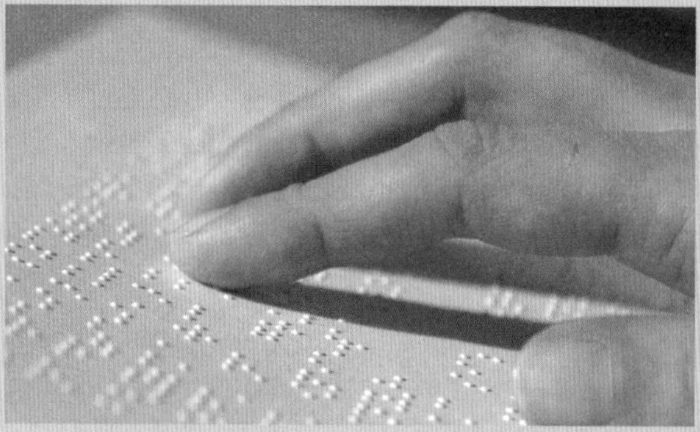

We have seen in this section that your brain has certain areas that are specialized to perform certain functions. We have learned from the examples of people with brain damage that missing important brain regions can have a serious impact on your behaviour. As humans, we have evolved a very complicated brain designed to keep us alive and safe. When parts of that very complicated organ do not work properly, our very survival may be in question.

It is not simply the physical structure of the brain that can influence behaviour. You are also full of all kinds of different chemicals that can influence your behaviour. The next section will look at how neurotransmitters and hormones can affect how you behave.

Neurochemicals—the chemistry of the brain and body

Hormones and neurotransmitters are chemicals in your body that directly affect your behaviour. In the previous section, we learned how damage to certain regions of the brain can change someone's behaviour. Here we will examine how increasing or decreasing the amount of a certain chemical in your brain or body can also cause changes in your behaviour. We will focus on two systems in your body: your nervous system and your endocrine system.

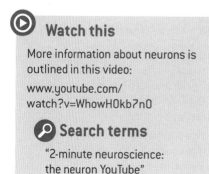

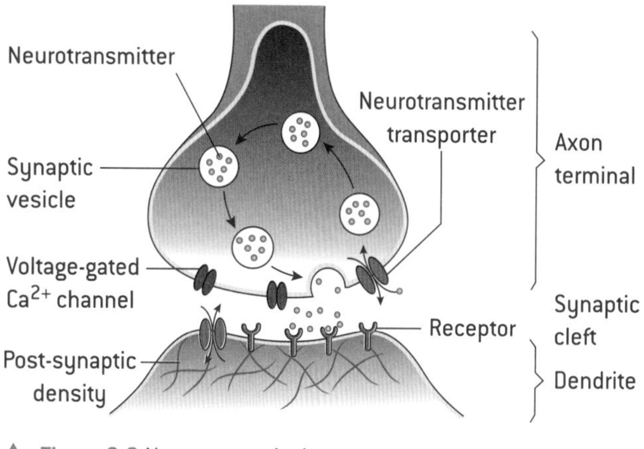

▲ **Figure 2.8** Neurotransmission

The nervous system—neurotransmitters

Neurotransmitters can influence your behaviour. They are chemical messengers that speed across the synapse between neurons. Each chemical carries a different message to the next neuron. One important neurotransmitter is acetylcholine.

Acetylcholine is a chemical in your brain that has many functions but one of the most important is that it helps you learn and remember new things. High levels of acetylcholine will help you learn new information and remember them later, whilst a lack of acetylcholine can hurt your ability to encode memories for recall later.

Watch this

More information about neurons is outlined in this video:

www.youtube.com/watch?v=WhowH0kb7n0

Search terms

"2-minute neuroscience: the neuron YouTube"

Key Study: Martinez and Kesner (1991)

The effect of acetylcholine on memory

Aim: to investigate the role of acetylcholine in spatial memory recall.

Procedure: the researchers used a laboratory experiment with rats in a maze. The rats first learned a maze in the laboratory by practising running through the maze. The rats were then put into three groups. One group was injected with a substance that would increase the amount of acetylcholine available in the rats' nervous system. One group received a substance that would decrease the amount of acetylcholine. A control group was not given anything to affect acetylcholine. The rats then ran the maze again and their behaviour was recorded.

Results: it was found that the rats with lower levels of acetylcholine made more mistakes and took longer to run through the familiar maze. The fastest group was the group with high levels of acetylcholine, the slowest group had low levels and the control group came in between the other two groups' results.

Conclusion: acetylcholine influences memory. The more acetylcholine that is present, the better the recall of spatial information.

Activity

Thinking critically about research is part of being a good psychologist. Can you think about anything in the Martinez and Kesner research that might cause you to question its validity in studying memory in humans?

DP ready ATL **Research skills**

Dopamine

Another important neurotransmitter is dopamine. Dopamine is associated with motivation and helps with encouraging behaviour by rewarding certain behaviours. Conduct some research to answer these questions.

- What role does dopamine play in learning? What role does it play in romantic love?
- What happens when our dopamine levels are too low?
- Is there a connection between dopamine and addiction?

The endocrine system—hormones

Like neurotransmitters delivering messages between neurons, hormones are chemical messengers—but hormones work in the endocrine system and travel in the bloodstream. Just like neurotransmitters though, they have many very significant influences on your behaviour.

Oxytocin is one of your hormones. Oxytocin plays an important role in trust and bonding. Like other hormones, it is made in the **hypothalamus** (in the limbic system) and released by the

What does it mean?

Oxytocin: a hormone made in the hypothalamus and then secreted by the pituitary gland; this hormone has been shown to be related to feelings of trust

Hypothalamus: part of the brain, it produces hormones for the endocrine system

pituitary gland directly below it. The hypothalamus is a great example of how the endocrine and nervous systems are separate but connected—that is, the hypothalamus is part of the brain but it produces hormones for the endocrine system.

Oxytocin is the same chemical and has the same role in most mammals, including the faithful family dog. In fact, research by Nagasawa *et al* (2015) has found that dogs and humans can increase each others' oxytocin levels. Nagasawa and colleagues had owners and dogs gaze into each others' eyes and then found increased levels of oxytocin in the urine of the dogs. Interestingly, they found that when dogs sniff the chemical oxytocin, they gaze longer into their owners' eyes, which in turn increases oxytocin levels in their owners. This seems to be evidence for cross-species trust and bonding.

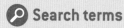

DP ready ATL **Thinking and research skills**

Oxytocin

In a presentation entitled "Trust, morality—and oxytocin", neuroeconomist Paul Zak calls oxytocin the "moral molecule". Watch the video then answer the following questions.

Watch this

www.ted.com/talks/paul_zak_trust_morality_and_oxytocin?language=en

Search terms

"zak oxytocin ted talk online"

- Do you think it is possible that one hormone is responsible for all of our morality and ethical behaviour? What makes you say that?
- Research methods: Zak talks about performing laboratory experiments to test for oxytocin. Can you think of a reason why laboratory experiments might lack validity in testing a "moral molecule"?

The nervous and endocrine systems are contrasted in Table 2.4.

Nervous system	Endocrine system	What this means
This has a role in: motion, movement, decisions.	This has a role in: growth, metabolism, digestion, reproduction.	The two systems have different roles.
Neurotransmitters are released in the nervous system.	Hormones are released in the bloodstream.	Hormones can reach areas not covered by the nervous system.
This system is associated with immediate, short-term actions.	This system is associated with ongoing processes.	Hormones act much more slowly than neurotransmitters.
This system is mostly under voluntary control.	This system is mostly under automatic control.	You can control things like your decisions but not things like your growth.

▲ **Table 2.4** Contrasting the nervous system and endocrine system

TOK link

Have you ever wondered: do you really have free will? How can you know for sure?

You may have heard people arguing about **free will** and **determinism**. One way to think about this debate is through the lens of psychology. If your behaviour is determined to a large extent by our biology, do you actually have free will?

Robert Sapolsky, a neurobiologist at Stanford University has said "I don't think there's a shred of free will out there. I think free will is what we call the biology we haven't uncovered yet." Robert Sapolsky (2018) 'The Biology Behind Evil, Free Will, And Everything Else' WGBH News. Marc Sollinger. *Innovation Hub*. May 11, 2018.

Do you think you have free will or is your behaviour predetermined? What makes you say that?

What evidence would convince you that you either have or do not have free will?

What does it mean?

Free will: the ability to choose between different possible courses of action

Determinism: the philosophical idea that all events, including moral choices, are determined completely by previously existing causes

Although they are separate systems, the nervous system and endocrine system are interdependent—that is, changes in one system affect the other system. In fact, some of the same chemicals act in both systems. For example, adrenaline is both a hormone and a neurotransmitter depending on which system it is in.

DP ready ATL **Communication skills**

Paragraph outline

How does your biology influence your behaviour?

Use the information in this section to write a paragraph outlining the main argument that your behaviour can be influenced by your biology.

Your paragraph outline should answer the question above using two main ideas. You should take one of these ideas from each of the subsections above: "Brain structures—getting to know your brain" and "Neurochemistry—the chemistry of the brain and body". Write a topic sentence that answers the question in one statement and follow it with the two main ideas. Your paragraph should end with a linking statement that restates your answer to the question.

Extension

Strong arguments often predict the criticisms they will receive. See if you can predict the criticisms of your arguments. This can take the form of a statement before your conclusion that may begin: "Some may disagree with this statement because ...".

Reflection Activity

Design your own concept map to help you to briefly explain one of the concepts discussed in this section.

Develop a list of ideas related to the concept. Write what you think are the most important ideas in the centre and the least important towards the outside. Draw lines between the ideas you think are connected. On these lines write notes to summarize how the ideas are connected. Use the remaining space around the outside to elaborate on any new ideas that extend your thinking.

Adapted from: Ritchhart, Church and Morrison (2011)

Brain imaging technologies

For obvious reasons, psychologists (and their patients) are not very interested in sawing into skulls and poking around in brains to learn new things. In the early days of scientific psychology, researchers were normally dependent on naturally occurring injuries or abnormalities from which they could learn about the brain and behaviour. Paul Broca for example had to wait until after his patient, Tan, died before he discovered the reason for Tan's speech problem. (See the Key study: Broca (1861) on page 42).

Today, researchers do not saw into many skulls or poke into living brains very often. Instead they rely on computer technology and advanced imaging to study the brains of patients while the patients are still using them. This has many benefits. With a dead brain you may be able to study structure but not processes—dead brains aren't thinking about anything. There are several ways to image a living brain and each one has its advantages and disadvantages. By far the most common brain imaging technologies are **magnetic resonance imaging (MRI)** and its close relative **functional magnetic resonance imaging** (abbreviated as **fMRI**). While MRI is like a photograph to study structures, fMRI is more like a video to study processes.

What does it mean?

Magnetic resonance imaging (MRI): a non-invasive structural imaging technology that produces three-dimensional detailed anatomical images without the use of damaging radiation to show the shape, size and density of brain structures

Functional magnetic resonance imaging (fMRI): a non-invasive functional imaging technology that produces three-dimensional detailed anatomical images without the use of damaging radiation to show processes in the brain

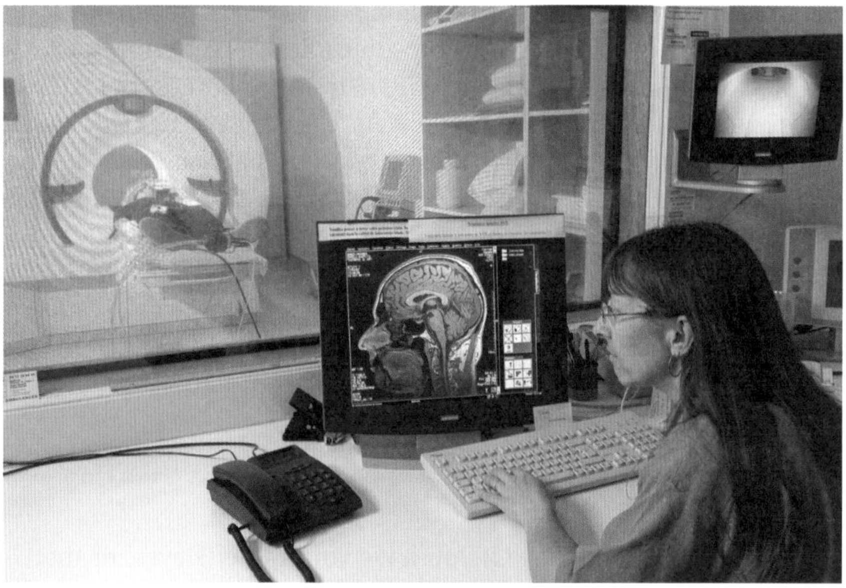

▲ **Figure 2.9** Functional magnetic resonance imaging

MRI and fMRI are not perfect technologies. The resolution is improving all the time but we are still unable to see individual neurons on these scans. Imagine you are flying in a commercial jet airplane over farmers' fields. You might be able to tell where one field ends and another begins, in fact you might even be able to identify what crops are growing where. You won't, however, be able to identify individual plants in the field. This analogy is similar to the limitations that psychologists have with MRI machines. They can identify regions but not individual neurons.

	CAT	MRI	fMRI	PET	EEG
Does it investigate structure or processes?	Structure	Structure	Processes	Processes	Processes
Spatial resolution	Up to 1–2 mm	Up to 1–2 mm	Up to 1–2 mm	4 mm	Very poor
Temporal resolution	NA	NA	1 second	30–40 seconds	Milliseconds
Major challenges	Radiation exposure	Up to 40 minutes spent without movement in a narrow noisy tube	Cancelling out random noise a lot of trials required	Radiation exposure	Cancelling out random noise

▲ **Table 2.5** Comparison of neuroimaging methods

Concept One

Concept Two

Conclusion: Concept One

This section has explained how your behaviour can be influenced by your biology. There are two main arguments.

- The structure of your brain and nervous system cause you to behave in a certain way.
- The chemicals in your nervous and endocrine systems both cause you to behave in a certain way.

You must be cautious here. Your biology does not *determine* your behaviour, it *influences* your behaviour. It would be reductionist to say that your biology is solely responsible for everything you do. **Reductionism** is the practice of analysing and describing a complex phenomenon in a simple way. The result of reductionist thinking is that you will have an explanation that is incomplete. As you will learn throughout this book, your behaviour is determined by your biology, your environment and your cognition (thinking) combined.

Concept Two: Behaviour can be inherited

Do your genes determine your potential?

Have you ever been told that you have your father's eyes, or that you have inherited your mother's good looks? Have you ever wondered how and why this happens? Psychologists are fascinated by these questions too. In this section you will start to look at the building blocks of what makes us human. You will learn about:

- genes and how they shape your appearance
- genes and how they shape your behaviour.

What is inheritance?

The study of **inherited characteristics** such as your eye colour, hair colour and hair type is called **heredity**. Characteristics that you pick up over the course of your life such as scars and tattoos are known as **acquired characteristics** because you collect them

What does it mean?

Reductionism: the theory that even complex behaviour can be explained by explaining the simplest, most basic physical mechanisms in operation during an event

Inherited characteristics: characteristics that you inherit from your parents such as eye colour

Heredity: the study of inherited characteristics

Acquired characteristics: characteristics that you acquire during the course of your life such as scars

Genes: genes are the most basic unit of heredity, made up of DNA and responsible for a specific trait or behaviour

DNA (deoxyribonucleic acid): hereditary material found in human cells

Alleles: a variant form of gene variation responsible for a specific trait such as hair colour

as you go. You cannot inherit a scar or tattoo from your parents. Psychologists studying genetics are therefore only interested in inherited characteristics.

DP ready ATL Research and communication skills

Genetics and inheritance

Uncover some of the amazing discoveries that have supported our understanding of genetics and inheritance using the interactive timeline at:

https://unlockinglifescode.org/timeline?tid=4

Search terms

"genome: unlockinglifescode timeline"

- Read about all the amazing discoveries made by scientists from 1865 to the present day.
- Select what you consider the five most important events on this timeline. Justify your choices to a partner.
- The timeline refers to the Human Genome Project. Conduct some of your own research into this project and uncover the researchers' latest discoveries. How far are they in achieving their goal of mapping out all genes in the human body?
- Create a poster for your psychology classroom that gives exciting information about genetic research.

All people start life as an individual cell with 23 pairs of chromosomes. One of the chromosomes in each pair is from your mother and the other from your father. You inherit biological information from each of your parents which means that you will inherit some of their characteristics. In fact, you can also inherit some diseases and even behavioural characteristics such as intelligence from your parents through their **genes**. Genes, made of a chemical called **DNA**, are present all along each chromosome. There are genes responsible for hair colour, eye colour and even your ear lobes. Ultimately, there are genes for everything—your physical appearance and all of your behaviours.

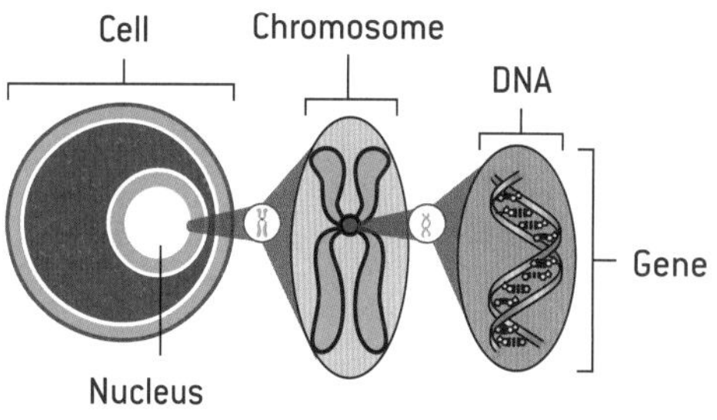

▲ **Figure 2.10** Gene, chromosome and cell

People are unique. They can have blue eyes or brown eyes, a big nose or a small nose, curly hair or straight hair. This is because there are different forms of genes. These variations of a gene are called **alleles** and they allow for the differences in a single inherited trait such as your hair colour. Alleles vary in length. Whether an allele is long or short results in the gene expressing itself differently. This influences the final trait or behaviour. As you can see in Figure 2.11, there are different alleles for the different eye and hair colour variations.

It may help you to think of one DNA molecule as an individual house on a street. The gene would be a whole street of houses. An allele accounts for variation in the type of houses on a street allowing some to have red doors and some blue doors. The chromosome would be a city that contains a lot of different neighbourhoods.

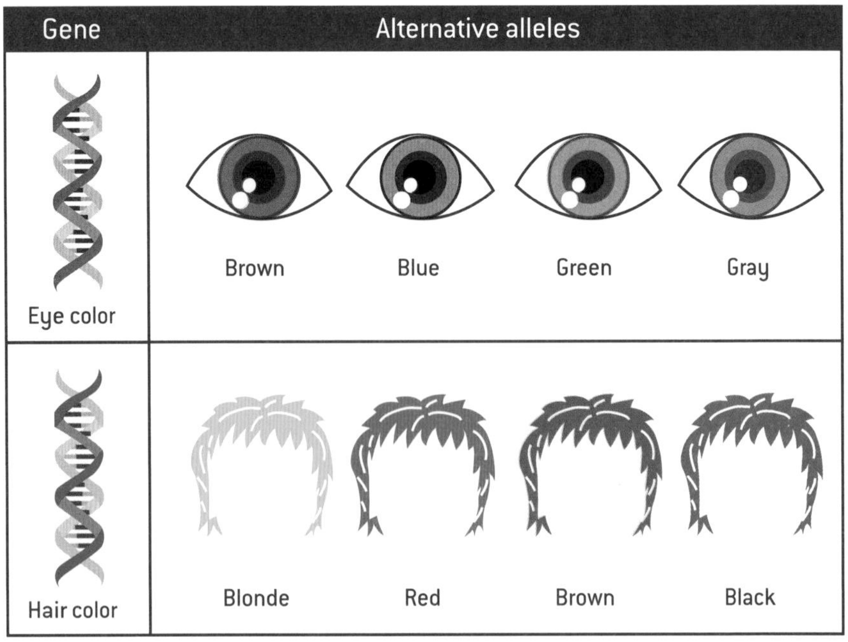

▲ **Figure 2.11** Allele variations for eye and hair colour

What does it mean?

Dominant gene: a gene that dominates over another gene

Recessive gene: genes that are dominated by other genes

Phenotype: a characteristic you can see such as ear lobes

Genotype: the set of genes that produce a phenotype

Epigenetics: the study of changes to a phenotype that do not involve changes to the DNA sequence

MOTHER \ FATHER	Black	brown
Black	BB (Black)	Bb (Black)
brown	bB (Black)	bb (brown)

▲ **Figure 2.12** Punnett square for hair colour

Whether you inherit a characteristic from your mother or from your father depends on the type of genes present in each pair of chromosomes. When a chromosome from a man pairs with the chromosome from a woman it brings the genes from each person with it. This means that pairs of genes are formed. If a gene for blue eyes pairs with another gene for blue eyes, then you will inherit blue eyes. If the two genes do not match though, the resulting eye colour will depend on which of these two genes is dominant. The gene for brown eyes may dominate over the gene for blue eyes. This would result in the final eye colour favouring that of the **dominant gene**. The gene that is dominated is known as a **recessive gene**. When a dominant gene pairs with a recessive gene, the final trait produced is always that of the dominant gene.

Let's look at an example involving hair colour. When teachers explain inheritance they often use diagrams called punnett squares that help to visually simplify the relationship between genes and inheritance. The genes are often shown as letters like those in the punnett square in Figure 2.12. The capital letters refer to the dominant genes and the small letters to the recessive genes. In this diagram, **B** is used to represent the gene for black hair and **b** is used to show brown hair.

If you have two identical genes such as BB then you will inherit black hair. If you inherit two different genes (Bb), then the hair colour that you inherit will be the same as that of the dominant gene. In this case, black hair (B). When two recessive genes come together (bb), you will get brown hair. In this example you would be three times more likely to inherit black hair than brown hair.

Hair, eye colour and ear lobes are all visible characteristics. Psychologists call these **phenotypes**. The genes that produce this characteristic such as Bb, BB are known as **genotypes**. Changes in gene expression can occur naturally over time through epigenesis.

Epigenetics—how your environment can influence your genes

Your environment and your lifestyle can also influence the way that your genes choose to express themselves. This means that the DNA sequence (genotype) underlying the characteristics remains unchanged, but the visible characteristics (phenotype) are affected. The study of these biological changes that turn genes on and off is known as **epigenetics**. These changes can be harmless, but can also have damaging effects such as causing cancer. This is a confusing topic and can be difficult to understand. Sometimes using an analogy can support your understanding. Let's try the analogy of a movie.

Think of your life as one very long interesting movie. Genetics in this example is like writing a movie. Consider Table 2.6 as an analogy for your genes.

The script	The actors	The director
Your DNA will act as the script and it provides the actors and actresses with their instructions for how they should perform. The DNA sequence would be the words in the script. The specific blocks of words on the script that inform actors of key events and actions to take place would be the genes.	Your cells are the actors and actresses in your movie, these are essential for a good movie.	Epigenetics, however, is like directing. You can have the same script but the director can choose to alter individual scenes that will make your movie better or worse. The final movie could be very different.

▲ **Table 2.6** Your genes—an analogy

A real-life example may include an individual who has been exposed to an extremely stressful event. The stress can have a significant impact on the body, causing the gene expression to change. This may result in a change in behaviour or appearance. Extreme stress has been known to cause both depression and weight gain.

If you would like to learn more about how you inherit your parents' characteristics, watch these videos. They give an easy-to-understand overview of genetic inheritance and punnett squares.

Watch this

www.youtube.com/watch?v=CBezq1fFUEA
www.youtube.com/watch?v=Mehz7tCxjSE&vl=en

Search terms

"crash course biology # 9"and "Mendel's pea plants Jimenez Diaz"

Activity

Now you have a better understanding of heredity, create your own punnett square for the inheritance of your nose shape and your eye colour.

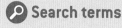

DP ready | ATL Thinking skills

The nature–nurture debate

When discussing the influence of your parents' genes on your characteristics it is impossible not to consider the opposite side of the debate too—nurture. This side of the debate states that your environment is also responsible for how you develop. There is little doubt that both your genes and your environment influence how you act and how you develop. There is debate, however, as to the extent of the interaction between these two factors in causing behaviours such as aggression.

Watch these videos to further your understanding of this debate and the influence that the environment and your actions can have on your gene expression.

Watch this

www.youtube.com/watch?v=k50yMwEOWGU

www.youtube.com/watch?v=kp1bZEUgqVI

Search terms

"epigenetics lucky lyle troubled tim" and "epigenetics SciShow"

In one video, a metaphor of a sentence and punctuation was used to explain epigenetics and the human genome. Can you think of your own metaphor to help explain epigenetics to a new psychology student?

What does it mean?

Twins: two children born from the same pregnancy

Twin studies: the study of heredity using twins as participants

Monozygotic twins: identical twins—twins that are born from the same zygote and share the same genes

Dizygotic twins: fraternal or non-identical twins: twins that are developed from one zygote but have developed from a separate eggs and fertilized by its own sperm cell

Concordance rate: the rate or probability that both members of a pair of twins will share the same trait

Genetic inheritance

Can you inherit your behaviour from your parents?

Psychologists can investigate the influence of our genes on behavioral characteristics such as aggression and intelligence by using a variety of research methods. A popular method used by psychologists to study genetic inheritance is the case of twins. **Twins** are offspring that share the same DNA because they developed from the same fertilized cell (zygote). **Twin studies** and adoption studies investigate the degree to which individuals share similar genes and behaviours. Identical twins, known as **monozygotic twins** share 100% of their DNA whereas non-identical or fraternal twins, known as **dizygotic twins**, only share 50% of their DNA.

We may therefore expect identical twins to not only look the same, but to act in the same way, more so than non-identical twins. The likelihood that a trait is inherited is known as a **concordance rate**. A high concordance rate indicates that a behaviour is genetically passed from parents to their children. Monozygotic twins should thus have a very high concordance rate if behaviours are indeed genetically determined.

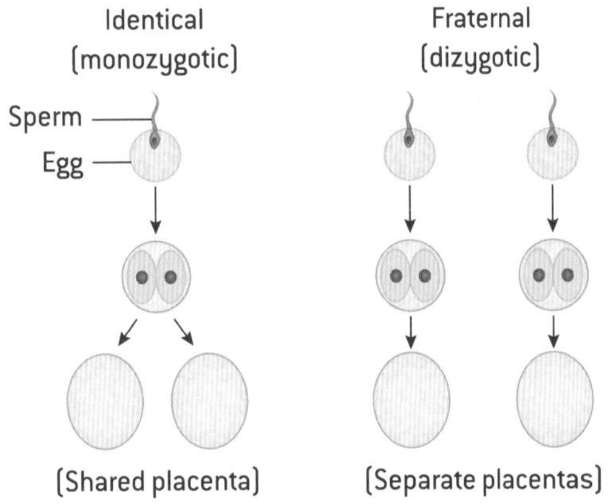

▲ Figure 2.13 The relationship between identical and fraternal twins

KS

Key Study: Bouchard *et al* (1990)

The Minnesota twin study

Aim: to investigate the relationship between intelligence and genetic inheritance.

Procedure: the researchers used a sample of monozygotic twins who had been raised together and compared them to monozygotic twins who had been raised apart. Researchers predicted that sharing 100% of their DNA and living in the same environment would result in higher concordance rates for the twins that were raised together.

Results: in terms of IQ, the twins raised together (88%) had a higher concordance rate than those reared apart (69%).

Conclusion: researchers concluded that IQ is influenced by our environment. Factors such as diet, schooling and parenting also play a part. According to the study it is our genetics, however, that are primarily responsible for our levels of intelligence (70%).

Twin studies are a useful source of data for psychologists when investigating the role of inheritance on behaviour. We must be careful, though, not to overestimate the importance of their findings as there may be alternative explanations. It is difficult to isolate environmental variables so there may be many differences in the way each participating twin has been raised even though the home environment was constant. This would undoubtedly influence the resulting behaviour of a child.

DP ready | **ATL Thinking skills**

Twin and adoption studies

Watch this video to gain a deeper understanding of twin and adoption studies, then answer the questions below.

> **Watch this**
>
> www.youtube.com/watch?v=bRKbZtpBcgl
>
> **Search terms**
>
> "nature and nurture study of twins YouTube"

- What are the benefits of using twin studies to investigate the influence of genes on behaviour?
- Why might a researcher choose to use adoption studies instead of twin studies when investigating inheritance?
- What are the limitations of using twin studies to assess inheritance and behaviour?
- What are the limitations of adoption studies to investigate inheritance and behaviour?

DP ready | ATL Research skills

Inheritance and behaviour

Conduct your own research into:

- the Dutch Hunger winter children and mental health
- the Warrior Gene and violence.

Answer the following questions.

- How did psychologists investigate these topics? Which methods did they use?
- What hypothesis were they testing?
- What conclusions can we make about inheritance and behaviour?

Alternatively, some psychologists focus on identifying individual genes that produce a specific behaviour. These studies investigate epigenetics or gene expression. A famous study investigating gene expression and depression is outlined below.

KS

Key Study: Caspi *et al* (2003)

Gene expression and depression

Aim: to determine the role of the 5-HTT gene in the onset of depression. The 5-HTT gene determines how we respond to stressful events. In order to understand this study it is also important to note that the shorter the alleles are on the 5-HTT gene, the more likely it is that the carrier will experience depression in response to stress.

Procedure: this is considered to be a natural experiment because the study investigated the number of stressful events an individual had experienced between the ages of 3 and 26. This was done using a life-events calendar. Participants were also interviewed to determine whether they experienced depressive symptoms.

Results: the participants with one or two shortened 5-HTT alleles experienced more depressive symptoms after facing stressful life events.

Conclusion: the researchers concluded that the 5-HTT gene influences the way individuals experience stressful events. Those with shorter alleles on this gene may experience more depressive symptoms.

DP ready | ATL Thinking skills

Onset of depression

Consider the study by Caspi *et al* (2003).

- What alternative explanations can you think of for the onset of depression in the participants?
- What limitations can you think of in relation to the research conducted in this study?

DP ready ATL **Communication skills**

Paragraph outline

How can genes affect your behaviour?

Use the information in this section to write a paragraph outlining the main argument that genes influence behaviour.

Your paragraph outline should answer the question above using two main ideas. You should take one of these ideas from each of the subsections above: "Genetic inheritance" and "Epigenetics—how your environment can influence your genes". Write a topic sentence that answers the question in one statement and follow it with the two main ideas. Your paragraph should end with a linking statement that restates your answer to the question.

Extension

Strong arguments often predict the criticisms they will receive. See if you can predict the criticisms of your arguments. This can take the form of a statement before your conclusion that may begin: "Some may disagree with this statement because ...".

Conclusion: Concept Two

To a large extent, our behaviour is influenced by our genes. Studies have found that 70% of our behaviour can be attributed to genetic factors. It is important, however, to acknowledge the interplay between genetic and environmental factors such as stressful life events. Human behaviour is therefore a result of a combination of biological, cognitive and social factors.

Reflection Activity

Sentence—phrase—word—share

1. Identify a sentence that you thought was key to understanding the concept that behaviour can be inherited.
2. Identify a phrase that caused you to question the truth of a claim.
3. Identify a single word that you thought was powerful or meaningful.

In small groups identify common themes that emerge from your understanding.

Adapted from: Ritchhart, Church and Morrison (2011)

Concept Three: Animal research

Animal research can teach us about human behaviour

What does it mean?

Animal model: a concept that refers to using animals in research to understand human behaviour

Doctors and researchers have used animals to study human biology for a very long time. An **animal model** is a concept that refers to using animals in research to understand human behaviour. It seems clear that since humans and animals share many biological traits, we could use animals to test products and treatments instead of using humans. We have a lot to learn from animals.

Reasons to use animals in research

You may have noticed that a lot of the research that psychologists do is on animals instead of humans. Animals have taught psychologists a great deal about human behaviour. There are three good reasons for using animals instead of humans, which are:

- ethics
- anatomy
- biochemistry.

DP ready | ATL **Research skills**

Famous animals in research

Do some research to discover at least three famous animal studies used in the history of psychological research.

- What did we learn from using these animals?
- Do you think the researchers needed to use animals? Could they have conducted the research on humans?
- Can you think of another method the researchers could have used to investigate the topic?

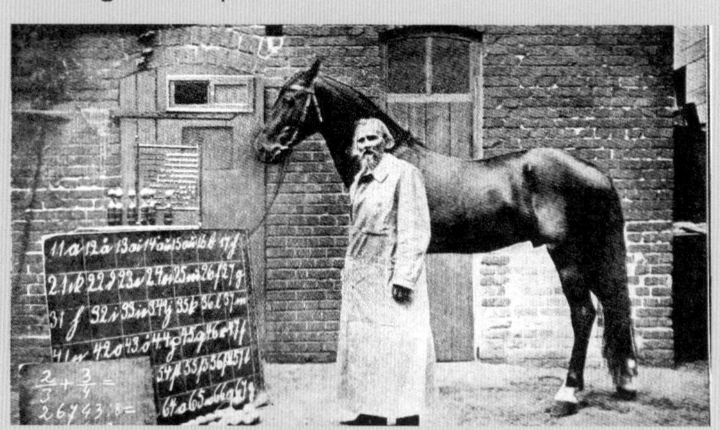

▲ **Figure 2.14** "Clever Hans", the counting horse

Ethics

The first reason is ethical: it is simply unethical to perform some studies on human subjects. This is a problem that does not have to do with the quality of the information we gain from animal studies. A study could be unethical and still deliver some very important, accurate and life-changing information. Ethical arguments simply try to answer the question: what is the right thing to do? It may be wrong to perform some research on humans but this does not mean that performing this research on animals is the right thing to do.

DP ready | ATL Thinking skills

Harmful research on animals

Is it acceptable to perform harmful research on animals? Consider this carefully. Could it be considered the "right thing to do" to harm or kill laboratory animals such as rats or chimpanzees if that research leads to a treatment that effectively ends depression or anxiety disorders in humans? These are some of the difficult ethical questions that researchers have to ask themselves.

- Do you think it is ethical to harm animals to ease the suffering of humans or save human lives?
- Test your thinking: would you consider it differently if it saved your own life, or that of a loved one?

DP ready | ATL Research skills

APA guidelines

Go to this section of the American Psychological Association (APA) website: www.apa.org/science/leadership/care/guidelines.aspx (Search for "Guidelines for the ethical conduct in the use of nonhuman animals in research")

According to the APA, what are the guidelines for the ethical care and use of animals in research?

Anatomy

The second reason for using animals in psychological research is that human and animal brains have similar structures. The idea here is that animals and humans share an evolutionary past. At some point in our evolutionary history, we shared ancient ancestors with all animals—even those that are now extinct. We share some relatively recent ancestors with chimpanzees and great apes. Some relatives are more distant such as octopus and pterodactyls. No matter how distant, if we all evolved from the same ancestors, we will share at least some biology with all animals.

Remember from the previous section that you can inherit your behaviour from your parents through your genes. It is also true that some animals can share a very large percentage of their genes with humans.

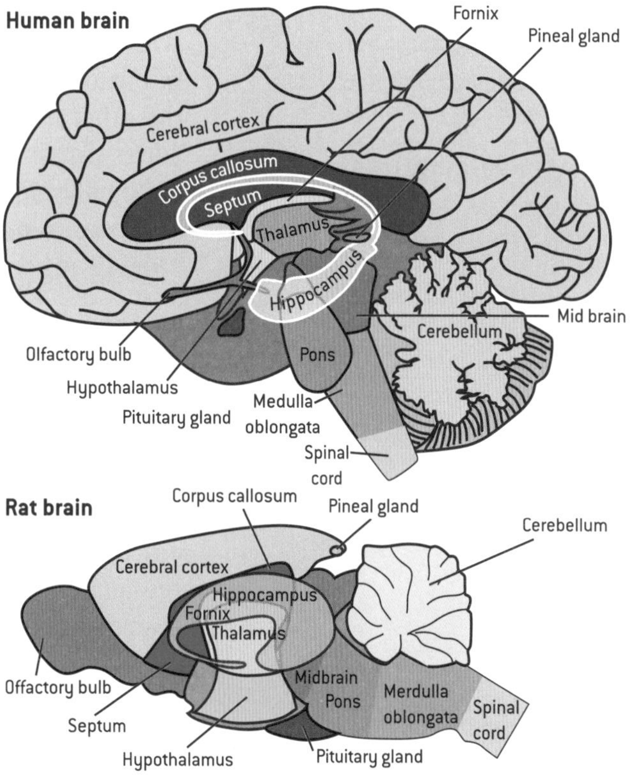

▲ Figure 2.15 The brain structure of a human and a rat compared

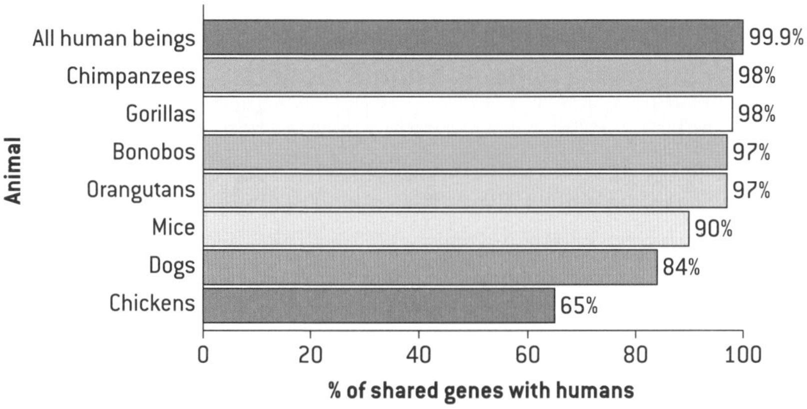

▲ Figure 2.16 Genes shared between humans and animals

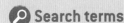

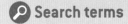

▲ Figure 2.17 *Aplysia Californica*

How far can we take the idea that animal models can help explain human behaviour? We can take it as far as the beautiful and majestic sea slug at least. Research performed by Eric Kandel has shown how much we can learn from seemingly distant animal relatives. The sea slug, *Aplysia Californica*, is able to teach us about some significant human things: learning and memory.

Through research on **aplysia** and later on mice, Kandel was able to show that neuronal synapses are essential in memory formation. Specifically, he showed not only how a few weak signals can cause chemical changes (neurotransmission) between neurons but that stronger signals delivered over a long period can cause different physical changes that can form long-term memories. Simply put: short-term memories are chemical changes in the brain (increase in neurotransmitters) while long-term memories are physical changes in the brain (dendritic branching and neurogenesis).

Watch this

This video will show you what a sea slug can tell us about learning:

www.youtube.com/watch?v=yLa-cXg8BwM

Search terms

"NOVAscienceNOW a memorable snail YouTube"

Aplysia Californica is actually a great subject for study because it is *not* like humans in very helpful ways. As mentioned earlier, you have billions of neurons in your brain—this makes you smart but also makes you a complicated animal to study. Aplysia, on the other hand, have only about 20,000 neurons, making them super simple by comparison. Add to this the fact that they have extremely large neurons and they become excellent subjects of study for **neuroscientists**. Fewer and bigger neurons make these animals much simpler than humans and easier to study.

Biochemistry

The third reason to use animals in psychological research is that humans and animals have similar chemicals influencing behaviour. Acetylcholine, dopamine, serotonin, adrenaline, oxytocin, vasopressin—all of these exist in both animals and humans. Since the same chemicals exist and influence the same structures, researchers assume that biochemicals will have the same effect on animals and on humans. Research has supported these assumptions.

Watch this

This video will show you what baboons can tell us about the hormone cortisol and stress in humans:

www.youtube.com/watch?v=sPS7GnromGo

Search terms

"stress response savior to killer YouTube"

There are important limitations to animal models. The value of animal models is limited by the extent to which we are different from animals. For example, if an animal has a brain structure that we do not have, that means the animal may have some abilities we do not have.

What does it mean?

Biochemistry: the branch of science that explores the chemical processes within and related to living organisms

DP ready | ATL **Thinking skills**

Counter argument to using animal models

Many animals have the ability to communicate chemically with each other by releasing chemicals (**pheromones**) through the air to deliver messages silently across distances—a kind of chemical extrasensory perception or sixth sense. Animals who have this ability also have a specific brain region most humans lack: a VNO or vomeronasal organ. In short, humans do not seem to be able to communicate chemically, so there appear to be clear limits to animal research.

Can you think of any more examples of the limitations of animal models for human behaviour?

Conclusion: Concept Three

The issue of using animals to further our understanding of human behaviour is a hot topic. The thought of harming animals for human gain is not one we like to consider. We cannot escape the fact, however, that in some cases using animals can be very beneficial for our understanding of human behaviour. It is very important that psychologists consider the alternatives to animal research before conducting their studies. If using animals is seen as the best option then the researchers should treat the animals as humanely and ethically as possible.

What does it mean?

Aplysia: a genus of medium-sized to extremely large sea slugs very useful in studying neurons

Neuroscientists: specialists in neuroscience, a multidisciplinary science concerned with studying the structure and function of the nervous system

Pheromones: a chemical substance produced and released into the environment by an animal, especially a mammal or an insect, affecting the behaviour or physiology of others of its species

Reflection Activity

Imagine that you could step into the mind of a person or animal impacted by the concepts discussed in this chapter. What do you think the person or animal might:

- know about, understand or believe
- wonder about
- question or challenge
- care about?

Adapted from: Ritchhart, Church and Morrison (2011)

Chapter conclusion

If a mad scientist found a way to switch your brain with someone else's would you be the same person with a different body? What if that same wacky scientist instead found a way to upload all your thoughts and memories from your brain to a computer? Now who would you be? These are interesting philosophical questions and they force you to consider deep questions of what it means to be you. The tendency is to think that "I" is the thing looking out at the world from behind your eyes, that the "I" you think is "you" resides in your brain. This is a universal idea and one that shows us how important biology is in thinking about what makes you "you". There is something unique and special about your brain that sets it apart and above the rest of your biology. For better or for worse, we associate ourselves with that organ more than any other.

Your biology plays an important role in determining your behaviour and who you are. However, it does not appear that you are a prisoner of your biology because your environment and your thinking contribute to your decisions and behaviours. Your brain is constantly growing and changing, and along with these changes come benefits and drawbacks. Your brain responds to the challenges you give it. Constantly challenging yourself to learn new things and to look through different perspectives can improve brain function and cognition.

Psychologists have learned a lot about humans from studying animals. From the simple aplysia to much more complex animals such as chimpanzees, we humans share a surprising amount of biology with our animal cousins. They can help us to learn more about ourselves but we should be careful about how similar we assume them to be.

Links to IB psychology topics

Biological approach to understanding behaviour

- **The brain and behaviour**
  - Techniques to study the brain
  - Localization
- **Hormones and pheromones and behaviour**
  - Hormones and behaviour
  - Pheromones and behaviour
- **Genetics and behaviour**
  - Genes and behaviour
  - Genetic similarity
  - Evolutionary explanations of behaviour

HL extension: The role of animal research in understanding human behaviour

Exam-style questions

1. **To what extent** can neurotransmission explain human behaviour?
2. **Discuss** the theory of neuroplasticity, making use of relevant research.
3. **To what extent** do hormones affect human behaviour?
4. **To what extent** does genetic inheritance influence human behaviour?
5. **Evaluate** one or more studies into research on how genetics may influence human behaviour.
6. **To what extent** are animal models useful in understanding human behaviour?
7. **Discuss** the ethical considerations of using animals in psychological research.

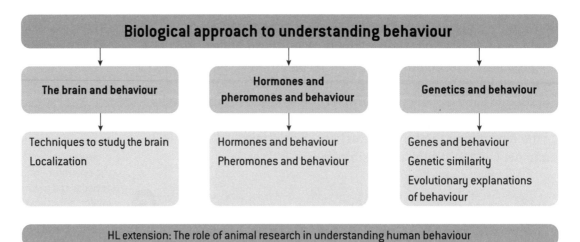

Big ideas

Concept One: There are biological reasons for behaviour

- Your behaviour is in part determined by your biology.
- Different locations in your brain have different responsibilities or functions.
- Your brain physically changes when you learn new things. Learning and consistent exposure to new things can make your brain thicker and bigger.
- Chemical levels throughout your body change your behaviours. Chemicals called hormones and neurotransmitters determine how you behave under certain circumstances.
- Brain imaging technologies are the main tool psychologists use to study brain structure and function. These technologies show, for example, blood flow, electrical signals and glucose consumption.

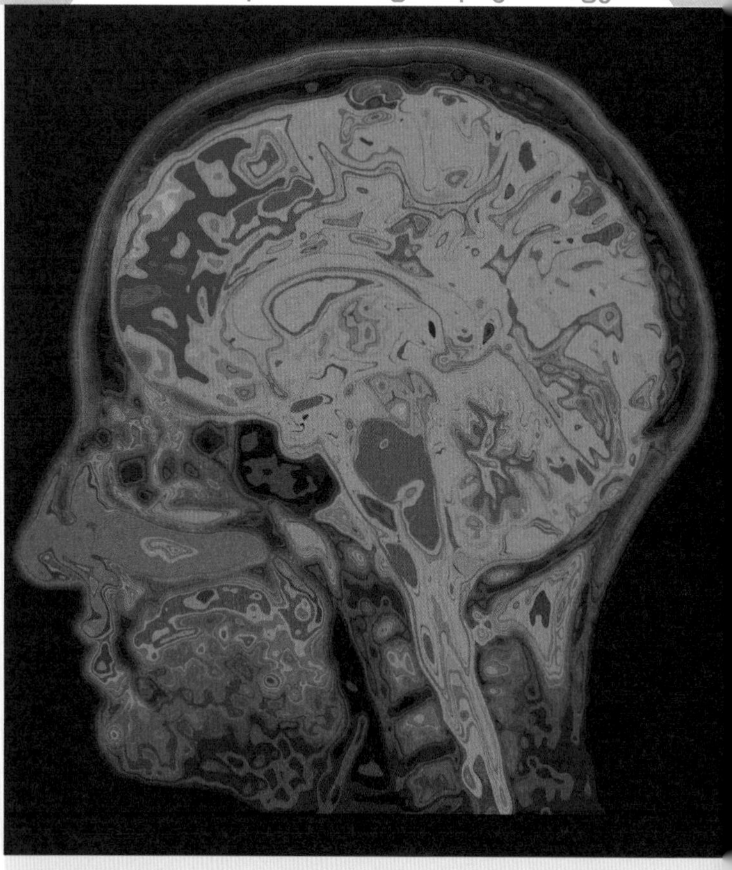

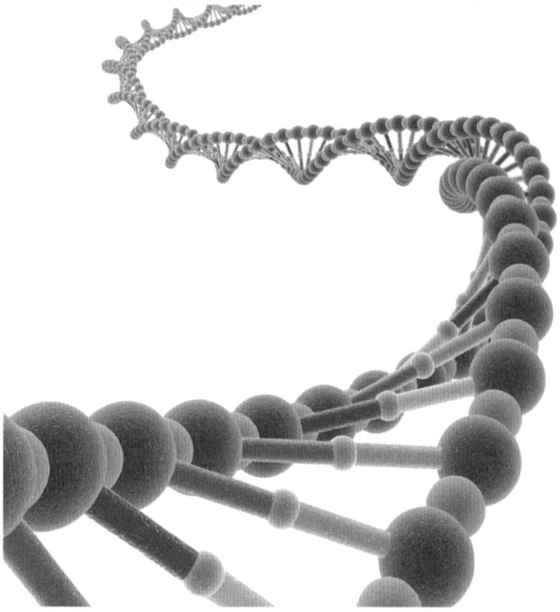

Concept Two: Behaviour can be inherited

- Genes are made of DNA. Genes are responsible for your physical characteristics and behaviour.
- One way in which psychologists learn about inheritance is by studying similarities in pairs of twins who had been raised apart.
- Individual genes that produce specific effects, such as depression and obesity, can be studied.
- Epigenetics is the study of how gene expression can be influenced by the environment.

Concept Three: Animal research

- Humans and animals have similar brain structure. All animals share distant relatives.
- Humans and animals have the same neurochemicals. The chemicals in our bodies are often identical to those in other animals.
- Humans and animals even share some aspects of culture.
- As a result of the similarities between the biology and cultures of humans and other animals, it is useful, to some extent, to use animals when studying human behaviour.

3 Concepts in cognitive psychology

In this chapter, you will learn the key concepts in cognitive psychology.

→ Concept One: Mental representations guide behaviour—how you interpret the world determines your behaviour
- schemas and schema theory
- the multi-store model of memory (MSM)
- dual process model of thinking and decision-making

→ Concept Two: Humans are active processors of information
- reconstructive memory
- perception
- biases in thinking and decision-making

→ Concept Three: Biological and sociocultural factors influence cognitive processes
- flashbulb memories
- social and cultural schemas

→ Concept Four: Digital technology is reshaping your brain—the internet is changing how you think
- selective attention

In this chapter you will also learn:

→ about important research studies in cognitive psychology

→ about ideas and theories related to
- how you understand the world around you
- the dangers of relying on memory
- sensation versus perception
- how your biology and your thinking are linked
- how using technology can change how you think and behave

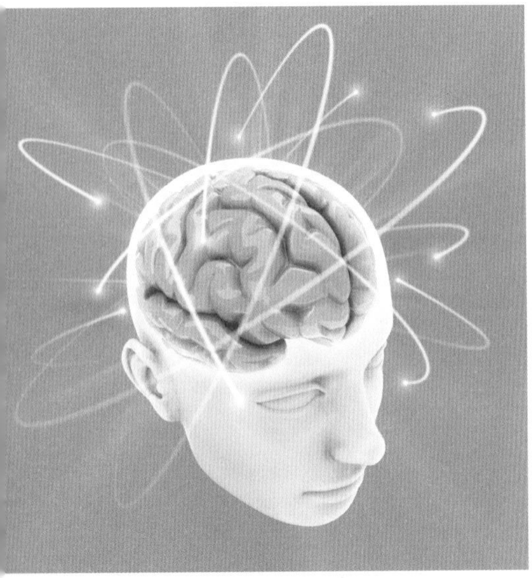

Introduction

This chapter explains four concepts behind cognition and behaviour.

- Mental representations guide behaviour.
- Humans are active processors of information.
- Biological and sociocultural factors influence cognitive processes.
- Digital technology is changing your thinking.

Cognitive psychology is the study of your mind. Your mind is responsible for mental processes such as memory, thinking, decision-making and attention. If you remember a birthday, forget a name or have to choose your best clothes for a date, your mind was responsible. Unlike your brain, your mind is not a physical thing. It cannot be touched or directly observed. It is a **hypothetical construct**. This makes studying the processes of the mind more difficult than studying the functions of the brain. Cognitive psychologists have therefore created **theoretical models** of mental processes, and psychologists use **scientific methods** to explain and study these models.

Concept One: Mental representations guide behaviour

How you interpret the world determines your behaviour

This section introduces you to the ideas of:

- schemas and schema theory
- the multi-store model of memory (MSM)
- thinking and decision-making system 1 and system 2 thinking.

Mental representations are used to represent information such as your skills, memories and ideas. These are cognitive structures or mental maps that represent something in your physical world that you have prior experience of. Mental representations are, therefore, created and updated as you experience the world. Mental representations allow you to think about complicated and abstract ideas after you have prior experience of them. This is because your mind has created a visual representation that becomes active when thinking. **Schemas** (or **schemata**), memory models and the dual-processing model of thinking are all examples of mental representations.

> **What does it mean?**
>
> **Hypothetical construct**: something that is not directly observable but created to try and explain human behaviour
>
> **Theoretical model**: a theory that aims to explain, predict and understand behaviour, often explained using a diagram
>
> **Scientific method**: a method of experimentation and observation that allows the formation and testing of hypotheses
>
> **Schema**: a mental representation or map based on life experience; (plural: schemas or **schemata**)
>
> **Script**: an event schema that prescribes a chronological order to a specific situation, such as going to a restaurant

Schemas and schema theory

Imagine that you are lying in bed after waking up in the morning. What do you do? What is your routine? Maybe you turn the light on, get out of bed, go to the bathroom, take a shower and then get dressed. How do you know what clothes are appropriate to wear today and how do you know how to put them on?

Most of these decisions were made easily and without much thought. This is because your mind has created a mental map of the layout of your house allowing you to find your way around, even when it is dark and the light is out. You also have mental maps in the form of **scripts** and social schemas that allow you to fill in the blanks and make decisions when you have limited knowledge about a situation. You may not know what the day will bring, but you do know what outfit is appropriate for an event you are attending. This is because your schemas are built using your past experiences, allowing you to create new scripts and make links between existing schemas.

Schemas are hypothetical constructs and so are not directly observable. This has led to some debate as to what a schema actually is. Psychologists cannot agree on a definition—but they do agree that without schemas you would struggle to make sense of the world.

What does it mean?

Self-schema: a mental representation of ourselves

Social schema: a mental representation of a group of people, often called stereotypes

The most common form of schemas include:

- **self-schema**—a set of beliefs or representations that influence your beliefs about yourself
- **social schemas** or scripts—representations of social concepts that allow you to make sense of your environment.

For example, you may hold the belief that you are a confident and outgoing individual. This belief may have developed as a result of many experiences that you have undertaken such as enjoyment of public speaking, socializing in large groups and meeting new people. Every time you engage in a similar activity your self-schema is reinforced and you maintain this belief that you hold about yourself. You also hold schemas for other people and your environment known as social schemas, one effect of which can be seen in the key study below.

KS

Key Study: Darley and Gross (1983)

Social schemas

Aim: to investigate the effect of social schemas on how participants interpret new or ambiguous information.

Procedure: this was a laboratory experiment. The first part of the experiment involves two groups of participants watching a video of a girl playing. Participants in one group observe the girl playing in a poor environment and the other group sees her playing in a rich environment. Then participants watch a video of her taking an academic test. Participants were asked to rate how they thought the girl would score on the test.

Results: participants who observed the girl in the poor environment believed that the girl would do less well in the test than the girl in the rich environment.

Conclusion: the researchers concluded that participants had used their social schemas when making their judgment. This judgment is based on pre-existing information that participants may have of people from each of the economic backgrounds. The situation is ambiguous and the judgment given may be incorrect. This study demonstrates how humans rely on pre-existing information when making judgments in unfamiliar situations.

Schemas can influence what information you remember from an event. A classic study by Anderson and Pichert (1978) discovered that the type of schema you use can influence how much information that you remember. Their study involved perception of a house: looking at a house as a potential buyer will cause you to remember different things about the property compared to viewing it as a potential burglar.

Imagine that you want to buy a house. What features would you look for in a suitable property? Maybe you would look for a garden, fence, burglar alarm and soundproof windows. This list would be fairly quick to compile. You have activated your house-buyer schema. In their study, Anderson and Pichert activated the house-buyer schema in some participants and then asked them to read a passage with information that would be of interest to those holding that schema. Twelve minutes later, after being distracted, they were asked to reproduce the story as accurately as possible. The house-buyer schema influenced the type and amount of information that participants recalled. Information that would fit well into a house-buyer schema was recalled.

Here's the twist. Participants were then told to recall the passage from a burglar's perspective. They then had to create a different schema. It may include easy escape routes, awareness of dogs and big windows. By accessing this schema after the first recall attempt, participants were able to recall more information. This time, information linked to the burglar schema. This study highlights that schemas influence someone's memory both during encoding and retrieval.

▲ Figure 3.1 Which schema are you using when you look at this image?

Your schema help you organize and make sense of information. They can help you in unfamiliar situations and guide your actions. They can also influence the type of information that you will remember. When you are unsure of how to act, making the best possible guess with the information you have is a sensible and logical thing to do. In fact, it is unavoidable. It may however, cause you to make the odd mistake. This is because you often adapt or replace unfamiliar information with an existing schema. You will learn more about these kinds of errors later in this chapter.

Watch this

Watch this video for a brief introduction to the concept of schema and the mind.

www.youtube.com/watch?v=8nz2dtv--ok&t=167s

Search terms

"Growth of knowledge Crash Course Psychology #18"

The multi-store model of memory (MSM)

Memory is a complex cognitive process. Atkinson and Shriffin (1968) created a very simple model of memory to help explain the **encoding**, **storage** and **retrieval** of information used in memory. The **multi-store model of memory (MSM)** splits memory into three separate and distinct memory stores. Each store varies in **duration** and **capacity**. This means that the length of time the information is held for changes, and how much information is stored varies between stores. The three memory stores are:

- sensory memory
- **short-term memory (STM)** store
- **long-term memory (LTM)** store.

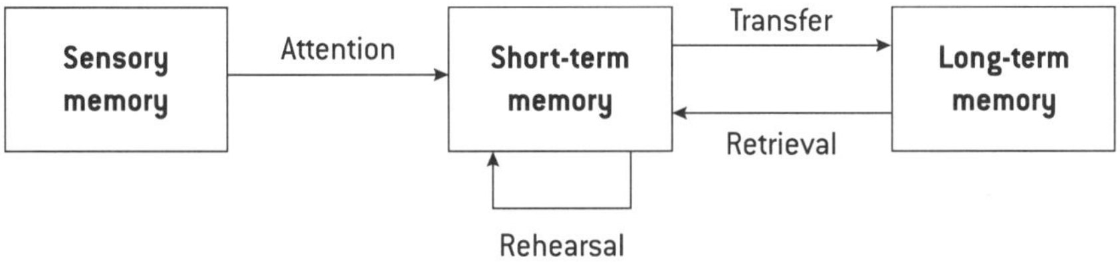

▲ Figure 3.2 The multi-store model of memory (MSM)

As memory is a cognitive process and the information travels through the memory stores in order, it can be useful to view this process as a sequence of events or stages. The process is outlined below.

What does it mean?

Encoding: allows information entering perception via the senses to be converted into a useable form for storage

Storage: the process of placing newly acquired information into your memory

Retrieval: re-accessing information that is already stored in your memory

Multi-store model of memory (MSM): a structural model of memory consisting of three memory stores

Duration: how long information can be stored for

Capacity: how much information can be stored in memory

Short-term memory (STM): a memory store of limited capacity and duration

Long-term memory (LTM): a memory store of infinite capacity and duration

What does it mean?

Attention: the process of selectively concentrating on specific pieces of information

Miller's magic number 7: evidence stating the capacity of short-term memory

Chunking: grouping similar types of information together

Reductionist: the process of simplifying complex phenomena in order to explain them

Encoding

- *Encoding* begins when information from the environment is detected by your senses.
- The sensory memory holds onto information just long enough for you to decide whether it is important enough to keep. This is done very quickly and much of the information is lost.

Storage

- If you pay **attention** to this information it moves from sensory memory to the short-term memory store.
- This has a limited capacity and can hold roughly five to nine items or 7 + /– 2. This limited capacity is often known as **Miller's magic number 7**. We can increase this capacity by grouping similar bits of information together. This is known as **chunking**.
- Information can be held in STM for roughly 30 seconds. If you want to keep this information for longer you must rehearse it. This means repeating it in your head. The information will then move to LTM which has unlimited capacity and duration.

Retrieval

- Information can be retrieved from the LTM when required.
- Sometimes this retrieval requires a prompt to help jog your memory. These prompts are called cues.

Internal link

The case of Henry Molaison is the subject of one of the Key studies in Chapter 2 on biological psychology: "Concept One: Biological reasons for behaviour".

DP ready ATL Thinking skills

Revisiting Henry Molaison

In Chapter 2 on biological psychology you were introduced to Henry Molaison, known as patient HM. This case study has provided psychologists with a lot of information about the nature of human memory. It has also been used as a common source of evidence to support the claims made by the MSM.

How do findings from the research conducted on HM provide support for the claims made by the MSM?

The MSM is a very simplistic or **reductionist** model of memory, and has been criticized for omitting some key parts of the cognitive process. However, it is useful in helping us to explain this complicated process and has been supported by a lot of psychological research.

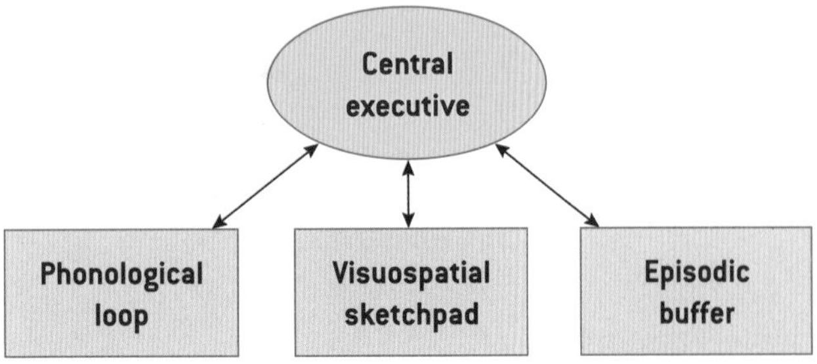

The working memory model is another memory model proposed by Baddeley and Hitch in 1974. This model concentrates only on short-term memory. It provides a much better explanation of how your short-term memory works, including the different modalities: the central executive, the phonological loop, the visuospatial sketchpad, and the episodic buffer. Each of these is a different section on your short-term memory and each has a specific role.

Psychology in real life

PRL

Extreme memory loss

Have you ever thought what life would like without memory? Probably not. We all tend to take memory for granted and losing it doesn't bear thinking about. We may anticipate some memory loss in old age, but typically we are expecting to rely on our memory for our entire lives.

Clive Wearing was struck down with a rare form of the Herpes virus. The virus attacked his brain and damaged his hippocampus, causing him to suffer from extreme memory loss. In fact, Clive cannot remember his past and he cannot create new memories. He lives only in the present.

This interesting documentary was made about Clive and how his amnesia affects his daily life.

Watch this

www.youtube.com/watch?v=k_P7Y0-wgos&t=625s

Search terms

"The man with the seven second memory (medical documentary)"

DP ready ATL **Thinking skills**

Build a supermodel of memory

Conduct some research on the MSM and on the working memory model. How did the working memory model improve on the MSM? Can you combine these two models and any others that you discover to create a new improved supermodel of memory? Try to provide a complete and comprehensive account of the process. (Tip: Two more models you may want to add are the levels of processing model and the long-term memory model.)

Start your research by watching this video.

Watch this

www.youtube.com/watch?v=bSycdlx-C48&t=129s

Search terms

"How we make memories Crash Course Psychology #13"

Thinking and decision-making—the dual process model

Look at the image opposite.

As you look at this image your mind is making sense of the information at lightning speed. Not only were you able to identify that the man has a brown shirt, you were also able to identify his emotion as angry. This was instinctive and automatic. You couldn't stop yourself doing it, even if you wanted to. You combined what you can see with your intuitive thinking. This is an example of what psychologist Daniel Kahneman calls fast thinking.

Concept One

Watch this

www.youtube.com/watch?v=UBVV8pch1dM

Search terms

"The science of thinking YouTube"

What does it mean?

Dual process model: Kahneman's model of thinking (see system 1 and system 2 thinking, below)

System 1 thinking: a fast, unconscious and automatic way of thinking

System 2 thinking: a slow, attentive and controlled way of thinking

Now try to solve this problem without using a calculator or paper and pen:

16×34

You are probably working through a series of steps taught to you in your mathematics class. This is quite difficult and requires concentration, unlike the intuitive task of reading emotions. The process is further impeded by not being able to write it down. This is an example of slow thinking. Taken together, thinking fast and thinking slow make up the **dual process model**.

Researchers refer to fast thinking as **system 1 thinking** and to slow thinking as **system 2 thinking**. System 1 is responsible for you being able to jump out of the way of an oncoming car. System 2 requires your attention. System 2 thinking is disrupted when you lose focus. You use system 2 thinking whenever you are required to complete a complicated task or form a reasoned argument. Table 3.1 gives a more detailed summary of system 1 and system 2 thinking.

System	Characteristics	Examples
System 1	automatic, fast, efficient and requires little energy or attention emotional prone to biases and systematic errors	stereotyping reading following familiar patterns
System 2	effortful, slow and requires attention and energy deliberate and rational less prone to biases and errors than system 1	solving mathematics problems interpreting difficult readings learning tasks

▲ Table 3.1 System 1 and system 2 thinking

Internal link

Localization of function in Chapter 2; Brain structures—getting to know your brain.

What does it mean?

Basal ganglia: a group of structures located deep within the brain responsible for motor control and memory

Amygdala: an area of the brain responsible for managing emotions.

Prefrontal cortex: the front part of the brain, responsible for decision-making and problem-solving

Research has discovered that the two systems are located in different parts of the brain. System 1 takes place in the older parts of the brain such as the **basal ganglia** and **amygdala**. The slower, more deliberative system 2 relies on the **prefrontal cortex**.

Representing your thinking using system 1 and system 2 has allowed psychologists greater understanding of your errors in judgment and choice. When you do something fast, you give up accuracy and attention and this causes errors. You will explore thinking errors later in this chapter in the section on biases in thinking and decision-making.

DP ready | ATL Communication skills

Paragraph outline

To what extent do cognitive models help to explain cognitive processes?

Use the information in this section to write a paragraph outlining the main argument that cognitive models support psychologists in explaining human behaviour and cognitive processes.

Your paragraph outline should answer the question above using two main ideas. You should take one of these ideas from each of the subsections above: "Schemas and schema theory", "The multi-store model of memory (MSM)" and "Thinking and decision-making—the dual process model". Write a topic sentence that answers the question in one statement and follow it with the two main ideas. Your paragraph should end with a linking statement that restates your answer to the question.

Extension

Strong arguments often predict the criticisms they will receive. See if you can predict the criticisms of your arguments. This can take the form of a statement before your conclusion that may begin: "Some may disagree with this statement because ...".

Conclusion: Concept One

Schema theory has given psychologists an understanding of how human beings come to represent their world. The multi-store model provides a simple explanation of how you encode, store and retrieve information. System 1 and system 2 thinking brings these processes together—system 1 thinking is automatic and utilizes your existing schemas in order to respond quickly, whereas system 2 requires that you access information from your long-term memory (LTM) to help you make a decision.

Concept Two: Humans are active processors of information

One of the earliest models used by cognitive psychologists is known as the computer analogy. This model claims that humans process information in much the same way as a computer does. It can therefore help you to understand how the mind processes information and influences your behaviour. In this analogy your brain is the computer hardware and the mind is the software. Fortunately, software can be updated.

Data enters a computer in the form of input and it is coded into a suitable form for storage. It is then processed, used and retrieved when needed (output).

Humans receive information in the form of sensory information. You are constantly receiving information from each of your senses and your mind has to transform this into a form that it can use, in this case, electrical impulses distributed throughout for brain. This information is then stored and retrieved when we need to perform a specific behaviour. The behaviour is your output.

However, humans are not computers. This model simplifies a complicated process but it allows us to consider how the information travels from one store to another. A model allows us to form hypotheses about cognitive behaviours and test them scientifically, even though we cannot *see* these cognitive behaviours.

Cognitive psychology continues to provide us with insight into human behaviour. The development of technology such as **fMRI** allow

What does it mean?

fMRI (functional magnetic resonance imaging): a process that measures brain activity by detecting changes in blood flow inside the brain

psychologists to monitor brain activity while engaging in a cognitive task. Fields such as behavioural economics explore economic decision-making and the cognitive biases we show when faced with unfamiliar situations. Most recently, cognitive psychologists are investigating the impact of digital technology on cognition.

DP ready ATL **Thinking skills**

Your mind as a computer

The computer analogy has proven useful to psychologists when trying to explain cognitive processes. It has, however, been criticized for being reductionist and for oversimplifying human thinking (Figure 3.3).

To what extent do you think the computer analogy is a suitable analogy for the human mind?

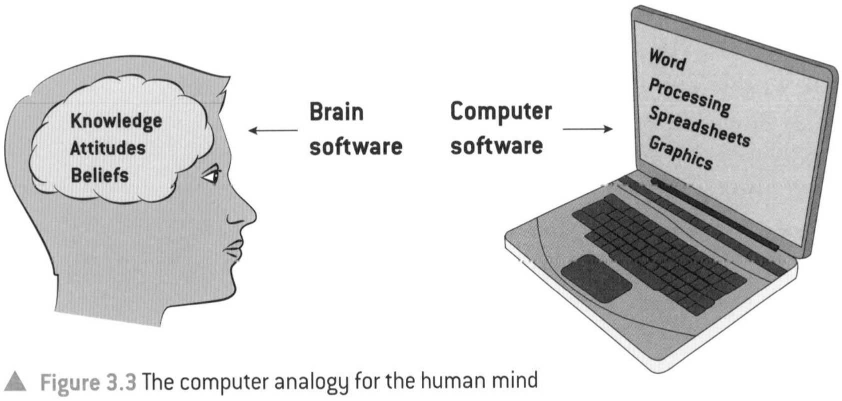

▲ Figure 3.3 The computer analogy for the human mind

Reconstructive memory

Think back to your first day in high school. What did you do? How did you feel? What lessons did you have that day? Who did you sit beside in your classes? Is the memory clear to you? As you read this you are actively processing your memories of that time and reconstructing information, sequencing it and developing a suitable account or story for your first day in high school. Are you 100% sure that your memory is accurate?

You are not perfect, and neither is your memory. The world is a busy place. You are constantly processing information and each bit is competing for your attention. Let's refer back to the MSM—you need to attend to a piece of information, store it and rehearse it before it will be moved into your LTM. Storing information in your LTM allows you to retrieve the information again when you need it.

Research has shown, however, that your memory retrieval is prone to error. In fact, you can distort memories and even create completely false memories based on information that you have received since witnessing the original event and having to recall the information. It is unlikely, therefore, that your memory of your first day at high school is 100% accurate. A lot has happened since then.

The chances are that you merged memories for different days together into a logical narrative that represents a typical school day. Many factors will influence your memory of events such as your emotions, attention, awareness, amount of sleep the night before and the occurrence of significant or unusual events. Your memory has in fact become distorted over time.

TOK link

Memory as a way of knowing

TOK considers memory a way of knowing. Memory is considered vital in all areas of knowledge (mathematics, human sciences, natural sciences, history, the arts, ethics and more). If your memory is not simply a recreation of the past, there are important implications for all areas of knowledge.

Take a moment to consider the following questions as you read through this section.

- Can we ever claim to know things that happened in the past?
- Is your memory a reliable source of information?
- Can beliefs or bias distort our memory of the past?

DP ready | ATL Thinking skills

Eyewitness testimony

Watch this video, which shows quick footage of an event. Once you have seen this footage, would you be comfortable giving eyewitness testimony to the police that could result in putting a person in jail?

Watch this

www.youtube.com/watch?v=RWO2UQ4MW7U

Search terms

"Brain games eyewitness inaccuracy"

Elizabeth Loftus is a cognitive psychologist who has spent her career studying human memory. More specifically, she studies **reconstructive memory**—the tendency for human beings to reconstruct or adapt their memories when they try to remember something.

The theory states that when you retrieve a memory, you are accessing both information from the past event itself and information after the fact—**post-event information**. The research suggests that memories are made up from things you remember from the past (the event as it originally happened) but also information that you automatically "fill in" to form the details you cannot remember. Interestingly, your mind fills in the blanks in your memory without you even knowing it—it is essentially guessing without your permission.

The key study below provided an example of this, when participants reported seeing broken glass but in fact there was none.

Helpful hint

Reconstructive memory can be thought of as a maths formula:

P + X = M

P is the actual past (the things that actually happened)

X is the bit you forgot but filled in with guesses (often using schema)

M is your memory

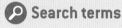

Figure 3.4 Elizabeth Loftus

Key Study: Loftus and Palmer (1974) (Experiment 2)

Memory recall

Aim: to study the effects of leading questions on memory recall.

Method stage 1: this was a controlled laboratory experiment. The procedure involved participants watching recordings of cars crashing and then completing a follow-up questionnaire. There were three groups of participants. Two of the groups were given a critical question in their questionnaire, and the question was slightly different for each of these groups.

- Group 1: "About how fast were the cars going when they smashed into each other?"
- Group 2: "About how fast were the cars going when they hit each other?"
- Group 3 received no critical question.

Method stage 2: in order to test the impact of delay and information received after the event. Loftus and Palmer asked participants to complete another questionnaire one week later. This questionnaire contained the critical question: "Did you see any broken glass?"

There was no broken glass in the films.

What does it mean?

Reconstructive memory: a theory that suggests memories can be influenced and altered due to a range of factors during recall including leading questions, emotion and perception

Post-event information: information received after an event

Results: participants who received the critical question asking "About how fast were the cars going when they smashed into each other?" were more likely to report seeing broken glass compared to participants in the other groups.

Conclusion: the word "smashed" invoked a higher intensity emotion that led participants to reconstruct the original memory when recalling it a week later. Participants believed they had seen broken glass when in fact there was none. Loftus and Palmer claim that the creation of this false memory was due to reconstructive memory.

Loftus and Palmer (1974) is just one of many experiments conducted on the reliability of memory. Loftus and her colleagues have been pivotal in creating an awareness in the general public of the reconstructive nature of memory. It is now accepted that your memory is not 100% reliable and you should be cautious when making important decisions based on the events that you have witnessed. Conversely, you should be forgiving of others when they make mistakes remembering something.

DP ready ATL **Thinking and research skills**

Reconstructive memory

Watch this

www.youtube.com/watch?v=PB20egI6wvI

Search terms

"How reliable is your memory? Elizabeth Loftus"

Conduct some of your own research into Loftus's research on reconstructive memory to answer the following questions.

- To what extent can we generalize the findings of Loftus's research to real-life settings?
- Can you think of any alternative explanations for her findings?

Perception—seeing is not perceiving

There is no sound and no light in your skull. Your brain floats in a dark, silent world between your ears. How then does it create the rich landscape of sounds, scents, tastes, sights and feelings that you experience as your world?

The answer in one word is **perception**. Note that perception is not the same as *sensation*. For example, when you see something, that means light has hit your retina which has sent a signal down your optic nerve. The signal eventually arrives at your visual cortex. Understanding what those electrical impulses mean requires you to interpret meaning from electrical signals in your occipital lobe. Interpreting sensory signals is what we call perception. In other words, your brain sees but your mind perceives.

Optical illusions are one way that your mind can be fooled by your senses.

What does it mean?

Perception: the process where humans make sense of the world around them using information gained via their senses

Cognitive misers: this refers to the tendency for people to solve problems and think in ways that use little time and energy

Heuristics: these are mental shortcuts or rules that support learning or problem-solving

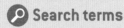

Optical illusions

It is difficult to tell exactly what you are looking at.

In Figure 3.5, are there three tongs or just two?

There are no curved lines in Figure 3.6.

The sides of the squares of the green-and-white checkerboard are horizontal and vertical.

In Figure 3.7 both lines are the same length but you perceive them not to be. The interesting thing is that even when you are told the truth of the illusion, you cannot help but misinterpret the image.

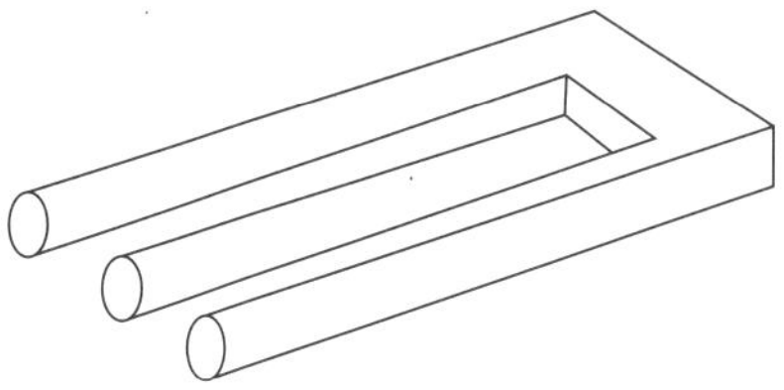

▲ Figure 3.5 The Blivet impossible object

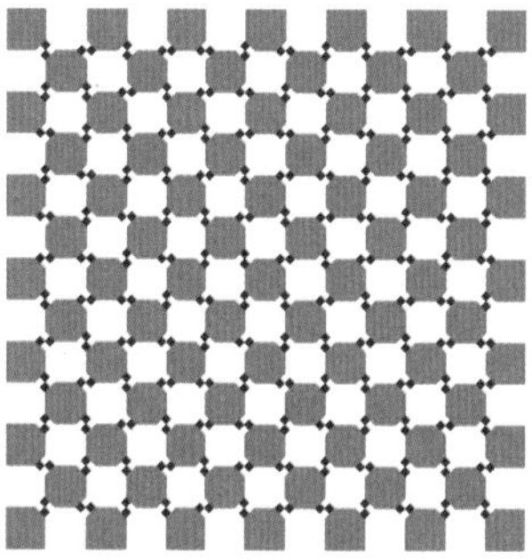

▲ Figure 3.6 Confusing checkerboard

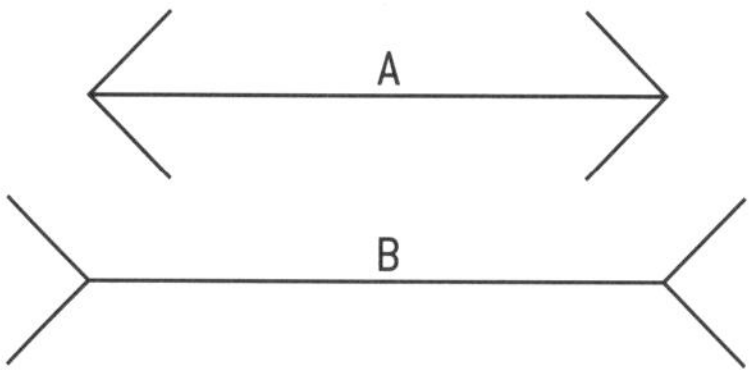

▲ Figure 3.7 The Müller-Lyer illusion

> **Activity**
>
> **There are thousands of perceptual illusions online. Search for "perceptual illusion" and you will find examples in both image and audio/video format. See if you can work out why you keep being fooled by these illusions.**

The interesting thing is that you do not only perceive with your senses. You have perceptions about causes of events and peoples' reasons for behaving a certain way. Your stereotypes and preconceptions are as automatic and difficult to change as your visual impression of the illusions above. It takes awareness and effort to overcome your misperceptions—and even when you are aware of them, they can still influence your thinking.

Knowing that you are prone to cognitive errors like the ones caused by these illusions is very important. If you know that you may make an error and you understand why, you will also understand that others are prone to the same mistakes. Similar to errors in remembering, this can make you more forgiving of your mistakes and mistakes made by others.

Biases in thinking and decision-making

You have biases in your thinking that result in consistent and predictable errors.

Human beings are often described as being **cognitive misers**. We need and want to make choices and find answers quickly so that we can carry on living our busy lives. People create mental shortcuts or strategies known as **heuristics** to help them with this, which can sometimes lead to cognitive biases. These errors are a form of system 1 thinking, often occurring automatically and at the subconscious level.

You are probably unaware that you engage in cognitive shortcuts every day in the form of habits, and that these habits have become part of your routine and help you to go about your life. For example, you will turn the light on when you wake up on a dark morning. This small action has become routine and you have come to depend on this behaviour. Becoming aware of some of your less useful habits and their triggers can help you to control your behaviour and allow you to lead an even more productive life.

> **TOK link**
>
> Are you a brain in a jar?
>
> This is a famous thought experiment designed to explore the limits placed on knowing due to our limited perception of the world.
>
> Imagine a brain in a jar filled with life-sustaining fluid. This brain is hooked up to a super computer that sends electrical signals to the brain, exactly like those that would normally be sent to the brain from the body of a living person. The question is that if the supercomputer were able to simulate reality perfectly, could the brain ever learn that it is only a brain in a jar?
>
> - Can you imagine a test that the brain could perform to determine its true reality? In other words, is it possible for the brain to learn it is in a jar and not experiencing the world as it perceives to be?
> - Do you think virtual reality technology could ever achieve total sensory immersion to the extent that a person could not tell reality from virtual reality?
> - You can find many different responses to this thought experiment online. Explore some responses to see what others think.

Not all biases however are easy to change. Like habits, you engage in them daily. Being aware of a perceptual illusion does not prevent you from seeing it, and unfortunately being aware of your biases does not prevent you from acting on them.

Table 3.2 outlines four of the most common cognitive biases.

Bias and thinking error	Explanation	Example
Confirmation bias	This cognitive bias involves seeking out information that reinforces or confirms your existing beliefs and behaviours.	A common example may be looking through the news headlines and seeking out information that confirms your beliefs about a certain person or social group, while ignoring any information to the contrary.
Self-serving bias	This is a common cognitive bias that involves attributing your successes to your own personal characteristics and your failures to other people or external factors. This error serves to preserve your own self-esteem.	If you score poorly on a mathematics test and you are unhappy about it, you may attribute the result to the poor delivery of the material by your teacher, or even accuse the teacher of not covering the test's content. If you score well, you may attribute this to your hard work, natural ability and thorough preparation.
Illusory correlation	This is a cognitive bias that involves making a connection or relationship between two unrelated things.	This bias is often associated with athletes and superstition. A football player may have put his right boot on first before a match and then gone on to score a goal. The player now correlates good sporting performance with putting on his boots in that order.
Implicit bias	This is a different kind of bias. It is an unconscious attribution of specific characteristics or a stereotype to a certain social group. This bias can affect your behaviours and beliefs towards that group.	You may have a subconscious expectation or belief about a certain race. For example, you may associate Asian students with being good at mathematics as you have heard about this in the media. As a result, when you struggle in school, you may be more inclined to ask an Asian student for help in mathematics and maybe even generalize this to all subjects.

▲ Table 3.2 Common cognitive biases

There are a number of factors that influence whether you will engage in a cognitive bias or an error in decision-making. These factors influence the amount of information you have to make sense of the information and/or your emotions. They include the following.

- The less detail you have about a person or situation the more the bias will influence you.
- Your focus of attention—you see your own behaviour differently from that of others. This is due to the difference in the amount of information you have available.
- Other influencing factors are:
  - the consistency and predictability of the situation
  - the presence of pre-existing schemas
  - your level of self-esteem.

DP ready | ATL Thinking skills

Habits and cognitive biases

Watch this

www.youtube.com/watch?v=0MbsGBlpP30
www.youtube.com/watch?v=wEwGBlr_Rlw

Search terms

"Power of habit Charles Duhigg at TEDxTeachersCollege" and "12 cognitive biases explained"

Watch these two videos and reflect on your daily habits. Create a list of good and bad habits using the following criteria: good habits help you achieve your daily goals and bad habits do not. Which of the bad habits can you erase from your daily schedule?

Reflect on your past week. How many cognitive biases do you think you are guilty of this week? Are they predictable? Can you avoid committing them in the future? What steps will you take to limit the cognitive errors you make?

You engage in system 1 thinking as behaviours become habitual or automatic. This can often lead to error as you pay less attention to what you are doing and rely heavily on previous experience. These errors often serve to preserve your self-esteem and maintain your existing view of the world. They can also cause you to develop unwanted prejudice and stereotypes.

Let's continue with our discussion on habit formation. Imagine that a student you know is trying to develop a healthier lifestyle, and has created a list of behaviours to avoid in order to get a toned body with well-defined muscle. One of these behaviours is their weekend trip to a local bakery to buy their favourite sugary cake. They know this food is bad for them, but they like it. It tastes good.

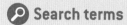

One day after a hard training session they start to get hunger pangs as they are walking past the local shops. In the distance they see the bakery and they know they can stop their hunger in an instant. They are conflicted, though, as they have just spent the last 90 minutes in the gym burning calories. Holding these two conflicting ideas and beliefs is a form of mental stress. It is stress we can do without.

Festinger coined the term "**cognitive dissonance**", which refers to an inconsistency between:

- two or more conflicting ideas or beliefs
- what you do and what you believe or say (acting out of your integrity or oneness)
- your existing belief and any new information.

What does it mean?

Cognitive dissonance: the feeling of mental discomfort experienced when someone holds two inconsistent ideas, values or beliefs

Concept Two

Watch this

www.youtube.com/watch?v=9Y17YaZRRvY&t=22s

Search terms

"Cognitive dissonance theory crash course YouTube"

Key Study: Festinger and Carlsmith (1959)

KS

Cognitive dissonance

Aim: to investigate whether participants engaged in a boring task would experience cognitive dissonance when asked to lie and say it was fun.

Method: a laboratory experiment was conducted on university students. Participants had to complete a series of very boring activities. These included turning wooden pegs for over an hour. Participants were then asked to tell someone waiting outside in another room that the activities were fun. Some were paid $1 to do this, and some were paid $20. Regardless of the payment, almost all people agreed to lie and say the experiment was fun.

Results: when evaluating the experiment, participants who were paid only $1 rated the experiment as more fun than those paid $20.

Conclusion: being paid $20 meant that participants had a suitable reason for engaging in the task, even if it was boring. This is why they were less likely to claim it was fun. Being paid $1 was not enough to lie, especially to themselves. Participants paid $1 had to modify their existing cognitions and reduce the dissonance by holding a new belief that the task was in fact fun.

When you experience cognitive dissonance, the feeling is so unpleasant that you seek to reduce it. In order to reduce the dissonance you must change one of the two cognitions. That is, you must convince yourself that you do not want a cake as you no longer enjoy it. Alternatively, you can eat the cake and convince yourself that this will not ruin your long-term health.

Activity

Use your knowledge of thinking errors and cognitive biases to create a health promotion campaign that is designed to stop teenagers from vaping. You must create cognitive dissonance in the teenagers if the campaign is to succeed.

DP ready | ATL **Communication skills**

Paragraph outline

Why it is possible for humans to make mistakes in their thinking and decision-making?

Use the information in this section to write a paragraph outlining the main argument that human beings are active processors of information.

Your outline should answer the question above using three main ideas. You should take one of these ideas from each of the subsections above: "Reconstructive memory", "Perception—seeing is not perceiving" and "Biases in thinking and decision-making". Write a topic sentence that answers the question in one statement and follow it with the three main ideas. Your paragraph should end with a linking statement that restates your answer to the question.

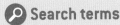

Extension

Strong arguments often predict the criticisms they will receive. See if you can predict the criticisms of your arguments. This can take the form of a statement before your conclusion that may begin: "Some may disagree with this statement because …".

Conclusion: Concept Two

You are an active processor of information. Your mind is constantly making sense of new information so that you can respond appropriately. Processing of this information can be automatic and unconscious, using system 1 thinking. When you engage in system 1 thinking you are prone to cognitive error. These errors include reconstructive memory, illusory correlations and cognitive dissonance.

Concept Three: Biological and sociocultural factors

Influence of biological and sociocultural factors on cognitive processes

Flashbulb memories

So far in this chapter you have learned about how psychologists use models to explain your higher mental process such as memory and thinking. These active processes are located in the mind; they are the result of conscious and unconscious thought and can influence your behaviour. However, while psychologists often study cognitive behaviours in isolation, there are often many factors at play. Your biology and your cognition often interact with sociocultural factors to produce a resulting behaviour, so it also makes sense to study this relationship.

An easy example to illustrate the **bidirectional** relationship between biological, cognitive and social factors relates to the feeling of being stressed or scared. Imagine that you have witnessed an emotional event that had a personal significance to you. This may have been a scary incident, a sad one or a happy one. Research has shown that emotion can cause a physical response (like a stress response to a fearful event), which can then influence your memory of that event. In the world of cognitive psychology, the relationship between emotion and memory has been the subject of much debate. **Flashbulb memories** are a unique form of memories of emotional and personally significant events. Flashbulb memories are vivid and highly detailed and often contain information such as where you were when you witnessed a significant or emotional event.

What does it mean?

Bidirectional: something can function in two ways or in two directions

Flashbulb memory: a highly detailed and vivid memory of a moment or situation in which you witnessed or heard about a surprising or emotional event

Overt rehearsal: the practice of deliberately recalling a memory (and often sharing it with another person)

Covert rehearsal: the practice of quietly recalling a memory as a thought or reflection

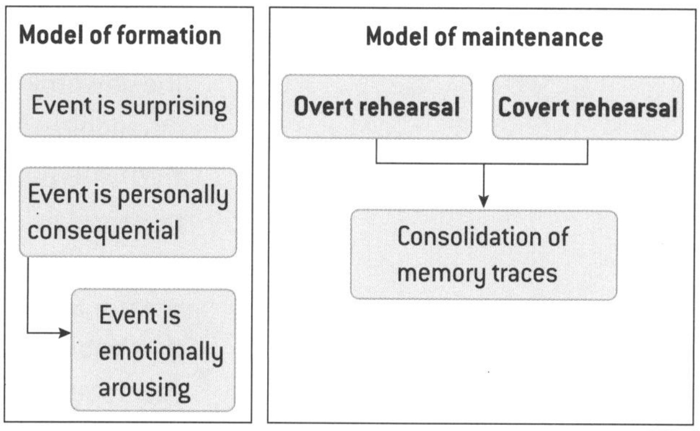

Figure 3.8 Flashbulb memory model

Brown and Kulik (1977) suggest that flashbulb memories are the result of a unique combination of brain regions (neural mechanism) triggered during the witnessing of an emotional event that is often surprising, and of personal significance to you. They claim that flashbulb memories are like a photograph imprinted in your memories. It is the emotional arousal that allows these vivid and long-lasting memories to be formed. You will often tell other people about such events and so the process of rehearsal plays a role in keeping the memory alive.

DP ready ATL **Thinking skills**

Your flashbulb memories

Create a list of significant memories. Think back to your early childhood and work forward to present day. How many of these do you think would count as flashbulb memories? Try to identify:

- where you were at the time of the event
- who told you or how you witnessed the event
- how it made you feel.

Consider these questions.

- Is the memory more detailed?
- How often do you think about this memory?
- How often have you told other people about this event?
- What information might be missing from your memory of the event?

Internal link

Refer to Chapter 2: "Brain structures—getting to know your brain" for a description on the role of the amygdala.

KS

Key Study: Sharot *et al* (2007)

Flashbulb memories

Aim: to determine whether there is a unique neural mechanism responsible for flashbulb memories.

Method: a laboratory experiment used participants who had witnessed the 9/11 terrorist attacks in New York. There were two groups of participants. One group was situated in downtown Manhattan during the attacks. This means these participants were close to the events of the day. The other group was situated midtown a few miles away from the attack itself. Participants were placed into an fMRI scanner and given words designed to trigger memories of the 9/11 attacks or a control event of their own summer in 2001.

Results: the left amygdala was activated when recalling the events of 9/11 but not when retrieving summer memories. Participants in the downtown group displayed an increased activation of the left amygdala when compared to the midtown group when recalling events of 9/11.

Conclusion: the left amygdala appears to play a role in the creation of flashbulb memories. Participants closer to the attack displayed greater activation of the left amygdala. The researchers concluded that there was a neural mechanism responsible for flashbulb memories. Results display that the more personally significant the event to the witness, the greater the activation of the amygdala.

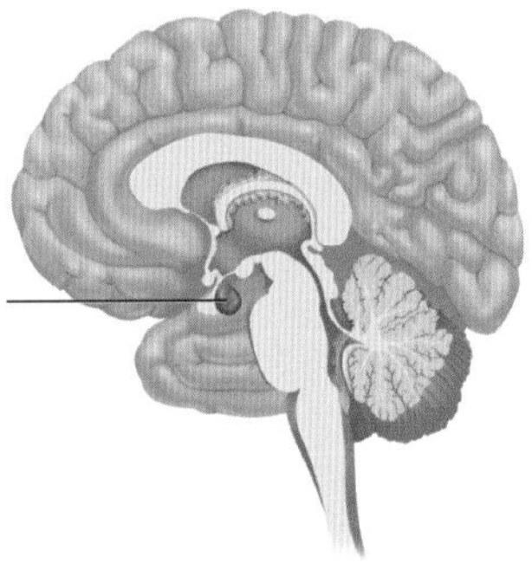

▲ Figure 3.9 The location of the amygdala in the human brain

Flashbulb memories continue to interest psychologists but we still have much to learn. While there seems to be some evidence of a unique biological mechanism responsible for flashbulb memories, there has been much scepticism. Some psychologists claim that it is the continued rehearsal and retelling of these emotional events that creates a vivid and long-lasting memory. This repeated exposure to the event increases your confidence in your memory and the subsequent retelling of the story. Here is an example of the bidirectional relationship of biology and cognition. Are flashbulb memories biologically unique and so essentially different (more vivid and reliable) than other memories, or is it the cognitive practice of rehearsal that makes these so vivid and reliable—or is it both?

The appeal of the flashbulb memory phenomena lies in the fact that all human beings have at least one event that could classify as a flashbulb memory. Let's hope the field of cognitive psychology continues to contribute to your understanding in this area.

Social and cultural schemas

You have just read about how your biology interacts with your cognition. Now you will learn about how sociocultural factors can influence your cognition—specifically, the influence of cultural factors on your memory.

Your environment is less predictable than your own behaviour. As a result, you develop schemas in the form of scripts to help you navigate the world and make it seem more predictable. **Scripts** are generalizations or stories that you have in your long-term memory that guide your actions in new or novel situations. A classic example of a script is that of a restaurant script cited by Schank and Abelson (1977). Here is an example of a restaurant script.

- Enter the restaurant, look for free table or signal waiting staff.
- Ask for the menu.
- Order some food.
- Eat the food.
- Signal the waiter and ask for the bill.
- The waiter brings the bill.
- Pay the bill and leave the restaurant.

Holding the restaurant script allows you to enter any restaurant and be able to act in a socially appropriate manner. If you enter a Sushi restaurant in Japan and this is a new cultural experience for you, your long-term memory will call on your restaurant script and use the information to help you. You may make a few mistakes along the way as you will be using your existing cultural knowledge to help guide you through the new experience. Making sense of this new information by updating your restaurant script has been named **effort after meaning** by Frederick Bartlett (1932). It is not surprising that you may be unsure of how to act in a novel situation; after all, you are relying on past experience to tell you how to act.

What does it mean?

Scripts: social schemas based on experience that provides a chronological order for events

Effort after meaning: the process of trying to make sense of unfamiliar information by changing it into something that is already known and understood

Watch this

www.youtube.com/watch?v=3kE1M-MfXxc

Search terms

"Your most vivid memories aren't as accurate as you think SciShow Psych"

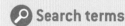

TOK link

Knowing the thoughts of others

TOK asks you to challenge your own assumptions about what you know and what it is possible to know.

Consider the ideas you are reading about here; this chapter is about the mind not the brain. The mind is an intangible thing—you cannot hold, weigh or measure it. At the same time, the nature of the mind means different things to different people.

Reflect for a moment on the nature of the mind versus that of the brain.

- To what extent can we truly know the mind of another person?
- Do you think the nature of the mind makes it impossible to know it scientifically?

If you answered "no" to the second question, you must read and examine the ideas in this chapter carefully and critically.

A classic example of the influence of cultural factors on your ability to recall memories can be seen in Bartlett's research. Participants in his "War of the Ghosts" study (1932) were asked to reproduce and retell a native American folk tale. The structure and content was unfamiliar to them and, as a result, they replaced unfamiliar cultural references with more culturally familiar information. The participants omitted or adapted information that they had no existing schema for, and replaced it with information from their existing schemas.

KS

Key Study: Bartlett (1932)

The War of the Ghosts

Aim: to determine the influence of existing schemas on recall of a culturally unfamiliar story—in this case, a native American folk tale.

Method: Bartlett asked university students to retell a native American folk tale. The story was unfamiliar to the students, both in its structure and its content. It contained references to the native-American culture such as seal hunting and war parties. Bartlett varied the times in which students would recount the story. Sometimes they would have to retell the story only 15 minutes after hearing it, but some participants had to recall the story months later.

Results: although the students could remember the overall theme or gist of the story, they altered the story to make it shorter and more coherent to their own culture. This was achieved by making it fit the typical Western structure of a fairy tale, for example beginning with "Once upon a time". Seal hunting was often replaced with fishing, and the final sentence was transformed into something more familiar such as "lived happily ever after".

Conclusion: cultural and social factors influence cognition (memory). The story was reconstructed by the students who applied their own social schemas so that the new, unfamiliar information fit with their existing Western experiences. This caused them to adapt it and make several errors when retelling the tale.

You can read the original story at http://penta.ufrgs.br/edu/telelab/2/war-of-t.htm

Conclusion: Concept Three

Your memory is a complex process and is influenced by many factors. If you have ever lived through a highly emotional event, it is likely that you have created a flashbulb memory. This is a highly vivid memory of the time and place where you received this information, which is caused by a unique neural mechanism. These memories are often considered to be more accurate than normal memories, but the increased accuracy may in fact be attributed to increased confidence in recalling the information due to frequent rehearsal of the memory. Culture can also influence your memory as you are more likely to remember information that fits with your previous experiences. In fact you are even likely to change unfamiliar information so that it fits with your existing knowledge. This can cause you to make errors when recalling information.

Concept Four: Digital technology is reshaping your brain

The internet is changing how you think

Life is getting busier. Many people use technology such as their smartphones, tablets and laptops to help them meet the demands of everyday life. Their phone is essential to their productivity. Social media has, however, been criticized for being a distraction, even addictive. Scrolling, texting and liking of Instagram posts has been accused of ruining your social relationships, your sleep and your memory. In this section you will explore the recent research in this area.

What does it mean?

Phubbing: the process of ignoring or snubbing people while looking at your phone

Psychology in real life

PRL

What is phubbing?

In 2016 the word "**phubbing**" was added to the *Oxford English Dictionary*. This recently introduced word is the combination of "phone" and "snubbing". Phubbing is the practice of ignoring a companion or companions in favour of your smartphone or other digital device. If you are someone who scrolls through Instagram while talking to a friend or relative, you are guilty of phubbing. The habit is becoming more prevalent in society.

Recent research has demonstrated that while digital technology has many positive effects on your behaviour, it is also having negative effects on your cognition and social relationships. We will explore this research throughout this section.

DP ready | ATL Thinking skills

Smartphone use

Watch this

www.youtube.com/watch?v=XCIDH1ZuY20
www.youtube.com/watch?v=R0xYCy2eft8

Search terms

"What is phubbing? Hannah Jewell" and "Simon Sinek Q & A: How do cell phones impact our relationships"

Watch the video on phubbing and consider the implications. Make a list of the positive and negative effects on behaviour caused by digital technology.

Now listen to Simon Sinek's argument on the overuse of smartphones. To what extent do you agree with his view? Create a counter-argument refuting his claims and attempt to find supporting research to back up your argument.

Selective attention

How constant distraction is killing your memory

A smartphone is a multipurpose device. It is a phone, first and foremost—but so much more: a camera, an alarm clock and a search engine to name just a few functions. As a result, many people will use their phone to help them wake up in the morning and then start to check their social media updates before getting out of bed. The effects of this continued connectivity is of great interest to researchers and is sparking much debate.

On one side of the debate there are those that feel technology is having a positive influence on your behaviour and productivity. Technology allows us to get more things done in one day than ever before.

On the other side, there are those who are concerned that technology is impacting not only your abilities but your brain functioning. These researchers believe that easy access to information is resulting in a different way of thinking—shallow thinking. It is also believed that constant connectivity limits your attention span and memory recall as you are constantly distracted by incoming information. This area of research is in its infancy, but the results are fascinating and very important.

Think back to a typical day in school. Where is your smartphone during your lessons? Do you keep it on the desk in front of you or do you place it out of sight in your bag. Recent research by Thornton *et al* (2014) has suggested that the mere presence of a smartphone on a student's desk can impair cognitive performance. Even just hearing the sound of an incoming notification or a phone vibrating was enough to interfere with the student's attention and reduce performance on attention-based performance tasks. It therefore seems that learning to manage your smartphone use may be more important that you think. Rosen *et al* (2011) studied the impact of cognitive distraction in an educational setting. The researchers concluded that receiving and replying to text messages in class caused participants to remember less information.

What does it mean?

Independent measures experiment: an experiment that involves using different groups of participants for each condition

Key Study: Rosen *et al* (2011)

KS

Cognitive distraction

Aim: to investigate the impact of attention hijacks (text messages) on memory recall in a classroom setting.

Method: the researchers conducted an **independent measures experiment**. Participants were students who were asked to watch a video of a 30-minute lecture and complete a test on the content afterwards. Some of the participants received text messages from the researchers during this period, and they were instructed to reply to these as quickly as possible. These participants received up to eight messages during the lecture. Other participants received no messages.

Results: academic performance (the test result) was directly correlated to the number of text messages received. Those participants who received the most text messages performed the worst on the test. The faster the participants responded to the text, the worse their performance.

Conclusion: texting in class influences memory recall. Delaying responding to text messages can reduce negative performance. The more general conclusion is that people find switching between cognitive tasks difficult.

As smartphone use is becoming part of everyday life, it has the potential to impact your cognitive abilities in many areas. One thing is certain: with more and more people owning smartphones it is becoming increasingly important to learn how to leverage technology for good and minimize any potential harm.

How your smartphone might ruin your relationships

Smartphone use has not only be linked to a decline in cognitive functioning, it has also been accused of ruining the quality of social relationships. Incessant phone use can cause you to divide your attention between your device and your friends and family. It is obvious that if you are looking at your phone, then you are not looking at the person you are supposed to be talking to. Not only is this behaviour often considered rude, it has been argued that phubbing can negatively impact the emotions of the other person.

DP ready ATL **Self-management skills**

Negative effects of smartphone use

Are you a phubber? Is your smartphone use causing your friends to feel lonely? Read this article:

www.theatlantic.com/magazine/archive/2017/09/has-the-smartphone-destroyed-a-generation/534198/

Search terms

"Atlantic Magazine smartphone destroyed a generation 2017"

To what extent do you agree with the claims that your smartphone use can negatively influence the emotions of others?

DP ready ATL **Research skills**

Positive effects of technology

It can be very easy to claim that technology is a negative influence on our lives—but there are two sides to every debate. Conduct some of your own research online to find the other side of the argument: "that use of digital technology has positive effects". It may help you to focus on some aspects of:

- virtual reality
- online gaming.

Concept Four

What does it mean?

Technoference: interference or distraction that is caused by technology

Social desirability bias: a bias that involves research participants acting in a way that will be viewed favourably by other people

McDaniel and Coyne (2016) conducted research to investigate the impact of what they call **technoference**—disruptions caused by technology—on married life. As the research was conducted through online questionnaires, it could be argued that it is likely that the results do not really reflect the participants' true emotions. Not being in the presence of a researcher may exclude any form of **social desirability bias** and encourage participants to give honest answers. The researchers concluded that when smartphones were allowed to impact social interactions it often signalled that the phone user was distracted or prioritizing someone or something else. Left unchecked, this could lead to unhappiness in the relationship or even feelings of depression. It is, however, interesting to question the cause and effect relationship here. Is the increased smartphone use hurting the relationship or is a poor relationship driving people to use their smartphone more often for social interactions?

Key Study: McDaniel and Coyne (2016)

KS

Technoreference

Aim: to investigate the effects of smartphone use on marital satisfaction.

Method: 143 married couples completed an online questionnaire.

Results: the majority of participants believed that technology was having a negative impact on their relationship, interrupting meal times, conversations and leisure time. The participants who reported higher levels of technoference were more likely to report depressive symptoms, as well as lower marital and life satisfaction.

Conclusion: by allowing technology to interfere with your social interaction such as conversations with friends, romantic time with partners and meal time with families, you are sending implicit messages about what you value most. This will lead to conflict and negative outcomes in social relationships.

DP ready ATL **Communication skills**

Paragraph outline

Explain positive and negative effects of digital technology on cognitive processes.

Use the information in this section to write a paragraph outlining the main argument that digital technology is influencing human cognition with both positive and negative effects.

Your paragraph outline should answer the question above using two main ideas. For your main ideas review your research on the positive effects of the internet; then refer to the subsections above on the negative effects of technology: "Selective attention" and "Psychology in real life" (on phubbing). Write a topic sentence that answers the question in one statement and follow that with your main ideas. Your paragraph should end with a linking statement that restates your answer to the question.

Extension

Strong arguments often predict the criticisms they will receive. See if you can predict the criticisms of your arguments. This can take the form of a statement before your conclusion that may begin: "Some may disagree with this statement because ...".

Conclusion: Concept Four

Digital technology can be good and bad. Recent research has focused on the negative impacts of the internet and smartphones on your ability to remember information and focus on tasks. While the research has produced varying results (relating to online gaming, for example), there is reason to believe that you should limit the amount of time you allow yourself to be connected to your device.

Chapter conclusion

Cognitive psychology is an important field despite being a difficult area to study. If mental processes guide human behaviour, then researchers must persevere in their quest for knowledge about the mind. Biological psychology has furthered our understanding of the brain and behaviour but this is only part of the story.

When you use your brain to think and remember, you are actively processing information in your mind. Psychologists represent these processes in cognitive models such as the multi-store model of memory (MSM). Models are simple and easy to understand, so they help psychologists to study complex behaviour.

Your cognitive processes are not perfect—you make predictable mistakes regularly. As more people begin to make a habit of using digital technologies, they will influence the types of mistakes they make. The use of digital technology is a learned behaviour and, as with any learned behaviour, there are implications for your brain and your mind. Research has shown that digital technology can influence your attention, memory and social relationships.

Reflection Activities

1. "I used to think .... Now I think ...."

   Reflect on your understanding of the concepts of dual process theory and thinking errors covered in this chapter. For each of the two concepts, complete the following phrases: "I used to think .... Now I think ...". This activity is designed to make you reflect on what you have learned and to practise putting your new understanding into writing.

2. Reflect and share ideas about schemas.

   Once you believe you have a clear understanding of the concept of a schema, join two other students and share your understanding. It is important that one person finishes sharing before others speak: each person is given a few minutes to share followed by a 30-second pause before another person speaks. When everyone has spoken, make connections between everyone's understandings—to do this, ask for clarification or identify the most important ideas shared.

Adapted from: Ritchhart, Church and Morrison (2011)

Links to IB psychology topics

Cognitive approach to understanding behaviour

Cognitive processes
- Models of memory
- Schema thinking
- Thinking and decision-making

Reliability of cognitive processes
- Reconstructive memory
- Biases in thinking and decision-making

Emotion and cognition
- Cognition and emotion
- The influence of emotion on cognitive processes

HL extension: Cognitive processing in the digital world

Exam-style questions

1. **Evaluate** one theory of one cognitive process.
2. **To what extent** is memory reconstructed?
3. **Evaluate** schema theory.
4. **To what extent** does emotion influence one cognitive process?
5. **Discuss** the influence of modern digital technology on one or more cognitive process or processes.

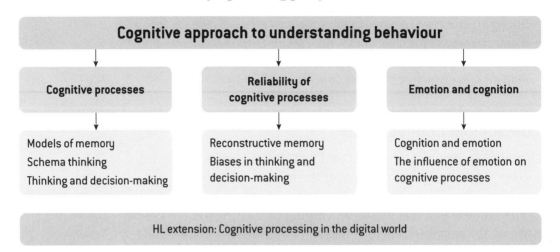

Big ideas

Concept One: Mental representations guide behaviour

- You have mental maps which allow you to fill in the blanks and make decisions when you have limited knowledge about a situation.

- You have an automatic, fast, and intuitive thinking system for easy decisions and a more effortful, slow and deliberate system for difficult tasks.

- The multi-store model of memory (MSM) states that memory can be broken down into sensory, short-term and long-term memory.

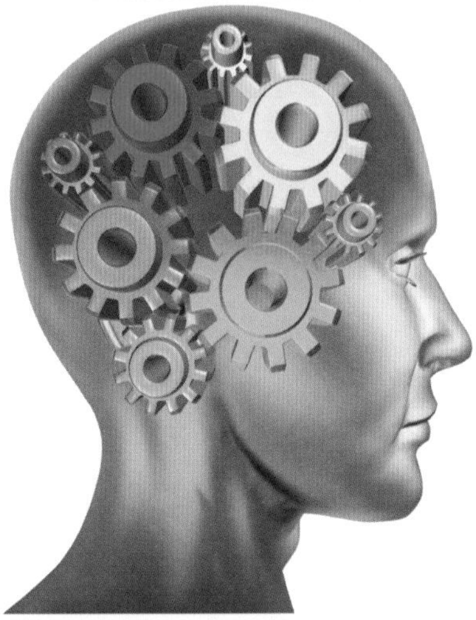

Concept Two: Humans are active processors of information

- The idea behind reconstructive memory is that when you retrieve a memory you are accessing both information from the event itself and information after the fact.

- You interpret the signals coming from your senses and make sense of them by accessing previous experiences and schemas.

- Biases in thinking and decision-making occur because you make consistent and predictable errors.

Concept Three: Biological and sociocultural factors

- Flashbulb memories are emotional memories that use a unique brain region and seem more vivid. You have more confidence in these memories than normal memories but in fact flashbulb memories are no more accurate.

- Social and cultural schemas are formed because your cultural background determines your expectations in unfamiliar situations and may affect how you reconstruct your memories of an event.

Concept Four: Digital technology is reshaping your brain

The internet is changing how you think.

- Selective attention refers to the way in which constant distraction is killing your memory.

- One of the negative influences of digital technology is that your smartphone might be ruining your relationships.

4 Concepts in sociocultural psychology

In this chapter, you will learn the key concepts in social and cultural psychology.

→ Concept One: Social influence—your thoughts, behaviours and attitudes are influenced by others
- where do you belong in your society
  - social identity theory
- social cognitive theory
- stereotyping

→ Concept Two: Culture and cultural norms—how your culture affects your behaviour
- culture and cultural norms
- enculturation and socialization
- dimensions of culture

→ Concept Three: Globalization and the interaction of cultures
- globalization and you
- acculturation

In this chapter you will also learn about ideas and theories related to:

→ how you learn from other people socially
→ why you stereotype others and why they stereotype you
→ how your cultural background shapes you
→ how psychologists compare cultures

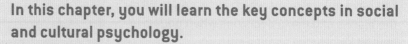

Introduction

Chapter 2 on biological psychology introduced the debate over nature or nurture. In that chapter we learned that your biology can determine who you are and how you behave—in short, you are the result of your biology. In this chapter we will add an important layer to that learning. You are not only the result of your biology, you are also the result of your environment and experiences. In addition, your cognition (your thinking) is partly determined by both of these. In this chapter you will learn about the influence that your friends, your family and your culture have on your thoughts, behaviours and beliefs.

Internal link

The debate over nature and nurture is introduced in Chapter 2 on biological psychology: "Concept One: Biological reasons for behaviour. The nature side of the debate is explored throughout Chapter 2.

This chapter explains three concepts explored by sociocultural psychology.

- Other people influence your thoughts and your behaviours, even when you are alone.
- Different cultures have different norms and these influence your behaviour.
- Globalization and the increasing interconnectedness of cultures is changing behaviours.

People are **tribal**—that is, they are social animals. People did not evolve to survive alone like a tiger or a leopard. Instead they evolved to live in complex social groups like whales and chimpanzees. The need to be part of a larger group is rooted in human psychology and has a very strong effect on your behaviour.

Concept One: Social influence

How are your thoughts, behaviours and attitudes influenced by others?

"Social influence" is a term psychologists use to describe how the desire to be a part of a group influences human behaviour. This section introduces three key ideas:

- social identity theory
- social cognitive theory
- stereotypes.

Where do you belong in your society?

Social identity theory and how you become your social self

Social identity theory (along with social categorization theory) tries to explain how and why groups form. It also tries to predict how two or more groups will behave when they interact with each other. The basic idea is that people identify groups as either being **ingroups** (groups they belong to) or **outgroups** (groups they do not belong to).

One main assumption of this theory is that people want to have strong **self-esteem**. You can improve your self-esteem through personal successes (such as scoring well on an exam or winning a race) or by being a member of a successful in-group (supporting a champion football team, for example). You may also want to be part of an outgroup you are currently not a member of because you see that group as successful. Different social groups define "success" differently but each of them strive to achieve success in their own way.

For example, if you are a boy football and tennis player, your in-groups would include: boys, football players and tennis players. You would also be part of a smaller, more exclusive group of boys who play both tennis and football. Your social groups can overlap with each other and so you have many social identities at the same time that influence your behaviour.

What does it mean?

Tribe: a social group often made up of related individuals characterized by strong social, economic and/or religious bonds

Ingroup: a group you are in

Outgroup: a group you are not in

Self-esteem: the opinion you have of yourself and your abilities

Minimal groups paradigm: a method used in sociocultural psychology to investigate the minimum conditions required for discrimination to occur between groups

Social identity can be broken down into different processes: social categorization, social identity and social comparison.

Thinking process	Explanation	Example
Social categorization	This is the process of grouping people together and categorizing them as a member of this group or that group. It can be used to explain racism, stereotyping and ethnocentrism, for example. When you do this, you tend to both exaggerate the differences between groups and also the similarities of people within groups.	Categories can be defined by any characteristic and so categories often overlap. Examples of categories are: conservative, liberal, gay, straight, male, female, caring, cruel, Muslim, Christian, Buddhist. "We" (the ingroup) are all similar to each other. "They" (the outgroup) are all the same. "They" are different from "us".
Social identity	This is the process of identifying as a member of an ingroup. You change your behaviour to act in the same way that you understand other members of that group behave. You can change your identity at any time but people are emotionally connected to their ingroups and do not change easily.	If you identify yourself as a liberal person, you will behave as a "normal" liberal would behave and you would hold similar beliefs and attitudes as "normal" liberals. You will also become emotionally connected to the group and your self-esteem will be partly determined by membership of that group.
Social comparison	People compare their ingroup with outgroups. In order to build and maintain self-esteem, members of an ingroup will see themselves favourably compared with outgroups. This can result in a bias or favouritism for the ingroup that can influence how you see outgroups and their members.	Ingroup favouritism may lead to discrimination and prejudice against outgroups. Unfortunately, we tend to perceive outgroup members more negatively in order to maintain or build our own self-esteem.

▲ **Table 4.1** Stages of social identity theory

Key Study: Tajfel *et al* (1971)

KS

Social identity

Aim: to investigate if boys placed randomly into groups would develop ingroup favouritism and outgroup bias.

Method: several similar experiments were carried out. The researchers used something called the **minimal groups paradigm** where participants are separated into groups based on unimportant or "minimal" differences. In the first experiment, 64 teenage boys from the UK were invited to a laboratory where they were asked to estimate the number of dots on a computer screen. They were then told that they were either in the "overestimator group" or the "underestimator group". The boys were then told to give points (which would later be turned into cash) to other boys from both groups. The researchers wanted to see how the boys would distribute the points.

Results: the boys showed a strong tendency to award more points to members of their ingroup than to members of the outgroup. This shows ingroup favouritism and outgroup discrimination.

Conclusion: the boys showed a preference for their own group members and discriminated against the boys in the outgroup, even though the reason for their group membership was meaningless. This study shows that we favour people in our own social groups even when the reasons for the social groups' existence are minimal. It also shows that we tend to discriminate against members of social groups to which we do not belong.

Activity

Many people use social media to edit photos of themselves carefully and to share only specifically chosen stories to try to show others how cool or how successful they are. They do this in an attempt to improve their own self-esteem and their reputation among their friends.

Ask yourself: why might this be dangerous? If you are comparing yourself to others' carefully edited photos and lives, what effect do you think this might have on your own self-esteem?

What does it mean?

Norms: ways of behaving that are considered normal in a society

Socialization: the process of learning to behave in a way that is acceptable to a particular group of people

Social cognitive theory: a theory that proposes you learn by observing the actions and consequences of others

Social cognitive theory and how people learn from others

Why do people love fairy tales and superheroes?

In the previous section we learned that people make decisions about what social groups they wish to be a part of and then adjust their behaviours, attitudes and beliefs to fit with the group's **norms** (normal behaviour). This section will explain the process of how people learn to behave in a way that is acceptable within a group. This is called **socialization** and it is how culture is learned.

DP ready | ATL Thinking skills

Are people born with a natural hatred for other races?

Nelson Mandela knew a lot about racism. He was jailed in South Africa for 27 years for fighting against the racism of the apartheid policies the South African government enforced from 1948 into the 1990s.

Mandela eventually rose to lead the South African state. He believed that hate is not something we are born with, but that hate of others due to skin colour, background or religion is something we learn. And if we learn to hate, we can be taught to love. He died in 2013.

- Do you think that Mandela's beliefs, stated above, are correct?
- Who is responsible for racism?
- Do you think we can solve the problem of racism? If so, how?

▲ **Figure 4.1** Nelson Mandela

Psychologists have long been interested in the process of learning. Early theories of learning were called behaviourist models because they focused on observable behaviour, not on thoughts and feelings. More recently, psychologists have become more interested in the cognitive or the "thinking and feeling" of learning. A theory of social learning was proposed by psychologist Albert Bandura. It is called the **social cognitive theory**.

Psychologists have developed a theory to explain how humans learn from each other socially. The theory is often called social learning theory but this name does not fit the theory well because it ignores the main point Bandura was making—that people are thoughtful learners not simple mimics. We do not simply imitate behaviours we see in our social group. We observe, we think, we act. It is the thinking that makes this a social cognitive theory.

This idea is explained further in Chapter 3 on cognitive psychology and is related to the concept that, "mental processes can be studied scientifically".

Internal link

This topic links to Chapter 3 on cognitive psychology: "Concept Two: Humans are active processors of information".

Behaviourist learning theories

Behaviourist theories describe changes in the behaviour of a learner as the result of things that happen in the environment of the learner.

Social cognitive learning theories

In addition to observed behaviour, social cognitive theories involve behaviours that cannot be observed, such as thoughts, beliefs, memories, motivations, and biases—in other words, cognitions.

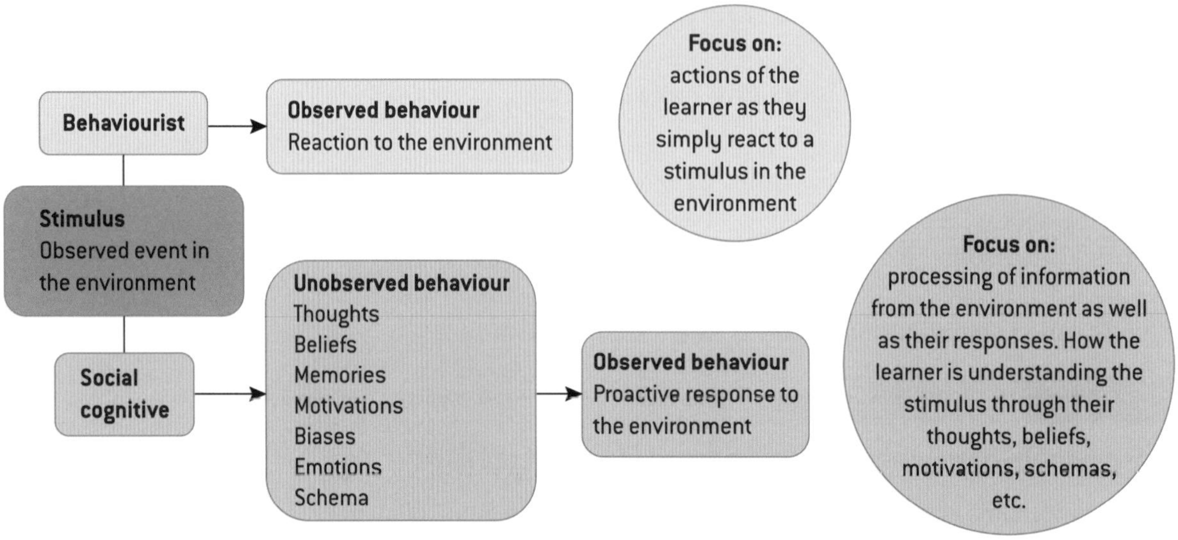

▲ **Figure 4.2** Behaviourist learning theories versus social cognitive learning theories

Out of his series of experiments, Bandura was able to make three main claims related to ideas about how people learn from each other.

- Vicarious learning—we can learn from others. We do not have to perform a behaviour ourselves to test the outcomes, we can learn from observing others doing it.
- Vicarious reinforcement—when we see others being rewarded for a behaviour, we are likely to also perform that behaviour or hold that belief or attitude.
- Similarity—we learn best from those similar to ourselves.

Key Study: Bandura, Ross and Ross (1961, 1963, 1965)

KS

The Bobo doll experiments

Aims

1. To investigate whether behaviours (aggression) can be learned through observation.
2. To investigate if similarity to a model played a role in learning.
3. To investigate the role of vicarious reinforcement and punishment on social learning.

Procedure: in a series of laboratory experiments, researchers arranged for children to experience one of three conditions. Children in condition 1 witnessed a model acting very aggressively and beating a Bobo doll. Children in condition 2 witnessed a non-aggressive model playing with the doll and surrounding toys. Condition 3 was the control— children in this group were not given a model to observe.

Children were then given time to play with the toys in another room and their aggression levels were measured.

Results

1. Children exposed to the aggressive model behaved more aggressively than children in the other conditions.
2. Children tended to imitate the behaviour of the model of their own gender (boys imitated the behaviour of male models and girls imitated female models).
3. Children were more likely to imitate the behaviour of a model who was rewarded, while not imitating behaviour that was punished.

Conclusion: children can learn socially from models, they do not need to perform the activity themselves in order to learn. This is why learning is sometimes called observational and vicarious learning.

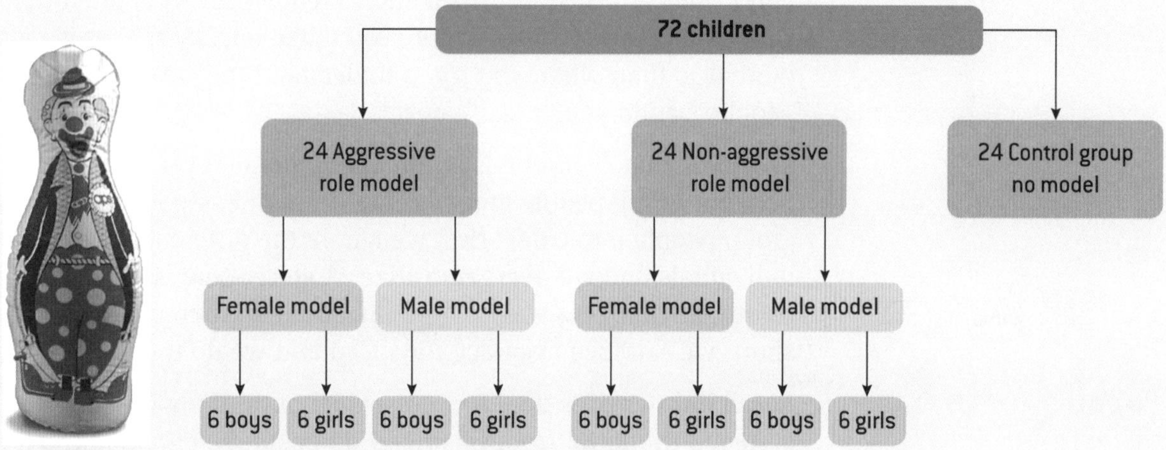

Figure 4.3 Method for Bandura, Ross and Ross (1961) Bobo doll experiment

DP ready | ATL **Research skills**

Mirror neurons

Research the theory of **mirror neurons**. Mirror neurons are unique neurons in the brain that fire both when you perform an action and when you see the same action performed by another person. In this way these neurons "mirror" the behaviour of another person. There is a theory that these neurons are responsible for empathy between people—in other words, this is how we can feel others' suffering.

Do you think mirror neurons play a biological role in social learning?

The theory of mirror neurons is still very controversial. Why do you think this is so?

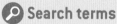

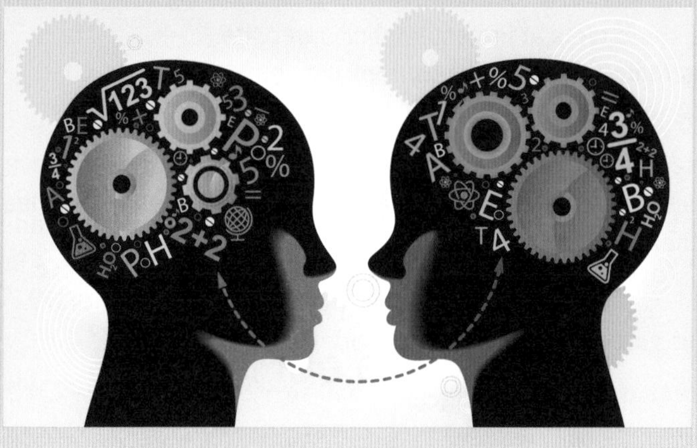

Watch this

www.youtube.com/watch?v=128Ts5r9NRE&t=4s

Search terms

"bobo beatdown: Crash Course Psychology #12"

What does it mean?

Mirror neurons: neurons that fire when someone acts and when they observe the same action performed by another person

What does it mean?

Cognitive misers: a theory that proposes people try to save their mental-processing resources by finding ways to save time and effort in understanding their world

Overgeneralize: when you apply what you learned in one situation to other situations where it may not be applicable

Stereotype: a commonly held and generally unchanging and oversimplified idea of a particular type of person or group

It is great to learn from your mistakes but even better to learn from the mistakes of others. Bandura's studies showed us that we learn much of our social behaviour from the people in life that we admire and respect (models). Good role models are very important for small children. This is why fairy tales have morals to their stories, and why parents have to be so thoughtful and careful around young people. Children are always watching and listening to others and are constantly learning behaviours, attitudes and beliefs.

Why do you use stereotypes?

As it turns out, people are all lazy thinkers or **cognitive misers**. We all take shortcuts in our thinking in order to save time and make quicker decisions in a complicated world. As is often the case when you try to save time, you make mistakes. This is never more true than when you try to understand the crazy variety of people around you.

We know that everyone is an unique individual yet we cannot help but group people together into types or categories. When we group people into categories, we ignore the differences between individuals and we **overgeneralize**. A **stereotype** is a generalized, mostly unchanging way of thinking about a group of people. In short, we sacrifice accuracy for speed and we do it automatically.

Internal link

Dual process thinking is covered in Chapter 3 on cognitive psychology: "Concept One: Mental representations guide behaviour".

Recall Kahneman's dual process model of thinking (system 1 and system 2 thinking) from Chapter 3 on cognitive psychology. Here is a quick reminder.

- System 1 thinking is automatic, fast, efficient, and requires little energy or attention.
- System 2 thinking is slow and requires effort, attention and energy.

Some of your thinking is deliberate—that is, it takes effort and all of your attention. This includes thinking such as completing a mathematics problem or learning a new skill. Some thinking is automatic and effortless, such as reading or using schemata.

Stereotyping is closely related to schema theory and system 1 and 2 thinking. Stereotyping is an example of system 1 thinking—it is an effortless, thoughtless connection between a group of people and some specific characteristic.

DP ready ATL **Thinking and self-management skills**

Discover your secret biases

Take some tests at Project Implicit's website:
https://implicit.harvard.edu/implicit/
(or search for "Harvard project implicit").

These tests will uncover some of the generalizations you have already accepted. Be honest with yourself when taking the tests—and bear in mind that you may not agree with the results.

Project Implicit®

DP ready ATL **Self-management skills**

Stereotyping

Managing your state of mind is important. This includes being aware of which system you are relying on for making decisions and judgments. Think of a time in the past month when you made a mistake in stereotyping someone.

- What mistake did you make, and how might your judgment have been different had you used system 2 thinking?

How are stereotypes formed?

As seen above, stereotypes are the result of our automatic thinking process. This does not explain the content of our stereotypes. Close your eyes and think of a "typical" French man. If you do not have much personal experience with this type of person you may have formed a picture in your mind like the one in Figure 4.4.

▲ **Figure 4.4** Stereotypical image of a French man

Despite never having seen a French man ever wearing this outfit, you might have had a similar image in your mind. That image is the result of gatekeepers, incorrect assumptions (illusory correlations), a grain of truth, and confirmation bias.

Table 4.2 shows how stereotypes originate.

Aspect	Role in stereotype formation	Example
Gatekeeper	A gatekeeper is a person in our society who controls what kind of information is shared. The mass media can play an important role in how stereotypes begin or continue.	• If you have no personal experience with a particular group of people, you may rely on what you have seen on television or the internet for your information. Unfortunately, these representations are often fiction because they do not reflect reality. For example, television shows such as "Homeland" and the news media often portray Muslims negatively and inaccurately.
Illusory correlations	Also called false assumptions, these correlations are formed when you believe two things or events are related when they are not in reality. These correlations are often created and reinforced in the mass media.	• "All Asian students are good at mathematics." • "Muslims are dangerous terrorists." • "Athletes are poor students."
Grain of truth	This refers to a situation when a single experience with one or only a few people causes a believed conclusion to be falsely generalized to a group of people. This means that many stereotypes are based (however loosely) on reality.	• Perhaps you sat next to an Asian student in a mathematics class who was very gifted (but you probably also sat near some who weren't). • There are some Muslim terrorists but there are more non-Muslim terrorists. Television programmes and movies often overrepresent terrorists as Muslim; news stories often emphasize Muslim terrorist acts.
Confirmation bias	People pay more attention to evidence that supports their beliefs (however rare) and ignores evidence against them (however convincing). This means that once you have made an overgeneralization, confirmation bias protects and maintains it.	• You simply did not notice the Asian students who struggled in mathematics. • You remember the news stories about Muslim terrorists but not those of non-Muslim terrorists.

▲ **Table 4.2** Formation of stereotypes

DP ready | ATL Thinking skills

Are stereotypes necessary?

Do you think it would be possible to live your life without using or forming any stereotypes? How would this affect you?

Stereotype threat

How stereotypes affect your behaviour

Unfortunately, stereotypes can affect the performance of a stereotyped person. For example, there is a commonly held assumption that girls are not as good at mathematics as boys. According to believers of this myth, this is why engineering departments in many universities have far more male students than females. The important thing to note here is that simply being the target of a stereotype can negatively affect your behaviour or performance of a task.

What does it mean?

Stereotype threat: when people feel they will conform to a stereotype

Stereotype threat is the anxiety and stress that people feel when they are asked to do something that may reinforce a negative stereotype. For example, girls taking a mathematics test did more poorly on the test when they were told beforehand that "girls are bad at maths". Other girls taking the same test did better on the same test when they were told that studies actually showed that girls are better at mathematics than boys. (Spencer, Steele, and Quinn, 1999)

DP ready | ATL Communication skills

Paragraph outline

How do other people influence our thoughts and behaviours?

Use the information in this section to write a paragraph outlining the main argument that your behaviour and thinking can be influenced by those around you.

Your paragraph outline should answer the question above using three main ideas. You should take one of these ideas from each of the subsections above: "Where do you belong in your society—how you become your social self", "Social cognitive theory and how people learn from others" and "Why do you use stereotypes?". Write a topic sentence that answers the question in one statement and follow it with the three main ideas. Your paragraph should end with a linking statement that restates your answer to the question.

Extension

Strong arguments often predict the criticisms they will receive. See if you can predict the criticisms of your arguments. This can take the form of a statement before your conclusion that may begin: "Some may disagree with this statement because …".

Conclusion: Concept One

This section has looked at social influence—specifically, how your social identity, social cognitive learning, and stereotypes can affect how you behave and how you think. There are many other influences such as conformity to normal behaviour and responding to direct requests from other people (compliance).

Reflection Activity

Sentence—phrase—word—share

1. Identify a sentence that you thought was key to understanding the concept of social influence.
2. Identify a phrase that caused you to question the truth of a claim.
3. Identify a single word that you thought was powerful or meaningful.

In small groups identify common themes that emerge from your understanding.

Adapted from: Ritchhart, Church and Morrison (2011)

Concept Two: Culture and cultural norms

How your culture affects your behaviour

Imagine yourself as a member of a different **culture**. You are still you, same body, same brain, same you. What would be different? Would you still be you? You may think, "yes, I would just be a Japanese me, or a Kenyan me." Exactly what that answer means is a very interesting topic; it reaches down to your most basic beliefs about who you are.

What does it mean?

Culture: the customs, art, social institutions and achievements of a particular group of people

DP ready | **Thinking skills**

Does your culture define who you are?

If you were raised in a different culture, do you think you would be a different person? How would you be different?

Culture and cultural norms

Culture is difficult to describe but we will define it here as the customs and beliefs, art, way of life and social organization of a particular group. Humans have a basic need to belong to a group of similar people with common beliefs and ideas. This is probably because, thousands of years ago, humans lived in small groups who needed to cooperate in order to survive in challenging and dangerous environments.

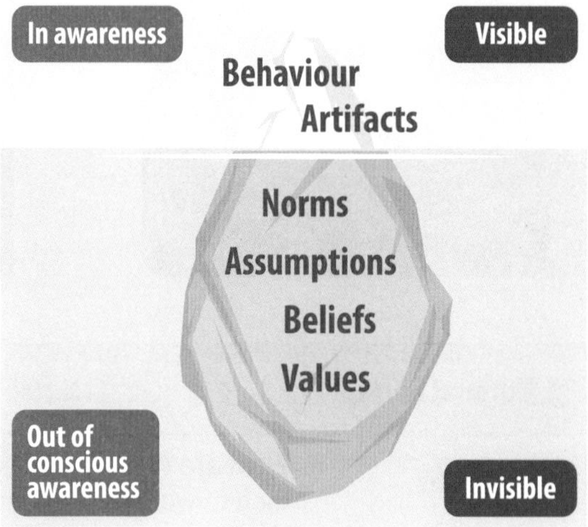

▲ **Figure 4.5** The iceberg model: surface and deep culture

Cultures are different from each other because different groups of early people were facing different challenges from their environments and therefore adopted environmentally specific customs, art, ways of life and social organizations in order to help them survive. For example, a group of early humans living in an environment where food and water were easy to find, such as the early African savanna or North American plains, would live in large, multi-family groups and have time for rich, artful cultures. These cultures were able to live in peace with neighbours and actively trade and intermarry with other tribes because they would not be in competition for food or resources.

TOK link

Everyone knows a fish lives in water except the fish.

Culture is one of the central ideas in TOK. It often seems easy to identify cultural habits of others, but it can be very difficult to identify specific ways that your culture affects your own behaviour. Consider these questions.

- In what ways does your culture determine how and what you think?
- Does your culture (or the language you speak) determine your knowledge?
- Are there ideas on which all cultures can agree? Try to list some ideas.

In contrast, early humans living in very difficult conditions, such as an arctic or desert region, would be forced into living in smaller groups of more closely-related members who spend much of their time in search of food and resources to survive. They may adopt an aggressive outlook to strangers who would be in competition for food and resources. It is easy to see how these two conditions could result in very different beliefs, art, ways of life, and so on.

DP ready ATL **Thinking and research skills**

Animal and human cultures

Internal link

The use of animals to study human behaviour is covered in Chapter 2 on biological psychology: "Concept Three: Animal research".

In Chapter 2 on biological psychology we learned that animal models can be used to study human behaviour. Do you think this remains true when studying cultures?

Many psychologists have used studies of animal societies to research human behaviour. One example is Robert Sapolsky, who studies baboon troops in Africa. Conduct some research on his work and use this to help you answer the question above.

Each culture has a unique set of norms. These cultural norms can be defined as expectations and rules for behaviour shared by a group of people. In essence, a cultural norm is simply a behaviour, belief or attitude that is "normal" among a group of people.

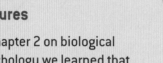

Cultural norm	Example
Gender roles	What are normal roles for men and women? Example: in which cultures is it normal for men to work while women stay home and look after children?
Marriage	Who decides who you will marry? Can you choose your own husband or wife?
Authority/power	How readily do people accept differences in power and authority? Is equality or authority valued?
Group versus Individual	Do members believe the needs of the group or the needs of the individual are more important?

▲ **Table 4.3** Examples of cultural norms

Cultural norms are important when studying how culture affects your behaviour because it is these "normal" behaviours, attitudes and beliefs that will influence the decisions you make when you think about the questions in table 4.3. Common norms will bind a group together but disagreement can cause tension and conflict within a group.

What does it mean?

Enculturation: the process of learning and conforming to the norms of a particular group of people

Enculturation and socialization

How you learn to behave

People are not born as a member of a culture, they have to become part of that culture as they grow older and learn from other members. This learning process is called **enculturation** or socialization. These two concepts are tightly related to each other. Enculturation is the process of learning and acquiring the characteristics and behaviours of a particular group of people. Once you have learned these characteristics and behave in the same way, you have been enculturated.

For example, enculturation may teach that different people have different roles in society while socialization teaches how boys and girls should behave differently in society, how people of different social status should behave or how younger people should treat older people. In Korean culture for example, respect for people older than yourself is very important. A younger person growing up in Korea is socialized to bow to older people but this is definitely not true in other cultures, such as in Germany or Brazil. A Korean person socialized in Germany may not be taught to bow to others as this is not a norm of German culture.

Concept Two

DP ready ATL **Thinking and research skills**

Socialization in different cultures

In 1962 an American soldier stationed in South Korea named James Dresnok was in trouble; he had lied to his superiors and forged documents. Instead of facing his punishment, he fled to North Korea. Once there he began a new life playing the American villain in North Korean government war movies and teaching English. He married and had two boys: Ted and James Junior. His boys were socialized into North Korean culture, they speak Korean perfectly and speak English with a North Korean accent. They have never left North Korea, that is the only culture they know. As a result, they think, believe and behave like normal North Koreans.

Watch this

www.youtube.com/watch?v=yd2dCk3N8cE&t=3585s

Search terms

"YouTube BBC4 North Korea Crossing the Line"

The question is: are these young men North Korean or American?

Take some time to think about your answer. Think about your own situation; how would you define your culture? Were you raised in your "home" country? Can you be socialized into two (or more) different cultures? In other words, can you be North Korean and American or does that make you a North Korean American who is different from other North Koreans and different from other Americans?

Watch the video to find out more.

Dimensions of culture

How to compare apples with oranges

What does it mean?

Etic approach: a way to study cultures as an outsider, used in cross-cultural studies

Cultural dimensions: measures of a culture that describe the effects of a society's culture on the values of its members

One of the problems with cultures is that they are all different. This is great for an amazing variety of music, food and ideas and it results in a rich and beautiful world but it is not very convenient for social psychologists. When not entertained by a Bollywood movie, enjoying a delicious Chinese meal, or listening to the latest music from California, social psychologists can be frustrated by diversity between cultures. Social psychologists often take an **etic approach** to studying cultures. This means that they study a culture (behaviours, beliefs and attitudes) from the outside. This approach allows psychologists to compare behaviour across cultures. Here is the problem: imagine trying to compare the length of two things without the help of a system of measurement. How do you compare length without the metre, for example, or the speed of an object without metres per second? The metric system allows scientists of different cultures the ability to share a common language in the study of physical objects.

Social psychologists needed a common measurement for cultures; luckily for them, a man named Geert Hofstede had an idea. Hofstede completed a huge study of over 70 cultures (more than 117,000 people) and found that all cultures shared certain trends or **cultural dimensions**. He describes these dimensions as the general preferences for one situation over another. (Hofstede, 2011)

For example, all cultures can be put on a spectrum between being accepting of inequality to not accepting of inequality, or very concerned about the needs of society versus very concerned about the needs of the individual. Hofstede realized that you could use these dimensions to compare differences between cultures. He delivered psychology its metre stick—or rather several of them. The table below shows one of Hofstede's cultural dimensions.

Collectivism (weak score)	All cultures exist on a spectrum between these two extremes.	Individualism (strong score)
Characteristics of the culture		Characteristics of the culture
• There are tight ties between members of strong ingroups. • The sense of "we" is stronger than the sense of "I" or the self. • "My group's needs are more important than my own". • Members are: cooperative, interdependent and relational.		• There are loose ties between individuals; all people are expected to look after themselves. • The sense of "I" or the self is very strong. • "I am most concerned about myself and my rights as an individual". • Members are: independent, autonomous, unique and self-sufficient.

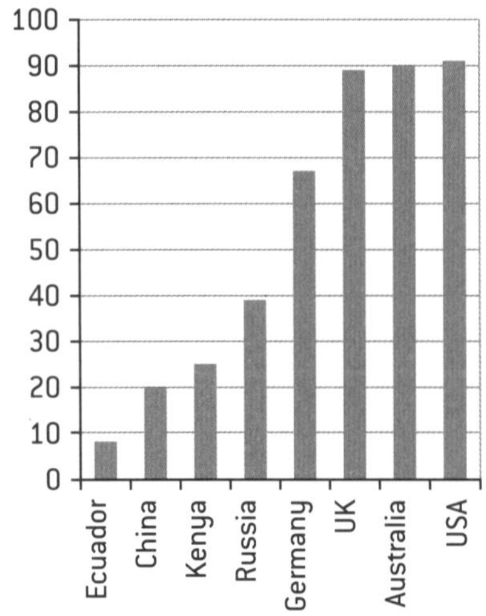

▲ **Figure 4.6** Individualism scores for various countries (low scores indicate a preference for community over individuality)

KS

Key Study: Berry and Katz (1967)

Effect of Hofstede's scores for individualism and collectivism on cultural norms

Aim: to investigate if a culture's score on Hofstede's individualism versus collectivism dimension would affect people's conformity to cultural norms.

Method: the researchers used samples from Eskimo (Inuit) people in Canada's Arctic region, who scored high on the individualistic dimension, and samples from Tenme people in Sierra Leone who scored low on the individualistic dimension. The researchers presented each group independently with a conformity test called the Asch Paradigm. This involves identifying which of three lines is the same length as a fourth target line. The participants were then given a "hint" which identified an incorrect line which they were told "most" others had chosen. The idea was that if the participant accepted the "hint" then the person was simply conforming to the group's (make believe) behaviour.

Results: the researchers found that the collectivist Tenme people were much more likely to accept the incorrect line as the correct one, simply because they were told that others had chosen that line. As one Tenme participant stated, "when Tenme people choose a thing, we must all agree with the decision ...".

Conclusion: members of collectivistic cultures will conform more to the group or cultural norm than will members of individualistic cultures.

The Power Distance Index (PDI)

The Power Distance Index (PDI)		
Low PDI (weak score)	All cultures exist on a spectrum between these two extremes.	**High PDI (strong score)**
Characteristics of the culture		Characteristics of the culture
• There is a relatively flat social structure. • "Everyone is equal to each other; no-one is naturally more powerful." • "People in authority should be challenged when this is needed."		• There are strict social structures. • "I think equality is OK. Some people in society deserve more power and influence than others." • "People in authority should be obeyed."

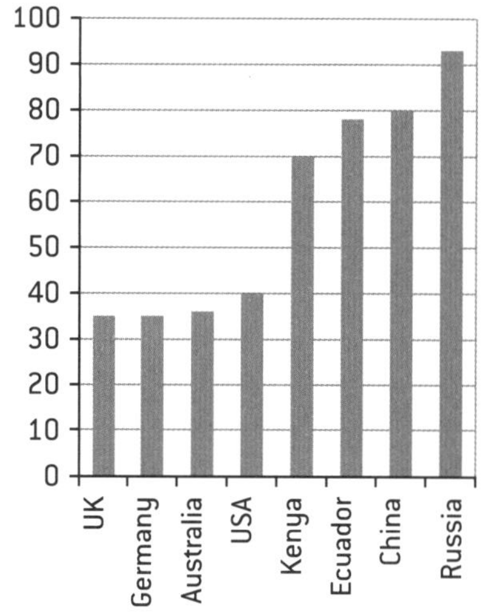

▲ **Figure 4.7** The Power Distance Index (PDI); a high score indicates strict hierarchy and respect for authority

Concept Two

Hofstede also included other dimensions of behaviour, each giving researchers another way to compare cultures with each other.

These dimensions are:

- masculinity vs femininity
- uncertainty avoidance
- indulgence vs restraint.
- long-term vs short-term orientation

DP ready | ATL Research skills

Comparing national cultures

Find out where your national culture fits compared to others, using the website www.hofstede-insights.com/country-comparison/

1. Research Hofstede's additional dimensions of behaviours (listed above) to find out what they claim to measure.
2. Research your culture using www.hofstede-insights.com/country-comparison/. Find out where your culture fits compared with the others that Hofstede has measured. Do you think Hofstede's measurement is accurate? What makes you say that?

DP ready | ATL Thinking skills

Categorizing diverse nations

Is Hofstede being unfair by treating diverse nations as one group? For example, he describes India as having a PDI score of 77—but India has over 22 official languages and a population of over 1 billion.

Imagine, for a moment, that you are Geert Hofstede.

- How would you defend using your dimensions to describe such a diverse group of people within a single culture?
- How might this kind of labelling lead to stereotyping?

DP ready | ATL Communication skills

Paragraph outline

How does culture influence thoughts, beliefs and behaviours?

Write a paragraph outlining the main argument that your behaviour and thinking can be influenced by those around you.

Your outline should answer the question above using three main ideas. You should take one of these ideas from each of the subsections above: "Culture and cultural norms", "Enculturation and socialization", and "Dimensions of culture". Write a topic sentence that answers the question in one statement and follow it with the three main ideas. Your paragraph should end with a linking statement that restates your answer to the question.

Extension

Strong arguments often predict the criticisms they will receive. See if you can predict the criticisms of your arguments. This can take the form of a statement before your conclusion that may begin: "Some may disagree with this statement because …".

Conclusion: Concept Two

This section has pointed out that culture is learned and that it has an important influence on your behaviours, beliefs and attitudes. What you consider normal is determined by the groups you are a part of and these in turn shape who you are. This is why it is so important to surround yourself with positive, caring people who look out for each other. If behaviours that benefit other people (prosocial behaviours) are normal, then the whole community wins; if the opposite is true (antisocial behaviour is normal), then everyone suffers.

Concept Three: Globalization and the interaction of cultures

Globalization and you

You have probably heard the term "global village". This is a way of thinking about the world as a result of an increase in telecommunications and interconnectedness with people all over the world. The world is getting smaller. Everywhere is now your own neighbourhood. The entire world is getting more familiar and more available. You can see an African safari in Kenya, you can experience Diwali in India, or even see what it was like to walk on the moon—all from your smartphone. This idea was originally shared by Marshall McLuhan in the 1960s when digital media was just starting to change the way people around the world think about themselves and others. He would be shocked to look around the world today to see just how far this digital connectedness has taken us. Even in the 1960s McLuhan believed that modern communication technology was moving people from individual experiences and identities to group experiences and identities. In short, he believed that the world was "retribalizing". In a way this is a return to how we lived on the African Savanna thousands of years ago. However, there is one main difference: our tribes today are no longer limited by space or time.

The argument goes as follows. Reading a book is an individual experience—you do not share it—you read alone and experience the world from one point of view only. As we move from that solitary experience of the world to one where all experiences are shared, we are no longer interested in self-identity. Instead we are more concerned about how the group is defined, what the group knows and feels and about acting with the group not without it. In addition, when you read a book, one thing happens at a time; when you are online, there are many things happening simultaneously and without geographical limits.

The global village is responsible for changing how people think, how we behave and how we connect to groups.

What does it mean?

Globalization: the increasing interdependence of world economies, cultures and people as a result of increasing trade, travel and digital technology

Watch this

The Global Village was first conceived of in the 1960s. This amazing interview from the early days of TV is way ahead of its time. Everything they are saying about television and radio is more true today with the internet.

Video link: www.youtube.com/watch?v=HeDnPP6ntic

Search terms

"marshall mcluhan cbc global village"

Do you think Marshall Mcluhan's "Global Village" is relevant today? Take a few minutes to make links from this interview to today's world.

DP ready | ATL Self-management skills

Online social interaction

Recall the section on digital technology from the Chapter 3 on cognitive psychology. Social media exactly matches what McLuhan was referring to when he wrote about returning to tribalism. We are increasingly defined by an online identity and this is changing how people experience social relationships. Reflect on the following.

> **Internal link**
>
> Use of social media is discussed further in Chapter 3 on cognitive psychology: "Concept Four: Digital technology is reshaping your brain".

- How many times a day do you check your social media accounts?
- How would stopping all of your social media activity affect you socially? How would it affect you emotionally?
- What percentage of your social interaction is now done online?

Imagine, for one moment, life without access to social media.

- How would life be easier?
- How would it be more difficult?

> **TOK link**
>
> **Globalization** is a powerful force. One effect of globalization is the increasing homogenization of the world's cultures—that means cultures are becoming more similar to each other as globalization continues. Some people think this is a problem because it means that the world is losing valuable indigenous knowledge and culture. Globalization overpowers the local traditions, diets, identities and knowledge of indigenous peoples. Consider these questions.
>
> - Can indigenous knowledge and cultures be protected from extinction?
> - What is the value in preserving these cultures and ideas?
> - Can aspects of indigenous knowledge be considered science? What makes you say that?

We no longer need a passport, or a lot of time or money to meet people from other cultures, religions or countries. This fact, combined with boundless human curiosity and our desire to meet other people has drastically increased intercultural communication and exchanges. This, in turn, has resulted in a process called acculturation.

Acculturation

> **What does it mean?**
>
> **Acculturation**: a bidirectional process of social, cultural and cognitive changes that occur as the result of the meeting between two or more cultures

Acculturation is the process of changes that happens both psychologically and culturally when two or more cultures interact. Globalization is increasing the number and frequency of interactions between the world's cultures so we are seeing more and more acculturation. When cultures come into contact with each other, changes always happen in both cultures but the influences may not be equal. The process of acculturation is like mixing paint. If you mix two different coloured paints together, you get a third colour that reflects the relative amounts of the other colours that were added. Even mixing a tiny drop of paint in a larger bucket of paint will change the colour of the entire mixture. The more colours that are mixed, the more complex is the resulting colour. The same is true for cultures. When two cultures interact, no matter how dominant one is over the other, they always affect each other. The relationship is bidirectional, meaning changes will occur in both cultures, not just the minority one.

DP ready | ATL Thinking and self-management skills

What is most important to you?

Reflect on your culture for a moment and imagine that your culture is a minority one with a dominant culture influencing it. What values and beliefs do you consider to be so important to your identity that you would be unwilling to lose them?

- Make a list of the values that you consider to be so important to you that you would never consider losing them as part of your identity and culture.
- Why are these things so important to you?

Generally speaking, you have four strategies when responding to acculturation. These strategies exist on a spectrum from open to closed attitudes toward change and integration.

Options for acculturation

Open to change and influence. Not worried about "losing their own culture".

Not open to change or influence of a new culture. Concerned about "losing their culture".

Assimilation

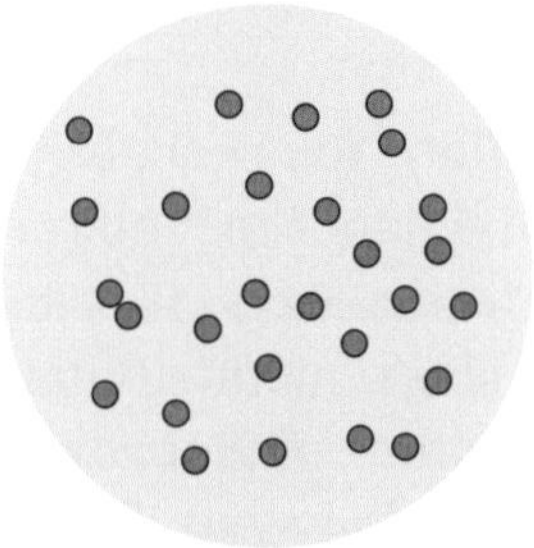

People want interaction with other cultures and are willing to change their behaviours, attitudes and beliefs.

Results in a "melting pot" of cultures. Where all in the culture share a similar single culture.

Integration

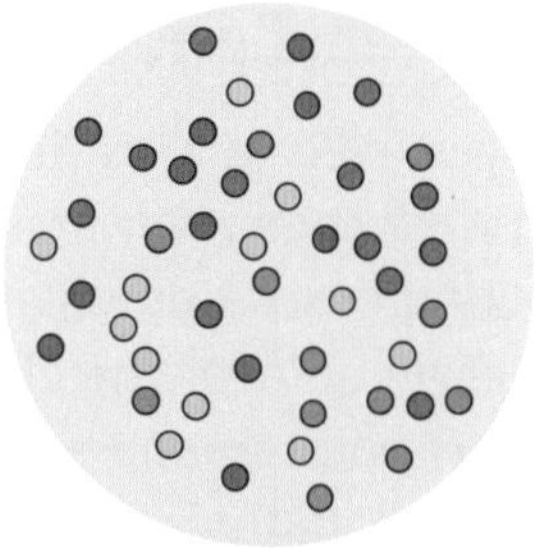

This is a middle option where people want to interact and be a part of a new or dominant culture but also want to keep their original culture identity as well.

The result is a dominant culture that is tolerant of the multicultural nature of many of its members.

Separation

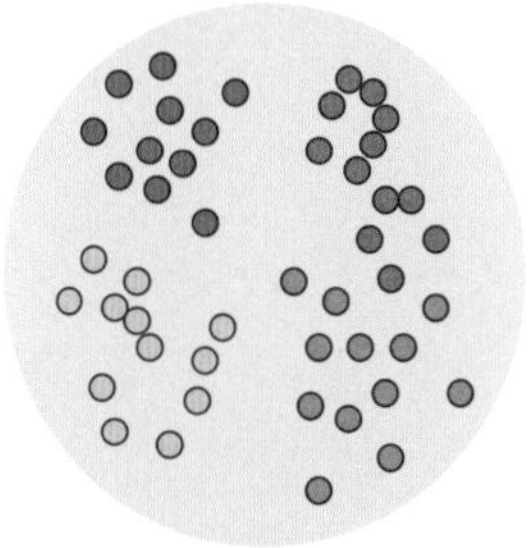

This option involves people typically avoiding contact with the dominant culture while living in communities defined by their original culture.

The result is a pluralistic society of different communities. This requires a dominant culture who accepts multiculturalism and little emphasis on group unity.

Marginalizations

This is a little different than the others because marginalization defines someone who has lost their own culture but also is not willing to integrate or assimlate. This often follows when someone forcibly loses their first culture. (for example: American First Nations and Australian Aboriginal People)

▲ **Figure 4.8** Strategies of acculturation

DP ready | ATL Communication skills

Paragraph outline

How does globalization influence your behaviour, attitudes and/or beliefs?

Use the information in this section to write a paragraph outlining the main argument about how your behaviour, attitudes and beliefs can be influenced by globalization.

This time use only two main ideas for your paragraph outline. You should take one of these ideas from each of the subsections above: "Globalization and you" and "Acculturation". Write a topic sentence that answers the question in one statement and follow it with the two main ideas. Your paragraph should end with a linking statement that restates your answer to the question.

Extension

Strong arguments often predict the criticisms they will receive. See if you can predict the criticisms of your arguments. This can take the form of a statement before your conclusion that may begin: "Some may disagree with this statement because ...".

Conclusion: Concept Three

You never lived in a world before globalization. You probably have a hard time even imagining the world without the internet connecting every tiny village with people, technology, ideas and values from all over the globe. There is no single moment that historians point to and say, "that is the beginning of globalization". Whenever it started, there appears to be no end in sight. In fact, it seems as though the pace of interconnection will increase.

Globalization has changed how people behave. As cultures come into contact with one another, they begin to influence each other. Some will grow dominant and some will, sadly, disappear. Some react in anger and feel threatened while others react with acceptance and friendship and seek a universal human culture that they hope will bring about world peace and understanding. Your reaction to globalization will be determined, to a large extent, by whether you feel threatened or not by the increasing interconnectedness of cultures and people.

Chapter conclusion

Nature or nurture?

Nature includes all of the things you were given before you came into the world while nurture covers all of the influences that have affected you since your birth and up to the point you are reading these words. In this chapter you have learned some ways in which nurture can influence your thoughts, behaviours and beliefs. In short, your biology does not 100% determine who you become. Much of who you are is determined by your environment and your culture. In Chapter 2 on biological psychology, you learned the importance of genetics and biology in determining who you are. You have now added the nurture part to the nature–nurture debate.

Internal link

Genetic inheritance and epigenetics—how your environment can influence your genes—are discussed in "Concept Two: Behaviour can be inherited" in Chapter 2 on biological psychology.

The thing to remember: the nature or nurture debate is not a debate at all. It is not "either/or". In reality both nature and nurture determine how you become yourself. Just as you would not be your same self with someone else's DNA, you would not be your same self raised in a different culture or raised by someone else's parents. You are the result of a very complicated mixture of biology and experience—so complicated, in fact, that each of the billions of people living on our planet is unique and unlike any other.

Reflection Activity

The Four Cs

In this activity you will reflect on **c**onnections, **c**oncepts and **c**hanges and you will **c**hallenge some ideas.

- Think about what you have learned about culture and behaviour and make connections to your own life.
- Challenge any ideas that you do not find convincing. Why are they not convincing?
- Describe some other concepts from this book or elsewhere that are connected to the ones in this chapter.
- Describe changes in thinking or behaviour that you believe are needed after your learning in this chapter.

Adapted from: Ritchhart, Church and Morrison (2011)

Links to IB psychology topics

Sociocultural approach to understanding behaviour

The individual and the group	Cultural origins of behaviour and cognition	Cultural influences on Individual attitudes, identity and behaviour
Social identity theory Social cognitive theory Stereotypes	Culture and its influence on behaviour and cognition Cultural dimensions	Enculturation Acculturation

HL extension: The influence of globalization on individuals' attitudes, identity and beliefs

Exam-style questions

1. **Evaluate** social identity theory.
2. **Evaluate** one theory of stereotype formation.
3. **Contrast** two strategies of acculturation.
4. **Discuss** research methods used in sociocultural psychology.
5. **To what extent** does globalization influence behaviour?

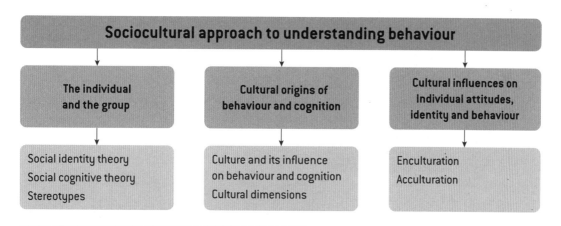

Big ideas

Concept One: Social influence—your thoughts, behaviours and attitudes are influenced by others.

- Social identity theory includes the idea that people understand the social world in terms of groups.
- Social cognitive theory states that people are active learners who build meaning from what they see in the world around them. People learn from the actions and the mistakes of other people.
- Stereotyping is seen when people categorize and generalize facts about the world and other people automatically and effortlessly.

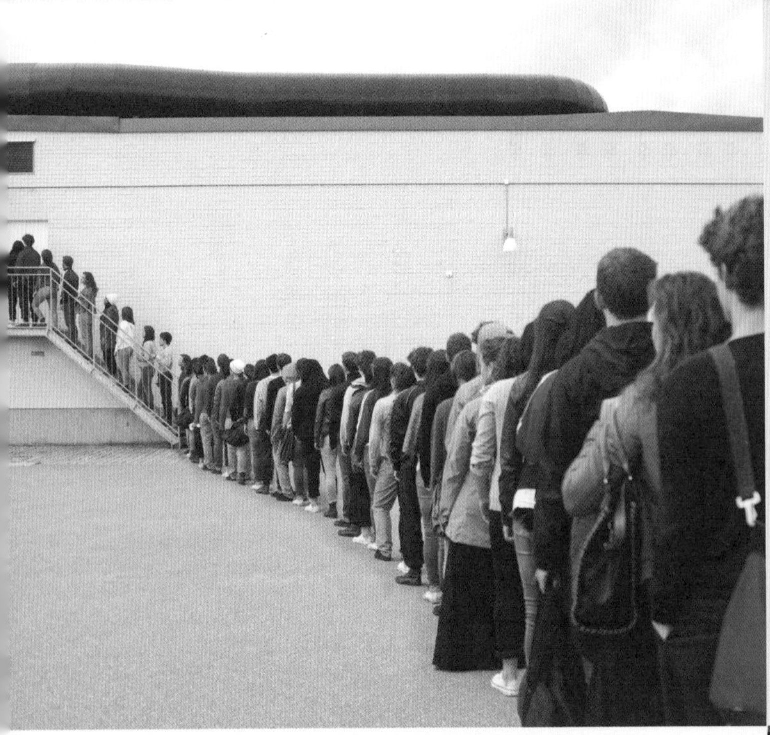

Concept Two: Culture and cultural norms—how your culture affects your behaviour.

- Each group or culture has a "normal" way to behave and this is expected of all members of the ingroup.
- Enculturation and socialization refer to how you learn how to behave as a member of your ingroup (or culture) from the people around you.
- Dimensions of culture are particular universal traits shared, to different degrees, by all cultures. They can be used to compare cultures.

Concept Three: Globalization and interaction of cultures—interconnection and acculturation.

- Digital technologies have made the world smaller and removed barriers to the interaction of cultures and people increasing communication, exposure and interconnectedness.
- Acculturation is seen when cultures change as they come into contact with other cultures. There are different ways to react when your culture comes into contact with another culture. Minority cultures may feel threatened by dominant cultures and try to resist their influence.

5 Concepts in applied psychology

In this chapter, you will learn about the options in IB psychology that focus on applied psychology.

Abnormal psychology

→ Concept One: Normality—are you normal? Is anyone normal?
- deviation from social norms
- inadequate mental functioning
- deviation from ideal mental health
- statistical infrequency
- the medical model of abnormality

→ Concept Two: Diagnosis—how do psychologists tell the difference between normal and abnormal behaviour?
- characteristics of a good diagnosis
- challenges in making a valid and reliable diagnosis

→ Concept Three: Etiology—what is the difference between a symptom and origin of an illness or disorder?

Developmental psychology

→ Concept One: Maturation—how does growth in a child's brain result in more complex thought and behaviour?
- neuroscience and babies
- Piaget's theory—linking biological and cognitive theories

→ Concept Two: Learning—how do children discover their world and other people in it?
- theory of mind—learning that others exist and have different beliefs and intentions

→ Concept Three: Attachment—how and why does attachment to others become important?

Health psychology

→ Concept One: Wellness—what does it mean to live well?
- determinants of health

→ Concept Two: Health problems—identifying and addressing issues preventing wellness

→ Concept Three: Health promotion—how do psychologists help people make healthier choices?
- the Health Belief Model—explaining unhealthy behaviours
- changing unhealthy behaviours

Psychology of human relationships

→ Concept One: Love—what binds us to each other?
- the biology of love
- Sternberg's triangular theory of love

→ Concept Two: Communication—how can communication build or destroy relationships?

→ Concept Three: Helping—why do you choose to help those in need?

Introduction

The options in IB psychology focus on aspects of applied psychology. As their name would suggest, they are applications of the approaches to behaviour studied in the core. That means they use a biopsychosocial approach to investigate one specific area of study in human behaviour. Students at standard level study one option, while higher level students study two. The following pages are meant as an introduction, not as a comprehensive explanation of the key concepts of each area of application.

The options in IB psychology are:

- abnormal psychology
- developmental psychology
- health psychology
- the psychology of human relationships.

ABNORMAL PSYCHOLOGY

What does it mean?

Abnormal: deviating from what is normal or usual, often understood to be in a way that is undesirable

Introduction

The central concept in this branch of psychology is "normality". The trouble is that arriving at a clear and accepted definition of "normal" is more difficult than you might think. Psychologists do not always agree on the best way to measure normality.

Concept One: Normality

Are you normal? Is anyone normal?

It is perfectly fine not to be normal. After all, who wants to be just like everyone else? Being **abnormal** means being unique. Psychologists try to define abnormality in order to determine when treatment might be necessary. Of course, not all abnormal behaviour is harmful, so not all abnormal behaviour needs to be diagnosed and treated. Abnormal psychology is focused on identifying and treating behaviour that is considered negative *and* abnormal.

Abnormal psychology is focused on the boundary of normal and abnormal. Is abnormality versus normality "black and white" or is it possible to be just a little bit abnormal? Where is the boundary between normal behaviour and abnormal behaviour?

- When does being sad turn into clinical depression?
- When does being shy turn into social anxiety disorder?

- When does being nervous turn into general anxiety disorder?
- When do poor eating habits turn into an eating disorder?

In the history of the study and treatment of abnormal behaviour, there have been many attempts to define abnormality. The most influential models have defined abnormality as:

- a deviation from normal social behaviour
- inadequate mental functioning
- a deviation from ideal mental health
- a statistical infrequency.

Deviation from social norms

This approach defines abnormal as any behaviour that falls outside what society or a particular social group would define as normal. Although this seems simple and intuitive, it quickly falls apart if you try to use it to determine whether treatment is necessary.

These are some of the problems with this approach:

- What is normal today may not be tomorrow.
- Who decides what is normal behaviour within a group?

Conclusion: this definition of abnormal does not help psychologists determine who needs treatment.

Inadequate mental functioning

This perspective is based on a theory by the psychologists Rosenhan and Seligman. They argue that you can use seven criteria to determine whether someone is healthy. The criteria are:

1. suffering: if a person feels as if his or her behaviour is wrong
2. maladaptiveness: when a person cannot achieve major life goals, such as not being able to have positive social relationships
3. unconventional behaviour: when a person's behaviour is different from most people's
4. loss of control: when a person cannot control his or her actions
5. irrationality: when a person's behaviour cannot be understood by others
6. causing discomfort: when a person's behaviour makes others feel uncomfortable
7. violation of moral standards: when a person acts in a way that is against the morals of a society.

Here is a problem with this approach:

- A person might display some of criteria 1–7 but not all of them. At what point does a person become abnormal? Rosenhan and Seligman defend their perspective by claiming that it is possible to be "just a little abnormal", they called this "degrees of abnormality".

Conclusion: this definition does not always help psychologists determine who needs treatment.

TOK link

How do we know what is normal?

Is it ever possible to know the difference between normal and abnormal? If so, who decides what the difference is?

Each person on this planet is the result of his or her own peculiar biology, experience and thoughts, which makes each of us unique.

Reflect on what you consider normal. See if you can come up with your own definition of normality.

What does it mean?

Medical model: sometimes called the "disease model", this is an approach to treating mental disorders in the same way that health professionals treat physical disorders; it often assumes a biological etiology of mental disorders

Deviation from ideal mental health

Humanistic psychologist Marie Jahoda proposed the following idea. She believed that psychologists should focus on mental health, not mental disorders. She identified six criteria for mental health. According to this perspective, you do not suffer from a mental disorder if you display:

1. efficient self-perception
2. realistic self-control
3. voluntary control of behaviour
4. an accurate perception of the world
5. positive relationships
6. self-direction and productivity.

Here are some problems with this approach:

- Achieving all of these goals consistently seems almost impossibly difficult for most people—so it is likely that most people would be considered abnormal under this model.
- Some of the terms ("efficient", "realistic", "positive") are difficult to define and measure so they are not very useful to psychologists trying to measure the health of a person's behaviour.

Conclusion: this definition does not always help psychologists determine who needs treatment.

Statistical infrequency

This perspective defines abnormality as something that does not happen very often (it is statistically infrequent). Under this model, if you are different from 95% of the rest of a population of people, you (or your behaviour) is considered abnormal. For example, if your IQ is less than 70 or more than 130, you are considered abnormally unintelligent or abnormally intelligent respectively. Unlike Jahoda's method, this method provides quantifiable measurement.

Here is a problem with this approach:

- Statistically infrequent behaviour can be desirable. Under this model, all Olympic athletes and geniuses are considered abnormal but they are not in need of treatment. It is not limited to undesirable abnormality.

Conclusion: this definition does not always help psychologists determine who needs treatment.

You are not the only one who has trouble defining normality. Psychologists have still not been able to develop a single definition for abnormal behaviour. In fact, it is unlikely they ever will. Instead they have adopted an approach called the **medical model**.

DP ready | ATL Communication skills

Making a metaphor

Create a simile or metaphor for the concept of normality. You might begin with "normality is like ..." or "being normal is ...".

Explain your metaphor in a few sentences and share with a friend.

The medical model of abnormality

This model of determining abnormality rejects the previous efforts of psychologists such as Jahoda and Rosenhan. As the name would suggest, this model treats abnormal behaviour in the same way as medical doctors treat illness. The medical model assumes that abnormal behaviour has a cause and that treatment focusing on causes will help patients who are suffering from psychological disorders. Instead of defining the vague concept of abnormality, the medical model looks at each disorder (negative abnormal behaviour) and establishes a set of symptoms that define it.

The medical model and biopsychosocial model are the current, and so far, the most effective method psychologists have to identify and treat negative abnormal behaviour (psychological disorders).

Here are some problems with the medical model.

- Treating psychological disorders in the same way medical practitioners treat physical ones can be difficult. Symptoms of psychological disorders are not as obvious or visible as physical symptoms.
- Since it is common for a person to have multiple disorders at the same time—which is known as **comorbidity**—it can be difficult to determine which symptoms belong to which disorder. This in turn makes treatment difficult.

Watch this

www.youtube.com/watch?v=wuhJ-GkRRQc

Search terms

"psychological disorders Crash Course Psychology #28"

Concept Two: Diagnosis

How do psychologists tell the difference between normal and abnormal behaviour?

Addressing each disorder separately rather than looking more generally at abnormality has required a massive effort of observing, measuring, categorizing and recording symptoms of disorders. This herculean effort has resulted in a huge book called the *Diagnostic and Statistical Manual of Mental Disorders-V*(DSM-V). The "V" stands for 5, because this is the 5th edition. The first edition came out in 1952. There have been some big changes between editions. For example, the first two editions considered homosexuality a disease. This is obviously no longer the case but does show us that what is considered a psychological disorder changes with culture and time. As mental health professionals learn more about a disorder, they can refine the criteria, change names, or remove a disorder from (or add a disorder to) the DSM. This book is used by anyone interested in **prevalence rates**, origins or treatment of psychological disorders.

Disorders each have their own prevalence rate. Very simply, this refers to how common a disorder is within a population of people. More specifically, it refers to the proportion of people in a population who have a given disorder at any one time or measured throughout their lifetime.

What does it mean?

Comorbidity: the simultaneous occurrence of two or more diseases or disorders in a patient

Prevalence rate: the number of cases of a disorder that are present in a population of people in a given time

What are the characteristics of a good diagnosis?

Arriving at a correct diagnosis is important for two reasons. Not only does the diagnosis determine treatment (which is important for recovery), there is also the problem of **stigma**. Stigma refers to a disgrace or shame that is felt by someone who is associated with a disorder.

For example, being diagnosed with major depressive disorder (commonly referred to as depression) or post-traumatic stress disorder (PTSD) could be seen by some as a sign of personal weakness. In reality, it is not a weakness any more than catching a cold or flu is a sign of weakness. Psychologists must be careful to get the diagnosis right to ensure the correct treatment and to avoid unnecessary stigmatization.

So, what makes a diagnosis a good one? As with research, **validity** and **reliability** are the keys.

Validity	Reliability
The correct diagnosis is made for an illness or disorder. This requires psychologists to examine the symptoms a person is suffering and correctly match the criteria to the DSM-V criteria in order to diagnose a particular disorder.	A diagnosis has reliability if different psychologists diagnose the same disorder from the same symptoms. This is why some people say you should always get a second opinion. In finding out whether other professionals agree with the diagnosis, psychologists can check for reliability and perhaps improve the diagnosis.

▲ **Table 5.1** Validity and reliability

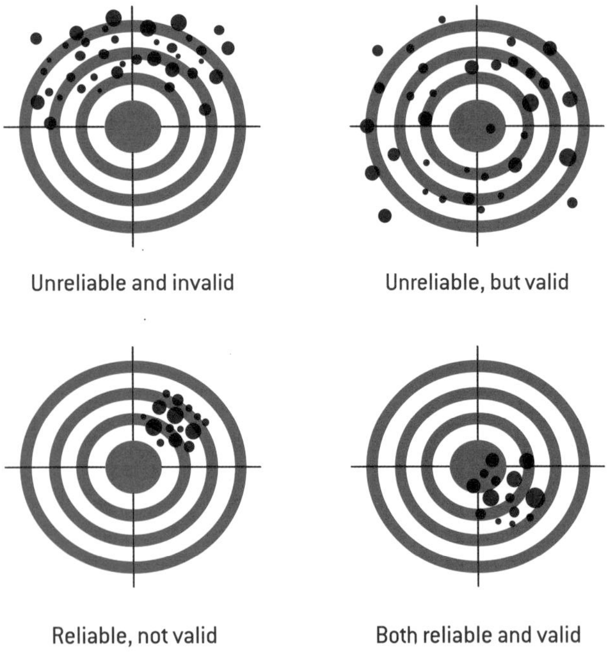

▲ **Figure 5.1** Validity and reliability represented as targets

Internal link

Cognitive biases are discussed in Chapter 3 on cognitive psychology: "Concept Two: Humans are active processors of information".

Challenges in making a valid and reliable diagnosis

Patients do not always display the same symptoms for a disorder, so different psychologists may give different diagnoses for the same person.

- When diagnosing a disorder, psychologists rely on symptoms and not causes for disorders. This is because our understanding of mental illness is incomplete. In diagnosing physical illness, doctors focus on things such as bacteria, viruses or genetic mutations—but mental health is not as advanced as physical health. A focus on symptoms means that two disorders with separate causes, but the same symptoms, may be confused and diagnosis may be wrong.
- Cut-off points are difficult to find. This means that it is difficult to tell when a behaviour has crossed the line between "normal" and "abnormal". Symptoms of a disorder may be present but it may be difficult for a psychologist to decide when these symptoms are "bad enough" to need a diagnosis and thus treatment.
- Psychologists may have biases in their diagnosis. Everyone, including mental health professionals, has biases. A diagnosing psychologist might be influenced by his or her attitudes and beliefs, abilities or cognitive biases.

KS

Key Study: Rosenhan (1973)

Being sane in insane places

Aim: to investigate whether psychiatrists could tell the difference between sane and insane people.

Method: the participants were 8 healthy people (including Rosenhan) who presented themselves at 12 psychiatric hospitals in 5 US states. All of the patients did the same thing: they made an appointment to see a doctor and complained of hearing voices that said "empty", "hollow" and "thud". Other than this they acted perfectly normally. Once admitted, the healthy patients acted normally and sought to be discharged from the hospital.

Results: all but one of the healthy people were admitted with the diagnosis of schizophrenia. None of the healthy people was identified by the hospital staff as not in need of treatment. The average stay was 19 days and the longest was 52. Each patient was discharged with a diagnosis of "schizophrenia in remission".

Conclusion: Rosenhan concluded that psychiatrists relying on the DSM-II could not reliably distinguish healthy people from the mentally ill.

Concept Three: Etiology

What is the difference between the symptoms and the origins of an illness or disorder?

You learned earlier that psychologists rely on **symptomatology** and diagnostic manuals such as the DSM-V to diagnose mental disorders. There is a danger that psychologists treat the symptoms but not the underlying causes or **etiology** of the disorder. For example, a common treatment for patients suffering post-traumatic stress disorder (PTSD) is selective serotonin reuptake inhibitors (SSRIs), which artificially increase the amount of serotonin available in the brain. SSRIs are very effective at treating many of the symptoms of PTSD such as emotional outbursts, hyperarousal and flashbacks. After taking SSRIs, patients appear to have recovered from the disorder—but only their symptoms have been treated. If you remove the SSRIs the symptoms will return.

PTSD has cognitive origins and those origins must be treated if a patient is going to recover from an illness. Although there is some evidence of a genetic link to PTSD (where your genes play a role in your development of PTSD), there is not yet any treatment for a genetic origin.

Psychologists have concentrated on a two-pronged treatment. First, they give SSRIs so that a patient does not suffer symptoms as severely. Increasing the amount of serotonin in the brain can improve the function of some brain regions such as the prefrontal cortex, which plays a role in emotional regulation. For example, SSRIs allow the prefrontal cortex to regulate the reaction of the amygdala to fearful or stressful triggers in the environment.

What does it mean?

Stigma: a mark or feeling of disgrace that accompanies a particular disorder or diagnosis

Validity of diagnosis: the degree to which a diagnosis is logically or factually sound or correct

Reliability of diagnosis: the degree to which a diagnosis is consistent across time, patients or health professionals

Symptomatology: the specific set of symptoms characteristic of a medical condition or mental disorder

Etiology: the cause or causes for a disorder, illness or disease

The treatment cannot be considered effective unless it addresses the underlying etiologies of the disorder. This is why once a patient has regained the ability to function, more or less regularly, that patient goes into the next phase of the treatment, which is often an exposure therapy. Exposure therapies are designed to eliminate the cognitive origins of PTSD, which means unlearning something that was learned. For example, someone may develop PTSD after a particularly violent car crash. The person then fears all cars and experiences a powerful fear reaction when seeing or entering a car. This is a learned reaction that must be unlearned.

Exposing individuals to the stimuli they are afraid of will trigger their PTSD (but the SSRIs should blunt the power of the reaction) then a mental health professional can talk sufferers through the anxiety and fear they feel. If this is done repeatedly, the association of fear that was learned (cars and violence in the example above) can be unlearned and the patient will no longer experience an unhealthy stress response when exposed to a car.

PRL

Psychology in real life

Exposure therapy—virtual reality therapy

Soldiers returning from war can suffer from PTSD due to the shocking, and often terrifying, experience of war. Much of the treatment breakthroughs for PTSD are therefore being made by researchers working with soldiers. Virtual reality therapy is a kind of exposure therapy that puts soldiers in game-like immersive re-enactment of a scenario that should trigger their PTSD. If people suffering from PTSD are repeatedly exposed to the negative stimuli without harm, it is hoped they will learn that the stimuli is not dangerous and should not be feared. Once they have unlearned their fear response, they can be said to be "cured" of their PTSD.

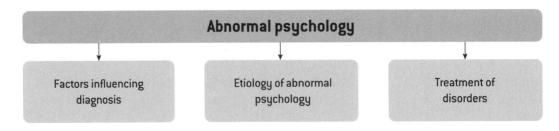

Etiologies can be tricky to discover. Symptoms are only signs that an illness is present, they are not the origin of the illness. Psychologists must search behind the symptoms and find the origin of an illness or disorder if they hope to find an effective treatment. This is why etiologies are a key concept in abnormal psychology—they are the reasons for an illness and therefore must be the target of treatment.

Links to IB psychology topics

Abnormal psychology

- Factors influencing diagnosis
- Etiology of abnormal psychology
- Treatment of disorders

DEVELOPMENTAL PSYCHOLOGY

Introduction

Do you remember when a good game of peekaboo just blew your mind? It probably feels like a long time ago, but before you turned 2 years old, you were probably a huge fan of this fascinating game. Nowadays, you might be more fascinated to learn that all babies, in every culture on the planet cannot get enough peekaboo. This universality is a hint that all people mature through roughly the same developmental stages.

The field of developmental psychology rests on the assumption that children all mature biologically in a pattern largely determined by their genetic make-up which allows for increasingly sophisticated learning from their environment. This interplay of a growing brain, a rapidly expanding mind and environmental influences combine to determine the mirror processes of **maturation** and **learning** that eventually result in a fully mature human adult.

This process takes time. In fact, if you are not yet in your mid-twenties you are likely still placing the final biological puzzle pieces into your brain. When you are around 25 years old your prefrontal cortex will have become a fully complete and functioning system. The prefrontal cortex is a hugely important brain region responsible for decision-making, reasoning, inhibition and emotional control. This also explains why babies cannot be trusted with important life decisions and why they have a hard time controlling their emotions.

The following pages will explore maturation and learning throughout the human lifespan.

What does it mean?

Maturation: the process of passing through stages of development

Learning: gaining knowledge or skills as a result of experience, studying or being taught

Structure–function relationship: the connection between brain development and cognitive function

Neurogenesis: the process of growing new neurons

Migration: a process that begins shortly after conception where a fetus' neurons begin to migrate to their "correct" positions

Differentiation: the growth of new neural connections

Pruning: the elimination of neural connections that are no long used

Concept One: Maturation

How does growth in a child's brain result in more complex thought and behaviour?

Neuroscience and babies

If you have been reading closely, you should know by now that "the mind is what the brain does". What and how you think is very much dependent on the physical make-up of your brain. It should be no surprise to you that as your brain grows in size and complexity, you develop new skills and abilities. This connection between brain development and cognitive function is called the **structure–function relationship**.

Structural changes in the brain can be summarized into four main processes explained below: **neurogenesis**, **migration**, **differentiation** and **pruning**. All of these happen throughout your lifetime but certain stages of growth can be linked to each process.

Neurogenesis is the process of creating new neurons from scratch. Although recent research has shown that this is possible

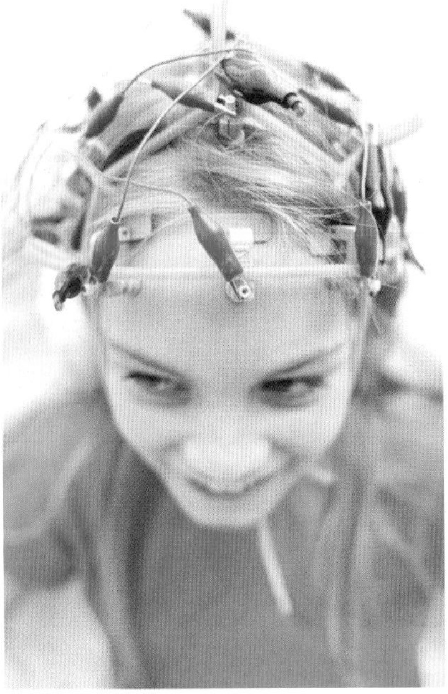

throughout your life, it is mostly done before you are born. By the time you are born, you had more neurons than you have now because you are designed to take maximum advantage of all learning opportunities. Your early learning was not stunted by a lack of neurons.

Before you are born, each of your neurons know exactly where they need to go and they migrate to that location and begin to grow dendrites to increase connections (differentiation) that are very important to learning. These connections between neurons (synapses) are exploding at a rate of 40,000 per second until you reach your prime peekaboo career at about 2 years old. This is the peak of synaptic growth—it's downhill from here—that is, your synaptic growth peaks and then declines in a process called pruning until the end of puberty. It's an incredible process.

Cell death is not random. The neurons that your brain finds a use for are retained while those not used are allowed to die. Researchers sometimes refer to this as the "use it or lose it" principle. Only cells that are not considered useful are pruned. Imagine sitting down to dinner with enough food for 1000 people. You cannot possibly eat everything but you will develop habits and eat what you like until you are full. Eventually, you can prune away all the excess and be left with only what you need while never worrying about going hungry. This is a very effective system that enables you to not only reach your potential but may also allow you to determine it very early in life.

DP ready ATL **Thinking and research skills**

Infantile amnesia

Babies are learning all the time and are also experiencing massive cellular growth in their brains so why can't you remember anything from before you were three years old? Some people claim to remember very early memories but this is likely caused by photos they saw of themselves as babies or stories told them by their parents. Find answers to the following questions:

- What kind of memories can babies remember?
- What kind of memories do they forget?
- What explanations can you find for infantile amnesia?

▲ **Figure 5.2** Jean Piaget

Piaget's theory

Linking biological and cognitive theories

Jean Piaget (1896–1980) was a Swiss psychologist particularly interested in how children learn. He believed that children's cognitive development was tied to certain stages of development that corresponded to their age. This is called Piaget's theory of cognitive development. He believed that as the brain grew in size and complexity, so did children's cognitive abilities. This theory is an excellent example of a researcher's focus on the interaction between the brain and the mind (or physical and cognitive).

Table 5.2 shows the stages in Piaget's theory of cognitive development.

Sensorimotor stage (birth to 2 years)
The focus in this stage is on sense and movement and includes touching and tasting everything in sight. This is when everything in reach heads for a baby's mouth. Reasoning has not begun.
This stage is characterized by: • object permanence: children begin understanding that things exist even when they are out of view • egocentrism: believing that the world centres on them and inability to understand other people exist independent of them.
Preoperational Stage (2–7 years)
Children are involved in lots of playing and pretending. This is a very imaginative stage with unbounded creativity. Children engage with symbolic representation of objects as something else—they are not playing with objects, they are playing with the meaning they attribute to an object. For example, a box is a spaceship, a stick is a magic wand, a doll is a baby.
This stage is characterized by: • centration: overly focusing on one small element rather than larger contexts • irreversibility: being unable to reverse a sequence of events • conservation: inability to understand that an object can change physical appearance yet remain unchanged in amount—for example, thinking that a single cookie broken in two becomes two cookies.
Concrete operational stage (7–11 years)
This is where logic and reason begin to take hold. Children can solve problems that relate to the world around them. They cannot solve abstract thinking problems. Inductive reasoning is achieved, but deductive reasoning is still absent.
This stage is characterized by: • successful conservation reasoning: recognizing that one cookie broken in two becomes two half cookies • recognition that others exist independent of themselves.
Formal operational (11–16 years)
Abstract thought, deductive reasoning and "thinking about thinking" become common in teenagers.
This stage is characterized by: • Nearly adult behaviour and cognitive abilities—some behaviours such as planning, risk management, emotional control may still be limited into the 20s. This is because the prefrontal cortex is still developing.

▲ **Table 5.2** Stages in Piaget's theory of cognitive development

DP ready ATL **Thinking skills**

Piaget's theory of cognitive development

There are some criticisms of Piaget's theory. Before you go any further, can you predict what some of these criticisms might be? Here's a hint to get you thinking: Piaget uses the concept of stages to outline child development. Do you think it is justifiable to use stages such as these?

Piaget's theory, based on stages of learning, laid the groundwork for controversial theories such as the **critical periods theory**. This theory argues that there are specific stages of development where a skill such as speaking a language must be developed. Some more strict versions of this theory claim that if a child does not develop language skills (verbal or signing) by a certain age, that child will be unable to develop language skills later in life.

Piaget's theory of cognitive development links biology and cognition into a theory of development. This theory makes a lot of sense because your mind and your brain are tightly connected to each other in structure, function and behaviour. However, this theory is missing something—the importance of learning and sociocultural influences in development. Vygotsky (1896–1934) attempted to describe these influences in his sociocultural theory of development and learning.

> **TOK link**
>
> When do babies know they are people?
>
> How can psychologists learn from babies who cannot speak or explain themselves? Can we ever really claim to know what is happening inside the minds of babies and young children?

Concept Two: Learning

How do children discover their world and other people in it?

Think back to Chapter 4 on concepts in sociocultural psychology. Recall that Bandura's social cognitive theory attempts to explain how children learn socially. Bandura was certainly aware of Vygotsky's research and would have used it as a starting point for his own theories.

Learning is the acquisition of knowledge and skills as a result of interaction with your environment. Vygotsky was particularly interested in high-order thinking (related to system 2 thinking from Chapter 3 on concepts in cognitive psychology). Vygotsky believed involuntary thinking (system 1 thinking) was driven by biology and therefore not relevant to sociocultural learning. Vygotsky's sociocultural theory does not therefore contradict Piaget's. In fact, they are complementary.

Vygotsky recognized that there were biological limits on a child's learning, but this was not his concern. He was interested in how society could help or inhibit learning. His view was that the role of adults, teachers and society at large was to ensure that children have access to their **zones of proximal development (ZPD)**. Sometimes children may be testing their limits and they reach beyond their abilities to attempt a new task. If they regularly experience failure this can result in frustration. This is sometimes referred to as **learned helplessness** and can result in low self-esteem. **Scaffolding** is the solution to helping young learners push their limits and move into their zone of proximal development. Scaffolding is when a helpful, knowledgeable adult or expert can help guide a student through the learning of a new skill. Parents, teachers and even older siblings seem to know this intuitively. They may break down a task into smaller parts, or guide a learner closely in the more difficult sections. The trick is to allow the learner to achieve as much as possible on his or

> **What does it mean?**
>
> **Critical periods theory**: the theory that children pass through stages of development that are limited to specific time periods that are crucial to the development of a particular skill or ability
>
> **Zone of proximal development**: what a child at a particular stage of development stage can do with the help of an adult
>
> **Learned helplessness**: a behaviour that results from repeatedly painful or otherwise negative stimuli someone is unable to escape or avoid
>
> **Scaffolding**: when a helpful, knowledgeable adult or expert helps guide a student through the learning of a new skill

> **Internal link**
>
> Bandura's social cognitive theory is discussed in Chapter 4 on sociocultural psychology: "Concept One: Social influence".

> **Internal link**
>
> Dual process thinking (system 1 and system 2 thinking) is discussed in Chapter 3 on concepts in cognitive psychology: "Concept One: Mental representations guide behaviour".

her own. Piaget famously believed that "when you teach a child something, you take away forever his chance of discovering it for himself". This will be old news to your teacher, who will have been trained in scaffolding and Vygotsky's zone of proximal development.

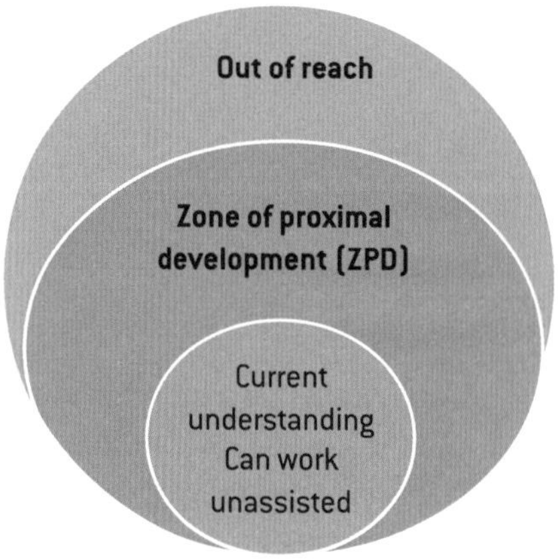

▲ **Figure 5.3** Vygotsky's zone of proximal development

DP ready ATL **Self-management skills**

Frustration during learning

Think of a time when you were frustrated while learning a new skill. It may have been trying to solve a mathematics problem, or learning how to ride a bike, or play a musical instrument. Vygotsky's theory suggests that your frustration is caused by reaching beyond your zone of proximal development or attempting to learn without expert help when you need it. Reflect on how you overcame that frustration. Did you persevere and test your boundaries of development or did your frustration overcome you so you gave up? We grow and learn by constantly testing our limits. Sometimes, without frustration you cannot have learning.

Current theories of development and learning such as Vygotsky's teach us that frustration is natural and can be a sign that we may have reached too far. If that is the case, the solution is to simplify the task a little and try again until we can accomplish our goal. Perhaps having someone hold the seat of your bike to get you started or attempting fewer notes of a complicated musical piece would help get you into your zone of proximal development.

Theory of mind

Learning that others exist and have different beliefs and intentions from yours

It seems strange to think about but one of the earliest things you learn is that other people exist. A child, when first introduced to the world, does not understand automatically the difference between people and things. **Theory of mind** is the learned ability to attribute mental states including things such as emotions, desires, beliefs, and intentions to other people. You know by now that other people have their own minds and their own wills—they want things that may be different from what you want and they can think and act differently from you. Young children have a difficult time with this concept. In fact, some of the greatest philosophers in history are not completely sure that anyone else exists—maybe the babies are right!

Researchers have developed an ingenious test for theory of mind. In order to understand whether a child can take another's perspective, researchers use something called the Sally–Anne task. The task is outlined in Figure 5.4.

What does it mean?

Theory of mind: the learned ability to attribute to other people mental states including things such as emotions, desires, beliefs and intentions

TOK link

Can you be sure that others actually exist? Solipsism is a philosophical idea that the only thing that exists for sure is your own mind. Everything you experience is simply a representation of your mind's perception—so how can you be sure that anything exists outside it? In short, in this philosophy it is impossible to prove that anything outside your mind is real.

Explore this idea and see if you can solve the problem that solipsism seems to present about the impossibility of knowing anything about your reality.

Concept Two

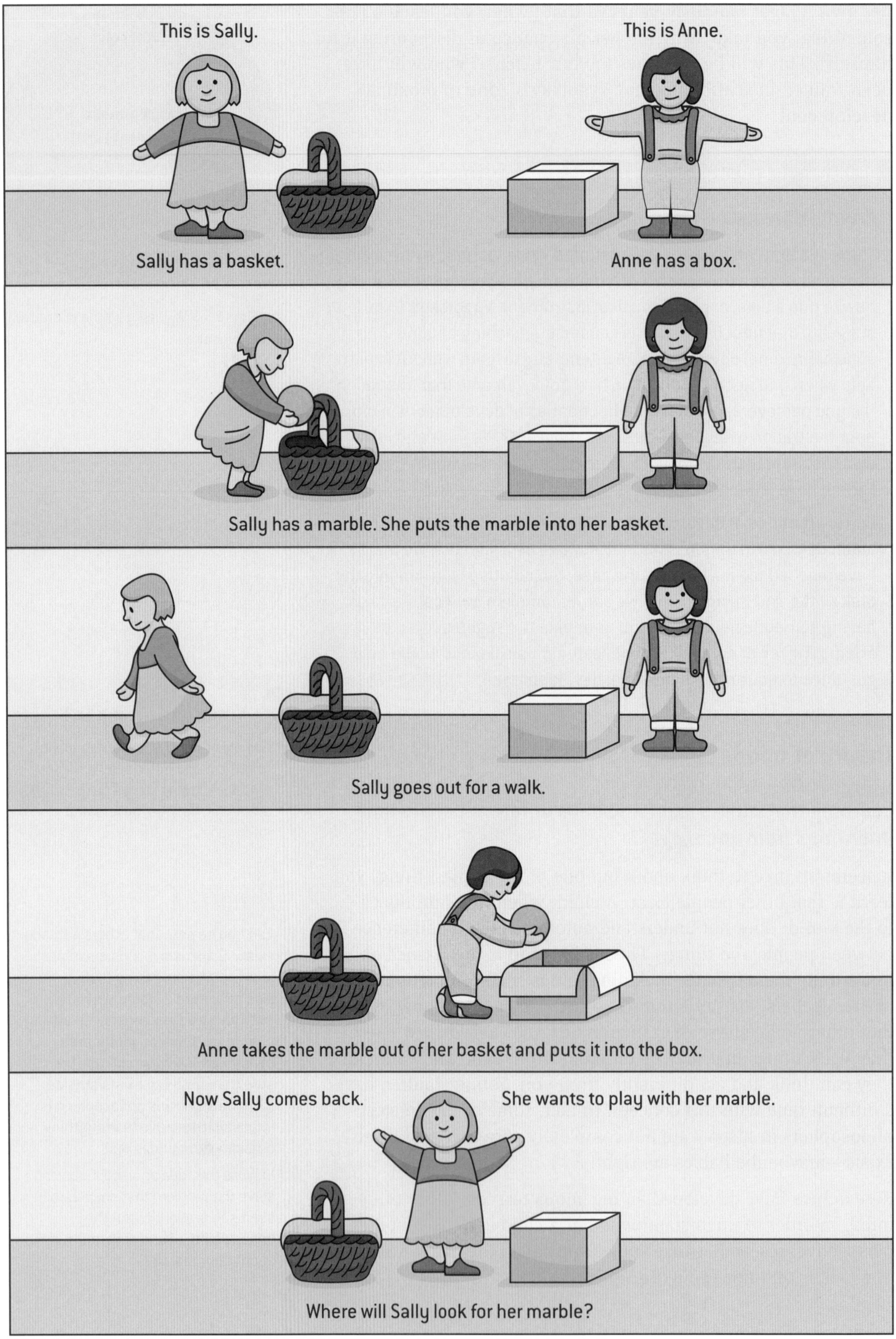

▲ **Figure 5.4** The Sally–Anne task (Baron-Cohen, Leslie and Frith 1985)

To pass the task, when Anne is asked where Sally will look for her marble, Anne must identify the basket. Anne has to understand three things:

- Sally is capable of having different beliefs from hers.
- Sally will base her behaviour on those beliefs.
- Those beliefs may be false.

In the case of the Sally–Anne task, a child has failed the task if he/she does not understand that Sally cannot know where the marble is, because Sally was not there when the marble was moved.

This is an ingenious and fun experiment. It can tell us a lot about the social understanding of children. In an experiment testing children with a mean age of 4.5 years, researchers found that 85% of Down syndrome children and 86% of clinically normal children passed this test, while 80% of autistic children failed.
(Baron-Cohen, Leslie, and Frith, 1985)

Concept Three: Attachment

How and why does attachment to others become important?

People are social animals with a basic need to belong—so it is not surprising that we seek attachment to other people. Negative long-term consequences can result if we fail to make social and emotional connections in childhood. One of the first researchers to discover the importance of contact and comfort was Harry Harlow.

KS

Key Study: Harlow (1958)

The nature of love

Aim: to investigate the role of early childhood experiences with one's mother on later development.

Procedure: Harlow used rhesus monkeys instead of human children for ethical reasons. Young rhesus monkeys are similar to human children in perception, memory, and learning capability. Researchers created two surrogate mothers for the rhesus monkeys. One surrogate was built using a block of wood and soft cloth, a milk-dispensing mechanism was installed near the breast area and heat lamp provided warmth. The second surrogate also provided warmth and milk but was made of wire mesh and did not resemble a female rhesus adult at all. In other words, the first surrogate provided comfort and had some physical resemblance to a mother rhesus monkey, but the second surrogate did not.

Findings: perhaps not surprisingly, Harlow found that the young rhesus monkeys preferred the cloth surrogate. What is surprising is that when the cloth surrogate no longer provided milk, the young rhesus monkeys would spend time with the cloth surrogate and go to the wire one only for feeding.

Conclusion: baby rhesus monkeys preferred to spend time with the cloth surrogate, maximizing contact comfort over basic needs (such as feeding). This was counter to the belief at the time that attachment prioritized basic needs over contact comfort.

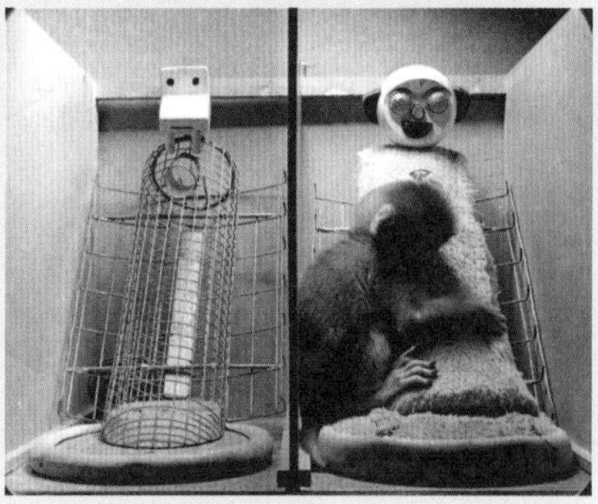

▲ Figure 5.5 Wire and cloth mother surrogates

What does it mean?

Bonding: the process of attachment between romantic partners, close friends, or parents and children. This bond is by affection and trust

Oxytocin: a hormone that plays an important role in bonding, trust and childbirth

Attachment, **bonding** and belonging are basic human drives and need to be discussed when considering motivation and human development. There are strong biological connections to human attachment and bonding.

Oxytocin is a bonding hormone that increases trust and bonding in humans and animals. During childbirth, mothers experience high levels of oxytocin, which is believed to play a role in increasing the strength of the bond between mother and child in the early moments and hours of life. Recent research has shown that there is an association between oxytocin and sensitive maternal caregiving (Kohlhoff 2017). This suggests that oxytocin is a biological mechanism to establish bonding between mother and child.

It seems that maternal care, bonding and attachment are very important in early childhood development. Different levels of oxytocin, different parenting styles and individual variations can lead to what developmental psychologist Mary Ainsworth describes as different attachment styles. In research involving short-term separation between mother and child, Ainsworth identified the attachment styles shown in Table 5.3.

Attachment style	Description
Type A (avoidant attachment)	The infant: • showed no distress when the mother left the room • showed no anxiety in the presence of a stranger • was indifferent to the return of the mother. This was shown by 20% of infants.
Type B (secure attachment)	The infant: • showed anxiety when the mother left the room • avoided the stranger when alone with him or her • showed a positive reaction to the return of the mother. This was shown by 70% of infants.
Type C (ambivalent/resistant attachment)	The infant: • showed very intense anxiety when the mother left the room • avoided the stranger at all times • reacted negatively, resisted contact and pushed away from the mother when she returned. This is shown by 10% of infants.

▲ **Table 5.3** Different attachment styles described by Ainsworth

An analysis of 32 research studies across eight countries and including 1990 participants showed that there were important similarities in attachment styles rather than differences across cultures. However, there were significant differences within cultures. This was attributed to differences in socio-economic status (wealth) between participating families. (Van Ijzendoorn and Kroonenberg, 1988)

PRL

Psychology in real life

Feral children

A feral child is a child who has lived isolated from human contact or social connection from a very young age. Fortunately these are rare cases but, when found, they provide researchers with an opportunity to study the role of sociocultural contact in development. Researchers must obviously be careful to protect the wellbeing of the children above all else.

Some of the more extraordinary cases involve children being raised by animals (Oxana Malaya lived with dogs for eight years) while others (such as the case of Genie) involve child abuse, confinement and neglect. Perform a search online for some of these case studies and make a judgment for yourself on how these experiences affected the child's later development.

Search terms

"Oxana Malaya" "Genie Wiley"

Links to IB psychology topics

Developmental psychology

- Influences on cognitive and social development
- Developing identity
- Developing as a learner

HEALTH PSYCHOLOGY

Introduction

Health psychology includes some aspects of mental health (although abnormal psychology concentrates on mental health issues). Health psychology is about mental, physical and social wellbeing. The goal of health psychologists is to study and promote wellbeing in individuals and in whole populations.

Concept One: Wellness

What does it mean to live well?

The central concept of health psychology is **wellness**. Health psychology investigates the determinants of wellness and illness. Wellness is not simply the absence of illness. Wellness can be defined as a positive state of physical, mental and social wellbeing that travels along a continuum over time. At one end of the continuum is wellness, at the other end is illness.

What does it mean?

Wellness: a positive state of physical, mental and social wellbeing

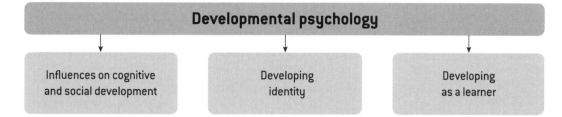

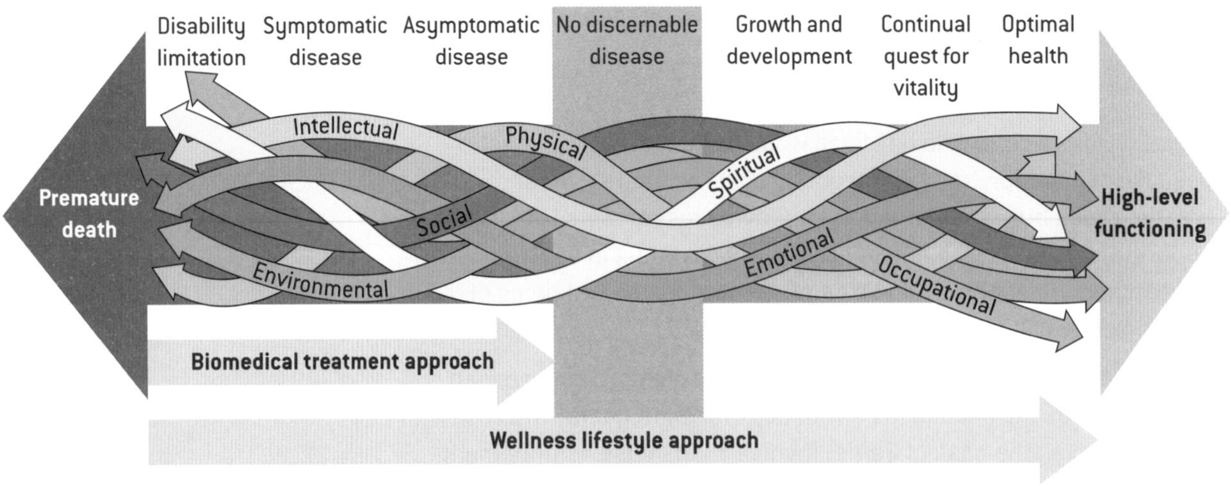

▲ **Figure 5.6** The wellness continuum

It should be clear to you by now that physical, social and mental health are all interrelated. Illness in any one of these areas can lead to severe illness and premature death, while wellness and balance between these areas can help you fulfill your potential and maintain optimal health and enjoyment of life. One relatively recent shift in psychology has been a shift toward positive psychology.

Positive psychology is the scientific study of what makes life most worth living. Martin Seligman, one of the founders of the modern positive psychology movement, lists wellbeing as being composed of five pillars: positive emotion, engagement, relationships, meaning and accomplishment. Positive psychology is not about making people less miserable but about making people healthier through the scientific study of wellness.

What does it mean?

Positive psychology: a branch of psychology that is concerned with improving the lives of people not currently experiencing any mental illness

Activity

In this activity you will be practising positive psychology.

Gratitude, optimism and kindness are key elements of positive psychology. Optimism and happiness are learned skills and it is important to practise them in order to improve your positive psychology. Here are some activities to get you started.

- Record gratitude.
  - Keep a gratitude journal. Simply spend five minutes during your day to record the things you are grateful for. Thinking about the negatives in life can get you down. Gratitude journals remind you of what is good and important and begin a pattern of positive thought.
  - Write one note of gratitude each day to someone you are grateful for. Give the person your note.
- Count kindness gestures.
  - Record all of the kind acts you perform in a day and read them at the end of the day. These can be simple things such as saying a kind word to someone or holding the door open for someone.
  - Sit somewhere and record the kind gestures you see being done in the world around you. This is an observation practice.
  - Gift your time. Think of your attention and time as a gift you give to others. Deliberately offer your time to others, see if you can improve their mood or their experience of their day.

Seligman states that positive psychology is:

- concerned with strength not weakness
- interested in building the best things in life, not just repairing the worst
- interested in making the lives of normal people fulfilling, by nurturing talent as well as treating illness.

Positive psychology is, in a sense, a counter to the disease model of mental health that seems to guide abnormal psychology. The goal of abnormal psychology is to identify and treat mental illness. This is, undeniably, a noble pursuit but it ignores the needs of the majority of "normal" people. Positive psychology is concerned with this majority of people. It must not be confused with "happyology" because being happy is not the goal of positive psychology. Seligman points out that it is about creating a balance between a pleasant life, a good life and a meaningful life.

Table 5.4 shows the characteristics of wellness relevant to positive psychology.

Flow	Mindfulness	Learned optimism
This is sometimes described as "being in the zone". It is a state of mind characterized by total absorption in an activity with a feeling of energized focus. This can give a feeling of meditation, peace and relaxation.	This is a state of active, intentional focus on the present moment. It is characterized by careful observation of your thoughts and feelings without judging them as good or bad.	This is the concept that optimism is not an innate trait or passing feeling but a skill that can be learned and mastered.

▲ **Table 5.4** Characteristics of wellness

Determinants of health

Some people experience illness that is taking away from their quality of life. In the past, a biomedical model was used to diagnose and treat these people. The biomedical model understands illness and disease as being the result of biological processes. This was a great improvement over previous models that could blame illness on witchcraft or bad magic. In the last quarter of the 20th century, a shift occurred and the biopsychosocial model gained influence.

In this model, the relative importance of each approach differs depending on the illness. For example, some illness may mostly have biological causes, social causes or psychological (cognitive) causes. Treating only one of causes can decrease illness but treating all of them will maximize wellness.

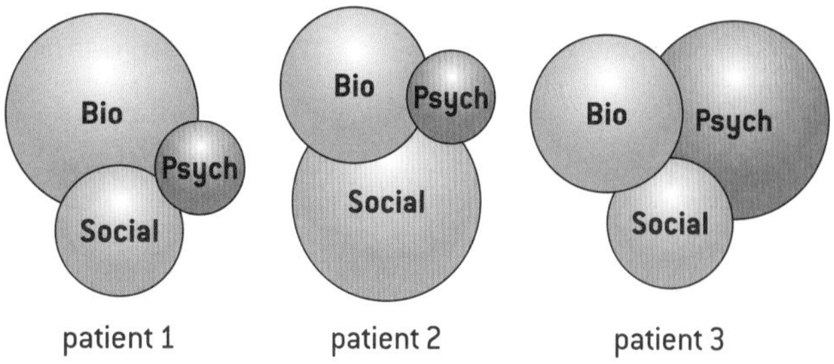

▲ **Figure 5.7** The importance of approaches is relative

The determinants of your health include all aspects of your life. Everything from how much you sleep, where you work, what you eat, who your friends are and how much money you have are all important. Generally speaking, determinants can be broken into two groups: social and personal. Each of these can be either a **protective factor** or a **risk factor** for your health. Health professionals commonly focus on illnesses affecting an entire group or population of people in order to achieve a positive influence on as many people as possible. This is called the **population health approach**.

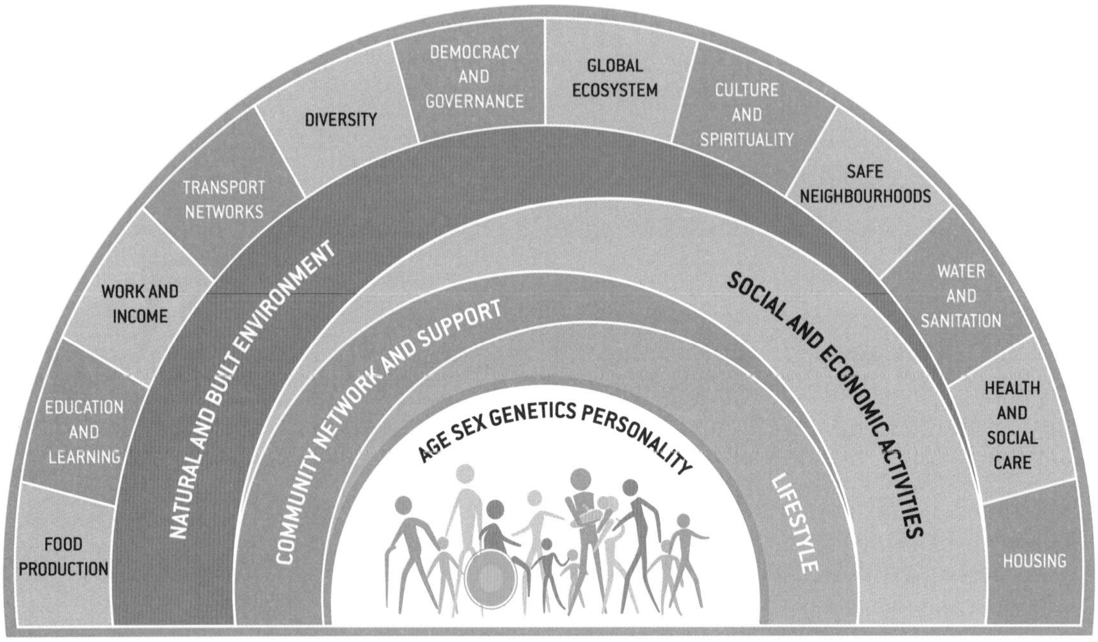

▲ **Figure 5.8** Determinants of health

What does it mean?

Protective factor: anything that decreases the likelihood of developing an illness or injury

Risk factor: anything that increases the likelihood of developing an illness or injury

Population health approach: an approach to improving health through policies that affect the entire population, rather than separate individuals

Psychology in real life

PRL

World Health Organization (WHO) Grand Challenges

On 8 February 2017 the World Health Organization (WHO) set out what it believes are the Grand Challenges to public health in the next decade. The WHO has identified non-communicable diseases as the biggest challenge. This is fertile ground for health psychologists in treating non-communicable diseases because these are often caused by misunderstandings and human behaviour more than biomedical causes.

Every year:

- 2 million people are newly infected with HIV
- more than 10 million people die before the age of 70 due to cardiovascular disease
- 800,000 people commit suicide
- 1.25 million die from road traffic injuries
- 800 million people are starving yet 70% of some of the world's richest countries are obese.

Stress and smoking are two common risk factors. Today:

- 1.1 billion people smoke tobacco
- 1 million people miss work every day due to work-related stress.

Concept Two: Health problems

Identifying and addressing issues preventing wellness

Positive psychology is concerned with improving the lives of healthy people but there are millions of people battling with health problems who also need help. Some health problems require treatment by medical professionals (cancers, viral and bacterial infections, and HIV/AIDS) but many illnesses can be prevented or treated by mental health professionals. Several areas where applied understanding of human behaviour can improve health and wellness include:

- stress
- obesity
- addiction
- chronic pain
- sexual health.

Obesity has become a global pandemic. **Overweight/obesity** is defined as a state where an individual has accumulated excess body fat to the point that it affects the person's health. If you are exposed to cheap, easily accessible junk food and you are allowed to eat these foods while living a low-activity lifestyle, you are susceptible to obesity-related diseases. Obesity itself is a risk factor for Type 2 diabetes, hypertension, some cancers and cardiovascular disease that can lead to heart attacks.

Here are some key facts about obesity.

- Worldwide obesity has more than doubled since 1980.
- Most of the world's population live in countries where being overweight kills more people than being underweight.
- In 2016, 41 million children under 5 years old were obese.
- Obesity is preventable.

There is no mystery about which foods or lifestyle choices are healthy and which are unhealthy. People have known for many years that eating processed, sugary foods that are high in saturated fats will damage your health. Despite this, many people eat sugar-saturated, energy-dense foods while sitting in front of the computer or television screen for hours on most days. Have you ever wondered why we love all the foods that are bad for us? Potato chips, french fries, doughnuts, sugary drinks, candy bars—we seem to love the foods that cause illness.

The answer may lie in our evolutionary past. At a time when humankind was still foraging for food, it was important to eat the most energy-dense foods because consuming maximum calories with minimal energy output was an advantage. An animal that spends its entire waking day consuming only enough calories for survival has no time for building social connections or in higher social pursuits such as art, music, and generally improving its life.

What does it mean?

Overweight/Obesity: a state where an individual has accumulated excess body fat to the point that it affects the person's health

▲ **Figure 5.9** A trolley of unhealthy food

> **What does it mean?**
>
> **Sedentary lifestyle**: a way of life that is characterized by too much sitting and too little physical exercise

Concept Two

Zoom forward to the 21st century and we are faced with a serious health problem. Two changes have occurred to many people's lifestyles and diets over the past 40 years.

First, millions of people around the world are consuming more calories than they need. In addition, the modern food industry is pushing highly processed foods, high in saturated fats, salt and sugar. You cannot blame food companies though, they are simply giving people what they want. They are providing what people are buying and consuming. Consider the findings of a 2015 report "Carbonating the World" on sugar-sweetened beverages (SSBs); following a study on the same topic by Ludwig, Peterson and Gortmaker (2001):

- "An extra 12-ounce (350-millilitre) sugary drink a day increases a child's risk of becoming obese by 60%" (where "extra" means in addition to the day's diet without the SSB).
- "Adults who drink one sugary drink per day are 27% more likely to be obese than non-SSB drinkers."
- SSBs "account for approximately 180,000 deaths each year."

Poor food choice is one reason for the obesity epidemic but poverty can also be a contributor to obesity. Healthier diets with calories gained from fresh fruits and vegetables, along with a healthy level of protein, can be more expensive than unhealthy calories. If you are living in poverty, the most calorie-dense foods are often the cheapest. Low-income families tend to purchase calorie-dense, high-sugar and fatty foods.

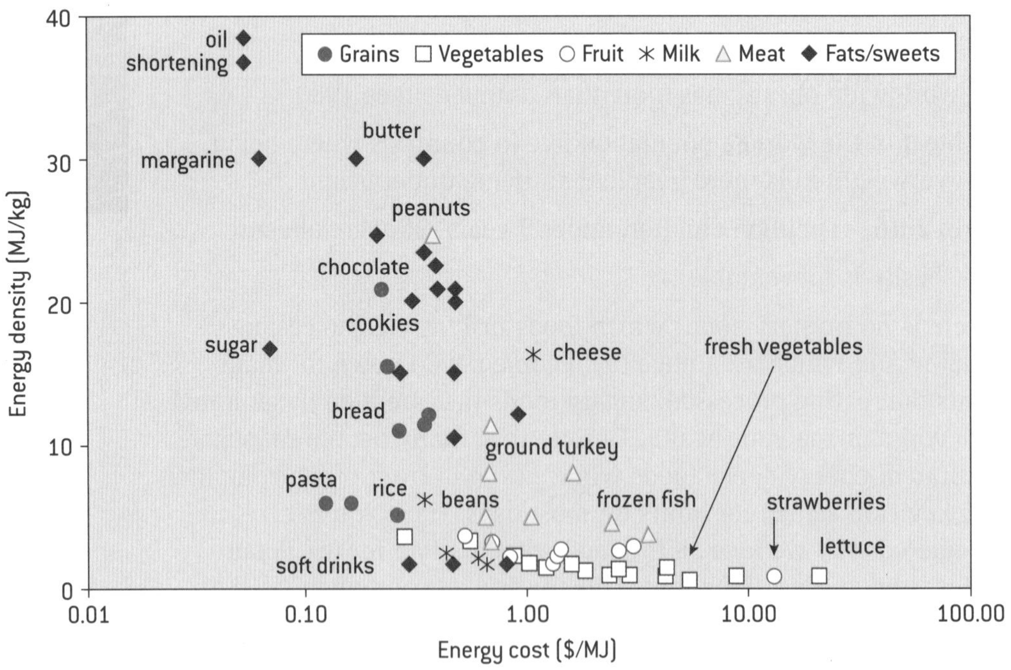

▲ **Figure 5.10** Relationship between energy density and energy cost of different foods

The second major change to occur is a lifestyle change. As far back as 2002, the WHO was warning that a **sedentary lifestyle** was a leading cause of disability and disease. Sedentary lifestyles use less energy than active ones. Habits such as screen-time activities (involving smart phones, television, computers, gaming) have dramatically increased in recent decades. At the same time,

consumption has increased and the types of foods consumed have worsened. So for most people, the most effective treatment for obesity is not a medical treatment. Instead, it revolves around lifestyle choices and food choices. These are treatments that can be supported by health psychologists.

It is important to understand that not all obesity is caused by lifestyle and poor diet. Some people are naturally heavier than what is considered normal. It is possible to be obese and not be in danger of the negative health effects such as diabetes and cardiovascular diseases. For the most part, people who are obese due to poor diet and lifestyle choices are the ones putting themselves at risk of ill health and premature death.

The obesity epidemic described by the WHO raises some very important questions for health professionals. If people understand what foods are unhealthy and at the same time they also understand that living a sedentary lifestyle is unhealthy, why do people choose both of these things? Understanding seemingly irrational behaviour is the art of psychology. Answering questions like this to determine why people make bad health choices can improve and lengthen the lives of millions of people worldwide.

Concept Three: Health promotion

How do psychologists help people make healthier choices?

Convincing people to change their behaviour can be difficult. For the most part, people do not make irrational decisions. Decisions that seem irrational turn out to be rational once you examine and understand the reasons for a decision. There are always rational explanations for seemingly irrational behaviour.

Psychologists study how people make decisions. Thinking and decision-making is at the heart of cognitive psychology. A clear understanding of how people make decisions can help psychologists find where cognitive biases or misunderstandings are causing people to make bad decisions.

These are some of the difficult questions facing health psychologists:

- Why do people smoke when they know it will lead to premature death?
- Why do people still engage in unprotected sex when they know they may contract a sexually transmitted infection or become pregnant?
- Why do people drink alcohol despite all of the negative health effects?
- Why do people use dangerous drugs when they know it will lead to ill health and possibly an early death?
- Why do people choose to work at high-stress jobs which they know lead to heart disease and premature death?

What does it mean?

Health Belief Model (HBM): a psychological model that describes how people form their beliefs surrounding health issues

The Health Belief Model—explaining unhealthy behaviours

Health psychologists have several models to describe the steps people take when they make a health-related decision. One example is the **Health Belief Model (HBM)** which is a model focused on decision-making—it is meant to explain and predict how people make decisions. It does this by breaking the steps down and isolating factors that determine the choices a person will make.

For example, the HBM uses "perceived threat" and "perceived effectiveness" of treatment and "cues to action" to explain and predict decision-making. Everyone is unique and we all bring our characteristics into each decision we make. The HBM recognizes this and includes demographic factors and personality traits in the model. Table 5.5 gives examples.

<table>
<tr><td>Demographic factors: age, sex, religion, education level</td><td colspan="2">Personality traits: extraversion, agreeableness, conscientiousness, neuroticism, openness</td><td>Other factors: peer pressure, self-efficacy</td></tr>
<tr><td colspan="2">Perceived threat</td><td colspan="2">Perceived effectiveness of treatment or prevention</td></tr>
<tr><td>Susceptibility
How likely am I to get this illness?</td><td>Severity
If I do get this illness, how bad will it be?</td><td>Benefits of action
What are the benefits of preventing this illness?</td><td>Barriers to action
What barriers might prevent action?</td></tr>
<tr><td colspan="4">Cues to action are things that are seen as a reason to act:
• internal: noticing symptoms of the illness in yourself
• external: educational health campaigns, advice from a friend, a loved-one's related illness</td></tr>
</table>

▲ **Table 5.5** Examples of factors in the HBM

The HBM suggests that people will make healthy decisions if they:

- believe they are likely to get an illness
- believe the illness is serious
- believe there are benefits to taking action
- believe they can overcome any barriers to action
- are exposed to something in the environment that triggers action.

Health professionals using the HBM may gain an understanding of why people seem to act irrationally in relation to health choices. Using the HBM can lead psychologists to answers for some of the big questions surrounding poor health choices.

DP ready ATL **Thinking skills**

Use the HBM to find an answer

Choose one of the difficult questions facing health psychologists (page 135) and apply the HBM to try to find an answer. Remember that people do not make irrational decisions—if you can work out their reasoning, you may be able to understand how to change their thinking and their decision-making.

Changing unhealthy behaviours

There are two basic strategies for changing unhealthy behaviours: the **personal health approach** and the **population health approach**. The personal health approach requires an individualized action plan designed by an individual and a health professional. These plans are very effective because they can target the specific, personal reasons a single individual is engaging in unhealthy decision-making. However, this approach is time-consuming and expensive. In order to enact change in an entire population, governments and health organizations often rely on the population health approach.

The population health approach uses research conducted on decision-making to enact policies and education programmes designed to change perceptions about health behaviour. The most effective health promotions use an ecological approach where multiple levels of a person's environment are targeted.

What does it mean?

Personal health approach: an approach to improving health that focuses on individualized action plans designed for a specific individual by a health professional

Advocacy group: a team of people who attempt to influence government policy or public opinion

Level	Examples of action
Individual	Education to change attitudes and beliefs, self-efficacy beliefs and subjective norms
Interpersonal	Social networking campaigns that encourage physical activity and healthy diets
Organizational	Healthy lunch initiatives at school or school-based, non-profit breakfast programmes and workplace exercise facilities
Community	Mass media campaigns
Policy level	Legislation on food labelling and the implementation of taxes or incentives on business

▲ **Table 5.6** Ecological approach

There are many strategies used by governments and **advocacy groups** to try to encourage people to make healthier decisions. The Centre for Science in the Public Interest (CSPI) is an agency in the United States of America that focuses on the food and beverage industry as it relates to the health of American citizens. The CSPI's main goal is to provide objective information to the public regarding food, alcohol, health and the environment. Organizations like this use a variety of strategies to encourage people to make healthier decisions. Table 5.7 gives details.

▲ **Figure 5.11** Fear appeals have been effective in anti-smoking campaigns

Strategy	Description	Link to the HBM
Education	This strategy is very simple and is meant to inform people of the actual threat to their health posed by a given activity. For example, it is possible that someone has misperceived the health risks of smoking or drinking. Education can clarify this misperception and perhaps change behaviour.	perceived susceptibility and severity perceived benefits of action
Fear appeals	Fear appeals are meant to scare people into changing their behaviour. Fear appeals are effective if they are delivered with a strong **self-efficacy** message. This means if you are going to scare people, you have to make them believe that they are capable of the required change in behaviour. Fear appeal without self-efficacy has been shown to backfire and reinforce poor health decisions.	perceived susceptibility and severity perceived benefits of action
Legislation	Governments can make laws that encourage people to make healthy decisions. For example, they can legislate regarding nutrition labels on foods. This is linked to education—legislation ensures that people understand the specific health benefits or dangers of foods, by having it displayed directly on the packaging.	perceived barriers
Taxation and subsidies	Governments can increase the cost of junk foods, cigarettes and alcohol in an effort to change people's behaviour. When the barriers to smoking (the cost) begin to get higher and higher, people may reconsider their choice to continue smoking.	perceived barriers

▲ **Table 5.7** Strategies used to encourage healthy decisions

Links to IB psychology topics

Health psychology

- Determinants of health
- Health problems
- Promoting health

What does it mean?

Self-efficacy: a person's belief in his or her ability to succeed at a particular task

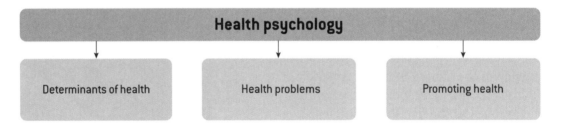

PSYCHOLOGY OF HUMAN RELATIONSHIPS

Introduction

The psychology of human relationships investigates everything having to do with interpersonal and intergroup relationships. This includes love and attraction, conflict and competition, prejudice and discrimination, as well as helping behaviour and the origins of kindness. As with the other applications, researchers examine biological, cognitive and social aspects of behaviour related to human relationships.

Concept One: Love

What binds us to each other?

What is love? This is a simple and a complicated question at the same time. Psychologists study love because it is one of the most powerful determinants of our behaviour. There are clearly different kinds of love; love for your favourite sports team, love for your parents, love for your family pet and love for a husband or wife. These are clearly different things but they also have some elements in common with each other. You cannot convince yourself to love someone you do not love. You cannot command someone else to love you. You cannot simply choose not to love someone you do love. These are painful truths that point out that whatever love is, it is not in our conscious control.

DP ready ATL **Social and communication skills**

Definition of love

Find a partner to carry out this activity.

Without any discussion, each of you should reflect for a moment about what the word "love" means. Again working separately, each make a mind map with "love" at the centre.

- Spend five minutes privately brainstorming words or ideas that you associate with the concept of love and write them on your mind map. Your partner creates a mind map in the same way. Exchange your mind map with your partner's. Do not talk to each other yet.
- Each of you examines the other person's mind map. Then each take a few minutes to write an interpretation of the mind map that summarizes the person's feelings about love. When you have finished your interpretation, read it to your partner. Your partner then reads his or her interpretation of your mind map.

Discuss the following.

Was your partner's interpretation of your concept of love accurate? What about your interpretation of your partner's ideas? What did you each get wrong? How do your concepts of love differ?

Love may simply be a biological drive; a part of a biological system evolved to form loyal pair bonds with other people in order to have children and pass on our genes. This may be a rather unromantic point of view but there are some strong arguments supporting it. Of course, as with all behaviour, it would be reductionist to argue that love is only biological, but let's examine this idea first.

The biology of love

There are two ideas for explaining love biologically: **evolutionary** explanations and **biochemical** explanations. These are not entirely different from each other because an evolutionary psychologist would simply claim that we evolved a particular set of chemicals and brain structures to support survival. Therefore, any biological explanation will have evolutionary connections, but for our purposes we will keep these separate for now.

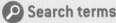

Evolutionary explanations for love focus not on romance but on procreation. Love is an evolved biological mechanism to ensure that we connect and bond to a mate in order to have children and pass on our genes to the next generation. Research into this idea has shown that women and men seek different things in mates.

One set of studies looked at 37 samples in 33 countries with over 10,000 participants. Researchers were interested in what people looked for in a romantic partner. They concluded that females valued older, financially successful men while men valued younger, healthy women (Buss 1989). Evolutionary psychologists would argue this is because young, healthy women are likely to have children successfully and older, wealthier men will be a strong partner for protection and support for raising a child.

What does it mean?

Evolutionary psychology: a branch of psychology that attempts to describe behaviour as a result of the process of natural selection

Biochemical: the system of chemical processes and substances that occur within living organisms

Dopamine: a neurotransmitter that plays a role in motivation and reward, sometimes referred to as the "pleasure chemical"

Mesolimbic dopamine reward system: a system in the brain responsible for regulating motivation and the desire for rewarding stimuli

In more recent research though, it has been shown that what men and women are increasingly looking for the same thing in mates: "mutual attraction and love"(Buss *et al* 2001).

The biological approach to studying love sees it not as an emotion but as a motivational drive that rewards certain behaviours with the pleasure hormone, **dopamine**. Helen Fisher has studied love in the brain using fMRI scans. She has found a connection between passionate love and an area of the midbrain known as the brain's reward system (the **mesolimbic dopamine reward system**). This is the part of the brain that is also associated with addiction. Fisher describes love as a desire, or a drive similar to the drive that addicts feel for their addiction.

In short, love may be an addiction, Fisher and her fellow researchers even go so far as to point out that romantic love and addictions, such as gambling, share many commonalities, for example, euphoria, craving, tolerance, dependence (emotional and physical) and withdrawal. Dopamine is blissfully ignorant of the reason why it is released—for all your reward pathway knows, you might be eating a chocolate bar, drinking alcohol, rock climbing, watching a funny movie or, if you're lucky, about to kiss the person of your dreams. Fisher argues that this is because love, addiction and some risk-taking behaviour are all handled by the same brain regions and neurochemicals—the midbrain and dopamine.

Watch this

www.ted.com/talks/helen_fisher_studies_the_brain_in_love

Search terms

"tedtalk helen fisher brain in love"

DP ready | ATL Thinking skills

Explaining love biologically

- Do you accept the biological explanations for love?
- If you are sceptical, what are your reasons for this?
- Put some thought into the idea that love is simply a biological process. What weaknesses could this theory hold?
- Why do you think it is so convincing to some people?

Sternberg's triangular theory of love

For many people, including Robert Sternberg, the biological explanation of love is unsatisfying because it fails to consider the many different kinds of love that exist. Sternberg has proposed the triangular theory of love. This theory takes a more cognitive approach to understanding how people experience different kinds of love. Four types of love are described in this theory.

- Romantic love: a passionate and intimate love without commitment—short-lived affairs fit in this category.
- Companionate love: an intimate, non-passionate love with long-term commitment—this is shown in long-term marriages with deep affection and commitment where the passion has passed.
- Fatuous love: a passionate and committed love—this is the classic "love at first sight" favoured by many poets and writers. This is characterized by a short courtship followed by marriage.
- Consummate love—this is the ideal relationship: it has balance between passion, intimacy and commitment. Couples experiencing this type of love are happy in their relationship and could not imagine a better partner. They overcome relationship difficulties and share experiences and goals.

The triangular theory of love is a cognitive one because it tries to explain how people understand love. Unlike the biological explanation, it does not attempt to explain the causes of love. This means that it is not seen as a challenge to biological explanations but as an addition to them.

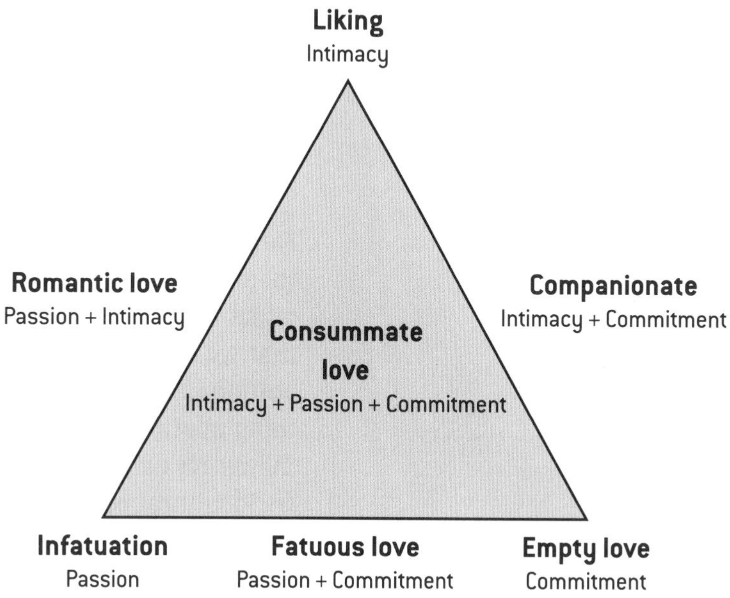

▲ **Figure 5.12** Sternberg's triangular theory of love

DP ready | ATL Thinking skills

What is needed in an explanation?

Biologists attempt to give reasons or causes for love (in other words to explain it) while Sternberg's theory is more descriptive than explanatory.

Do you think it is useful to simply describe a behaviour or must a theory explain something in order to be useful? What makes you say that?

What does it mean?

Reciprocity: exchanging things or favours with other people for mutual benefit

The final pieces to the love puzzle are sociocultural explanations. As you can imagine, there are several social theories relating to love and attraction. These tend to deal with who you find attractive rather than giving an explanation of how love works or a description of different kinds of love. The social theories also tend to be a mixture of sociocultural and cognitive explanations for behaviour. We will consider two theories here and you will have the opportunity to explore and evaluate a third on your own. As you read about these theories they may seem very obvious. This means two things—the theory explains human behaviour and you are human.

Reciprocity is a very simple theory based on social exchange theory. This kind of theory looks at relationships as a "give and take" where balance is sought between partners. In short, you like people who like you. People who like you are actually telling you with their behaviour that they admire the choices you have made in building your social self. In this way, they are validating your choices and this makes you feel good. Very often you will return the favour of liking someone. This explains the idea that if you like someone, you should ask the person to do you a favour. This way, you have established a "give and take" relationship where you have the next move!

Familiarity theory states that you like things that you see more often. It is closely related to the mere-exposure effect. Together, these ideas mean that simply talking to and being with someone you like will increase how much you like the person and how much the person likes you. That is, of course, unless you have some detestable traits that will be uncovered in time. The happy fact is however, that few people hide these detestable traits very well. An initial liking of someone will more likely lead to more liking than less. It turns out the old proverb that "familiarity breeds contempt" may be wrong after all.

Familiarity is also linked to a more obviously social psychology theory called the proximity principle—a very simple principle but which has profound implications. The proximity principle states that we tend to form relationships with people who are nearby. If you do not find that shocking, you are not alone. The interesting thing about this principle is the fact that space and distance matter less and less in our world. As discussed in Chapter 4 on sociocultural psychology, the internet and online social media have largely eliminated space and time as a limiting factor in human relationships. This principle was originally suggested in the 1950s—long before the internet began to shape our social lives. A 21st-century interpretation of this principle might require a redefinition of proximity from "being in close proximity to someone" to "being in close proximity to an internet connection".

Internal link

There is discussion on how the internet and social media affect human relationships in Chapter 4 on concepts in sociocultural psychology: "Concept Three: Globalization and the interaction of cultures".

DP ready ATL Thinking and research skills

Additional explanations

There are other social and cognitive explanations for love.

- Research the attraction similarity model or the matching hypothesis.
- Write a summary of their hypotheses.
- Consider the social and cognitive theories examined in this section. Place the theories in rank order from the most convincing to least convincing. (Rank the most convincing as 1.) Explain your rank choices.

Concept Two: Communication

How can communication build or destroy relationships?

People communicate in many ways. Subtle looks, touch, speech and body language can all convey complex messages to the people around you. What you say and how you say it is vitally important to your relationships. Two ways psychologists can describe the style of communication you use are attribution style and patterns of accommodation. These can both be either positive or negative and so can strengthen a relationship or erode it. At the beginning of any relationship, there is a gradual increasing level of sharing and communication. It can take time to be comfortable enough to share—you probably would not walk up to someone you had just met and share your deepest emotions and desires.

Social penetration theory explains the gradual process of moving from shallow talk about the weather, for example, to a deeper disclosure of your thoughts and feelings. Not only does this theory argue that you move from shallow to deeper discussions and sharing but it also states the following:

- You tend to like people who share thoughts and feelings at a more intimate level.
- You will share more deeply with people you like.
- You like those that you have shared most deeply with.

This is interesting because although it seems obvious that you will share more with those you like, it is not as obvious that you will in turn like people more if you share more with them. Self-disclosure (sharing your thoughts, fears, insecurities and feelings) may play an important role in the formation and strengthening of relationships.

The thing to remember from social penetration theory is that talking with people while sharing thoughts, feelings and emotions can strengthen bonds as well as build relationships. This is true for listeners and for those sharing.

Your **attribution** style can also have an impact on your relationships. Essentially, attribution is about how you interpret the actions

What does it mean?

Attribution: the act of assigning a cause or reason to a particular behaviour

of others. You have reasons for your behaviour. According to attribution theory, these reasons can be either attributed to your situation or your disposition. Your situation refers to what is happening in your environment, while your dispositions are the essentially unchanging elements of your personality. How couples, friends and family members communicate using these attributions can affect relationships.

People in healthy relationships tend to interpret positive behaviours to a person's disposition and negative behaviours to temporary environmental situations beyond the control of the other person. Positive communication often uses universal statements like "always" for positive traits, and "never" or "rarely" for negative traits. For example, the following is a hypothetical interaction of a positive attribution style and a negative one.

- Negative: why are you late? You are always taking too long to get ready!
- Positive: why are you late? The traffic must have been terrible!

Researchers argue that communicating with a negative attribution bias can damage a relationship.

Remember that it is the communication of these negative attributions that is the focus of attention. The attribution itself is not the problem. In order for attribution to affect a relationship, it must be communicated.

What does it mean?

Accommodation: the practice of using positive, constructive strategies to maintain a relationship

DP ready ATL **Thinking skills**

What comes first?

One criticism of the theory of attribution styles is that it assumes that attribution styles in relationships are consistent and they do not change. Some questions are raised by this assumption.

- Can how people communicate their attributions change over time?
- What do you think: does the negative attribution lead to relationship decline—or does a worsening relationship lead to negative attribution?

Active

Constructive	Destructive
VOICE: acknowledge dissatisfaction and actively attempt to improve the situation	**EXIT:** acknowledge dissatisfaction and actively work to end or abuse the relationship
LOYALTY: not necessarily acknowledge dissatisfaction and passively wait for situation to improve	**NEGLECT:** not necessarily acknowledge dissatisfaction and passively allow the relationship to deteriorate

Passive

▲ **Figure 5.13** Relationship conflict strategies

You will have failed relationships in your life. Perhaps you are experiencing some conflict recently and are now reflecting on how you communicated during that time. Another idea that underscores the importance of communication in relationships is that of patterns of **accommodation**. When positive strategies are used in communication it is called accommodation. Psychologists Rusbult and Zembrodt (1983) have identified two positive (constructive) strategies and two negative (destructive) communication strategies.

These strategies are meant to describe how people communicate during times of conflict in a relationship. Destructive patterns may lead to the end of a relationship, while constructive ones help resolve conflict and build trust and love. It is interesting to note that women are more likely to accommodate than men.

John Gottman and Julie Schwartz Gottman are psychologists and relationship therapists. The Gottmans have spent decades studying communication patterns in couples. They claim to be able to predict whether a couple will divorce with 90% accuracy. They collect longitudinal qualitative and quantitative data and then analyse the data to determine the likelihood of divorce. Over decades and analysis of thousands of couples, they have identified four communication behaviours that can erode a relationship. They call these behaviours the four horsemen of relationship apocalypse. Table 5.8 below gives details.

Criticism This is a statement that attacks the character of a person—it is more than a simple complaint. This is a negative attribution bias towards the partner.
Contempt This is treating someone with disrespect or mocking sarcasm. The Gottmans consider this the worst of the four behaviours and the number 1 predictor of divorce. It includes behaviour such as name-calling, insulting, eye-rolling or mocking behaviour.
Defensiveness This a self-defence mechanism where the victim of an attack claims to be innocent and under attack for no reason. This often takes the shape of deflecting blame onto others in order to hide blame or guilt.
Stonewalling A listener shows this behaviour by withdrawing from a conversation and refusing to communicate with the partner. Often the only communication is a closed or disinterested body language such as turning away, crossing the arms and avoiding eye contact.

▲ **Table 5.8** Gottman's four horsemen behaviours

Gottman's four horsemen theory connects well to patterns of accommodation and negative attribution. All relationships, even healthy ones, see these behaviours sometimes. It is not the presence of these behaviours that predict the end of a relationship, but the frequency with which they appear, that is most important.

DP ready ATL **Self-management skills**

Communication with your family

Reflect on how you communicate with your family. Can you think of a time when you used one of Gottman's four horsemen while communicating with a family member? Was it intentional or do you think you sent an unintended message?

Think back to what you learned about phubbing in Chapter 3 on cognitive psychology.

- Do you think that phubbing is a new form of stonewalling?
- How could you avoid sending the wrong message to your friends and family?

Internal link

Phubbing is discussed in Chapter 3 on cognitive psychology: "Concept Four: Digital technology is reshaping your brain".

What does it mean?

Prosocial: any behaviour or action that helps others or society in general

Antisocial: any behaviour or action that causes harm to others or society in general

Karma: the idea that the intentions or actions of an individual will influence the future of that individual—in other words, if you do good things then good things will happen to you

Egoistic helping: helping behaviour motivated by self interest

Empathetic helping: helping behaviour motivated by a desire to ease the suffering of others

Social desirability effect: the tendency for people to speak or act in a way that makes them look good

Concept Three: Helping

Why do you choose to help those in need?

Helping is almost universally seen as a positive and socially beneficial behaviour. We honour superheroes as "super helpers" and tell children stories of the great deeds they do to help people in need. Superheroes are a great example of how nearly all cultures try to socialize children into a culture of helping others. Behaviour that helps society is beneficial to society in general and the individuals within it. Most behaviour can be classified as either **prosocial** or **antisocial**.

Pro-social behaviours are any behaviours that benefit other people or society while anti-social behaviours are behaviours that cause harm to others or that generally go against social or cultural norms. The table below shows some examples of each of the two types. Psychology has long sought to explain what drives people to commit either prosocial or antisocial behaviour. Criminology and criminological psychology are fields of study into antisocial behaviour. In this section we are interested in prosocial behaviours—that is, why do people choose to do the right thing when it is not necessarily the easiest thing to do?

Prosocial behaviour	Antisocial behaviour
helping behaviour	violence
volunteering	abusive language
honesty	vandalism
fairness	intimidation
responsibility	threatening others

▲ **Table 5.9** Prosocial and antisocial behaviours

Social exchange theory provided one explanation for love and attraction but it can also be useful in explaining why people perform prosocial behaviours. Trivers (1971) proposed the reciprocal altruism model in an attempt to explain helping behaviour between strangers. Trivers' idea was simple: people help others in the hope that in the future the favour will be returned when they themselves are in need. If an entire society believes that their good deeds will be repaid, then it may create a norm of helping behaviour where everyone helps and everyone is helped in return. This is similar to the Hindu and Buddhist idea of **karma**. Karma can be defined as a belief that your behaviour at any given time will influence your future.

In contrast to the reciprocal altruism model (and with decidedly more optimism in human nature), Batson proposed the empathy/altruism hypothesis as a cognitive alternative. This hypothesis understands helping behaviour as either **egoistic** or **empathetic**.

- Egoistic: this is helping behaviour where the goal is to increase positive feelings for the helper or to gain some other benefit. This could include acting in order to end some negative state of mind or discomfort. For example, it could be soothing a crying baby simply because you cannot stand the sound of a crying baby.

- Empathetic: this is helping behaviour driven by a genuine concern for the wellbeing or safety of others. For example, this would be soothing a crying baby because you want ease the baby's suffering.

Batson seems to believe that people are inherently good and giving. His theory claims that helping behaviour is caused by empathetic concern for another's wellbeing. The benefits to the person helping are not the ultimate goal but instead are an unintended consequence.

To test his idea, Batson had to devise a way to control levels of empathy and to determine the difference between empathetic and egoistic helping. This is no easy task. Think back to the example above about the crying baby. Which do you think is more socially acceptable: helping a baby only because you find the crying annoying or helping a baby because you are moved to end the suffering? Most people would tell you they helped the crying baby out of concern and empathy, not self-interest. The tendency for people to answer in a way that makes them look good is called the **social desirability effect**. Batson devised the empathy-escape paradigm to distinguish between reasons for helping without the need to ask participants why they were helping.

Key Study: Toi, Batson and Steiner (1982)

KS

Empathy and helping behaviour

Aim: to investigate the effect of empathy on helping behaviour.

Procedure: female psychology students were played a recording of an interview with a fictional student named Carol who had broken both her legs and could not attend lectures. Participants were divided into two groups: high empathy (told to focus on Carol's feelings during the interview) and low empathy (told to focus on the facts of her story). The researchers then made two more conditions: easy and difficult escape. Half of the participants in each group were told Carol would be attending their class and half were told she would stay at home. "Easy escape" was the condition where Carol stayed at home because participants would not have to experience meeting the person they declined to help.

Results: participants in the low empathy group were much less willing to help in the easy escape condition than they were in the difficult escape condition. In contrast, the high empathy group was not affected by the change in escape condition and had a high rate of helping in both difficult and easy escape conditions.

Conclusion: empathy must have been the motivating factor for helping because those in the high empathy condition helped regardless of whether escape was easy or difficult.

What does it mean?

Bystander effect: the effect on behaviour when the presence of other people leads to an individual deciding not to help a person in distress

There are many researchers interested in the reasons for helping behaviour. Researchers either believe helping behaviour is determined by egoistic helping (Cialdini) or empathetic (Batson). This has turned into one of the great debates in psychology as researchers keep publishing research to refute the evidence most recently published by their intellectual opponent. Some might say that it is similar to a slow-motion argument where the findings of a study seem to be dependent on what researchers are trying to find.

DP ready ATL **Research skills**

Research bias

Research must be unbiased and above all seek to find truth, but this is not always the case. Sometimes research bias can reduce the validity of research findings.

- To what extent do you believe that researchers find whatever it is they are setting out to find? In other words, do you think that findings are dependent on the design of the study?
- Where there seems to be research bias, do you think this prevents any real conclusions being made regarding the origins of human behaviour?

In contrast to helping behaviour, many psychologists have spent their careers looking into why people choose not to help when someone is in need. The **bystander effect** is defined as the phenomenon that individuals are less likely to help in a given situation if there are other people present. In many ways, this is the flipside of helping behaviour. It is tempting to label non-helpers as especially callous or uncaring but research has shown that most people will fall victim to the bystander effect. This effect has been observed in real life and in experimentation.

Psychology in real life

PRL

Bystanderism in the case of Wang Yue

In October 2011, a 2-year-old in Foshan, China called Wang Yue wandered into the street behind her father's store and was struck by a van. The driver of the van initially stopped but then continued driving, running over the child again. What happened next is shocking and challenges notion that people will naturally feel empathy and help in emergency situations. As Wang Yue lay injured in the street, 18 passers-by ignored her. She was run over again before eventually being dragged out of the street by a garbage collector and taken to hospital. She died eight days later.

The witnesses and passers-by were normal people, not heartless robots, so how did this happen? Researchers are interested in studying why people choose not to help in situations where others are in need.

Table 5.10 offers different explanations for bystanderism that arose from two important studies.

Social explanation	Cognitive explanation
Factors affecting bystanderism Latane, Darley, McGuire (1968)	The good Samaritan study Piliavin *et al* (1981)
Diffusion of responsibility: this is the belief that others will act so you do not have to. Ambiguity: you are unsure if help is needed. Group inhibition: others are not acting so inaction must the right thing to do.	Arousal: you notice someone in need and your body readies itself for action (arousal). Cost/Reward Analysis: you weigh the costs of helping. If the costs of helping outweigh the rewards, you choose not to help.

▲ **Table 5.10** Social and cognitive explanations of bystanderism

As with everything else in human behaviour, bystanderism is a complex phenomenon that has a mixture of biological, cognitive and social explanations. A deeper understanding of both bystanderism and helping behaviour may be useful in nurturing communities of individuals that care for each other and take responsibility for each other's wellbeing.

Links to IB psychology topics

Psychology of human relationships

- Personal relationships
- Group dynamics
- Social responsibility

Chapter conclusion

This chapter introduced the main concepts in only a few fields of applied psychology. There are many more fields and each of them contributes to a growing body of knowledge on how and why people behave as they do. All fields of study rely on the core components of psychology: biological, cognitive and sociocultural origins of behaviour. As our understanding of these three areas improve, so will our understanding of all the areas of application. Applied psychology is limited only by humankind— wherever there are people, applied psychology will be useful in explaining behaviour.

Fields of study in psychology include:	
abnormal	sport
developmental	criminal
health	organizational
human relationships	school/educational
business	consumer
economics	forensics
clinical	personality

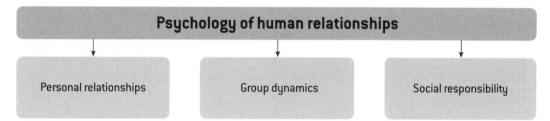

Reflection Activity

Create your own concept map for each of the main sections in this chapter on applied psychology: abnormal psychology, developmental psychology, health psychology and the psychology of human relationships.

To create your concept map, generate a list of ideas or concepts related to each specific area of psychology. Sort the ideas by placing what you think are the most important ideas in the centre and the least important ones towards the outside. Connect linked ideas with lines and write notes on the lines to describe the connections. Use the remaining space around the outside to elaborate on any new ideas that extend your thinking.

Adapted from Ritchhart, Church and Morrison (2011)

Exam-style questions

Abnormal psychology

1. **Evaluate** biological treatments for one disorder.
2. **Discuss** concepts of normality.
3. **Discuss** the etiologies of one disorder.

Developmental psychology

1. **Discuss** one theory of cognitive development.
2. **To what extent** do biological factors influence cognitive development?
3. **Discuss** one theory of attachment and development.

Health psychology

1. **Discuss** prevalence rates for one health problem.
2. **Discuss** one risk factor and one protective factor for one health problem.
3. **Evaluate** two health promotion strategies.

Psychology of human relationships

1. **To what extent** can biological factors explain interpersonal relationships?
2. **Discuss** the role of communication in personal relationships.
3. **Evaluate** one model of prosocial behaviour.

Big ideas

Abnormal psychology

- Normal behaviour is not the same in all cultures and not all abnormal behaviour is considered a problem.
- The way mental health professionals diagnose symptoms of psychological disorders is similar to the way doctors examine symptoms of other medical conditions.
- Etiology refers to the underlying causes of a disorder.

Developmental psychology

- As children mature, their brain grows and they become capable of more complicated thinking and decision-making. They learn more from the environment and the people around them.
- Humans are social animals who seek attachment to others. Psychologists have identified different attachment patterns in children.

Health psychology

- Health psychology is about wellness. It is not enough to simply be free from psychological disorders to be well.
- Health problems such as obesity can have psychological origins as well as social or biological ones.
- Studying how and why people make health choices can help mental health professionals to promote healthy behaviours.

Psychology of human relationships

- There are biological, psychological and social origins of love and attraction.
- You can chose to communicate in ways that encourage good relationships or in ways that can damage or end relationships.
- Many people are willing to help even when helping might lead to personal danger or loss. Why people help is determined by social as well as psychological factors, some researchers even argue there are biological origins of helping.

6 Assessments—how to show your understanding

In this chapter you will learn:

→ the purpose of assessments
- gauging your understanding using external and internal assessments

→ command terms in IB psychology
- short answer command terms
- extended response (essay response) command terms

→ what counts as evidence in IB psychology
- describing research—abstracts

→ how to show your understanding
- formulating responses to prompts in psychology

→ taking it to the next level—critical thinking
- opportunities for critical thinking

→ the differences between short answer responses and essay responses

Introduction

Why does my school have tests and assessments?

You probably don't enjoy writing assessments or tests. School is about curiosity, character, searching and discovering. If that is true, why do schools insist that students take tests and other assessments? The answer is simple: assessments give you a chance to show what you have learned. In other words, you are given the opportunity to showcase your understanding of a new concept. Most often this is done without the help of texts or the internet—just you, your memories and your understandings.

Knowing something is not the same as *understanding* something. Knowing something involves asking "what", "when", and "where" questions. Understanding something is more difficult and requires asking "how" and "why" questions. Of course, you need to know things before you can understand them. For example, you need to know the causes and symptoms of an illness before you can understand how to cure that illness. Finding a cure involves understanding the connection between causes and symptoms.

In IB psychology you will be asked challenging questions that go beyond knowing. You will be asked questions that are specifically written to allow you to show how well you understand a concept. These are sometimes referred to as "concept questions" and they require you to explain connections between ideas.

Some examples of questions are given in Table 6.1.

Approach	Knowledge question	Concept question
Biological	**Can** animal research be used to explain human behaviour?	**Why** is it possible to use animal research to understand human behaviour?
Cognitive	**What** kinds of biases do we have built into our thinking and decision-making?	**Why** do we have biases built into our thinking and decision-making? How can these be explained?
Sociocultural	**In what ways** is globalization influencing your behaviour?	**How** does the interaction of local and global culture influence your behaviour?

▲ **Table 6.1** Examples of knowledge questions and concept questions

Assessment

External and internal assessments

Your teachers are constantly assessing your understanding. These assessments are meant for your teacher to gauge how well you are learning the concepts and will determine the grade your school gives you, but when you reach the DP, they do not count toward the grade the IB awards. The IB uses a combination of internal and external assessments to determine your grade in IB psychology. Table 6.2, taken from "IB Psychology Guide: Assessment" shows assessment arrangements at standard level (SL) and higher level (HL).

Paper 1 (2 hours) 50% of grade at SL 40% of grade at HL	**Paper 2 (1 or 2 hours)** 25% of grade at SL 20% of grade at HL	**Paper 3** Not assessed in SL 20% of grade at HL	**Internal assessment** 25% of grade at SL 20% of grade at HL
• A two-hour exam at the end of the two year course • Section A: three short-answer questions on the core approaches to psychology (27 marks) • Section B: one essay from a choice of three on the biological, cognitive and sociocultural approaches to behaviour* (22 marks) *HL can be tested on "extensions" in each approach	SL (1 hour) • A one-hour exam at the end of the two-year course • One question from a choice of three on one option (22 marks) HL (2 hours) • A two-hour exam at the end of the two-year course • Two questions; one from a choice of three on each of two options (44 marks)	HL only • Three short-answer questions from a list of six static questions on approaches to research (24 marks)	• A report on an experimental study undertaken by the student (22 marks) • This is assessed by your teacher and your grade is confirmed externally by the IB at the end of the course

▲ **Table 6.2** (Taken from the IB Psychology Guide: Assessment)

Command terms in IB psychology

Questions in IB psychology are worded very carefully to make sure that you show your understanding of a concept or connection. You should think of questions as opportunities to show your understanding but you need to pay close attention to exactly how your teacher is asking you to show your understanding. Command terms are keywords in every question that tell you what to do. Before you can understand how to write an answer, you need to know what the command term is asking you.

Short answer command terms

Command term	Meaning	Notes
*Explain	Give a detailed account including reasons or causes.	This is the most important command term. All of your responses will require you to explain yourself. When you explain you give someone more information to help them better understand a statement or idea that you have made or described. When you outline and describe you also need to explain.
Outline	Give a brief account or summary.	This command term will often be used with a theory. You may be asked to outline schema theory, for example. This means you will have to give all of the relevant details of the study and explain the link between the theory and the behaviour it is trying to explain.
Describe	Give a detailed account.	Describing is similar to outlining in that it requires you to show your understanding of something by explaining details of the theory, study or behaviour.

*See below for additional notes on the importance of explaining.

▲ **Table 6.3** Short answer command terms explained

Explaining

The most powerful word in your answer is: "**because**".

Explaining something is the most important thing you can do in any question. Make sure that you do not just state something—you must always state a fact, then explain it. Stating a fact might be enough to show that you know something but it is not enough to show that you understand it.

Remember, in IB psychology your goal is to show that you *understand* human behaviour—it is not enough to show that you *know* about human behaviour. This is why explaining is necessary for all of your responses. Giving the reasons or causes of something shows that you understand it.

Explanations often come after specific words such as "because," "therefore," "in other words ..." or "this means that ..." If you have these words in your response it normally means you are explaining your statements and showing understanding.

Extended response (essay response) command terms

Command term	Meaning	Notes
Contrast	Give an account of the differences between two (or more) items or situations, referring to both (all) of them throughout.	Contrasting is tricky. You will be asked to contrast two things. Do not simply describe each and then write about how they are different. Instead, identify at least two ways the things are different and then spend roughly half of your response explaining each of the differences.
Evaluate	Make an appraisal by weighing up the strengths and limitations.	Evaluating means to look at the things the theory or study does well *and* to point out some of the things that are not done well. It is not enough simply to describe the theory or study and then list the pros and cons. You must explain why you think each one is either a strength or limitation of the theory or study.
To what extent	Consider the merits or otherwise of an argument or concept. Opinions and conclusions should be presented clearly and supported with appropriate evidence and sound argument.	This command term is essentially asking you "how much or how little". You should be on one side or the other. Do not pick the middle road. Your response should argue "to a great extent" or "to a small extent". To say that something has merit or otherwise to "some extent" is really saying nothing at all.
Discuss	Offer a considered and balanced review that includes a range of arguments, factors or hypotheses. Opinions or conclusions should be presented clearly and supported by appropriate evidence.	Imagine you are sitting at a table with several specialists in the area you are studying. What would the conversation sound like? The individuals would probably be sharing their theories and pointing out problems with the theories of the others. This is what a response to a "discuss" command term looks like. You lay out different ideas and discuss the relative merits of each.

▲ **Table 6.4** Extended response (essay response) command terms explained

What counts as evidence in psychology?

Theories and **studies** are not the same things. A theory is an idea that tries to explain the reasons or causes for behaviour, while a study is a real-world test or examination of a **hypothesis**. This means that theories on their own are just an educated guess about the relationship between a cause and a behaviour—they are not evidence, they are a proposal. Studies are what count as evidence for or against a hypothesis. A hypothesis that is supported in experiments, observation or interviews (these are all kinds of studies) is considered to be a good theory.

As in the natural sciences, knowledge in psychology depends on research and studies that use the scientific method. Chapter 1, on research in psychology, provides an outline of the common methods used to learn new things about human behaviour. These methods include formal laboratory experiments, quasi-experiments, interviews, observations and case studies.

TOK link

The difference between a hypothesis and a theory

The nature of knowledge is different in different fields of study. A hypothesis is a suggested possible outcome of an event and is testable—that is, it can be verified or falsified by research. A hypothesis is made before any evidence is gathered. Theories are supported by evidence. In the natural sciences, once enough evidence has been gathered to support a theory, it can be claimed that the theory is proven.

- Why do you think psychologists do not claim that research ever *proves* a theory of human behaviour?
- Does this mean that psychological research can never have certainty?

Psychologists observe human behaviour and then create a hypothesis to explain that behaviour. Once they have a hypothesis, they can design experiments to test their idea to see if it can accurately explain or predict human behaviour. Once they have evidence, they call it a theory. Psychologists do not use the word "prove" when talking about their theories. Instead, they say things such as "this study supports the theory of ..." or "this study illustrates the theory of ..." Likewise, you should not use the word "prove" in your answers.

Nonetheless, you will be expected to use psychological studies and research to support claims that you make in your responses in psychology. This is a very important part of your answers. Studies are always tied to theories. In your responses you should never talk about a study without first describing the theory it is testing.

Internal link

Review Chapter 1 on concepts in psychological research.

Describing research—abstracts

Aim—Procedure—Results—Conclusion (APRC)

APRC stands for things you must include when you describe a study. The key is to be brief.

Aim: what was the purpose of the study? An "aim" statement normally starts with "to investigate ..." and normally investigates the relationship between a variable and a behaviour.

Procedure: this is the step-by-step description of how the researcher investigated the relationship described in the "Aim." If the study is an experiment, you are required to identify the Independent Variable and Dependent Variable as well as the experimental and control conditions. The sample is often briefly described in this section.

Results: the results are also sometimes called the findings. Results are often stated in relation to what is specifically being measured (the effect of the Independent Variable on the Dependent Variable—in other words, what happened to the Dependent Variable when the researcher changed the Independent Variable).

Conclusion: this is a statement about the relationship between the variables or the variable and behaviour under investigation. The conclusion is different from the results because it is about what can be learned from the results, not just the results themselves.

You can find examples of APRCs throughout this book.

DP ready | ATL Communication skills

Citing sources

In psychology you will often see citations when a study is used as evidence. You are expected to remember and give credit to researchers for their research. This is normally done after the first mention of the research. Citing is easy to do in psychology; simply give each researcher's last name and the year the research was published. This has been done throughout this book and looks like this: (Bandura 1962); (Darley, Gross 1983). If there are one, two or three researchers give all their last names. If there are more than three researchers, it is acceptable to give the first researcher's name then use "*et al*", which means "and others": (Loftus *et al* 1974).

How to show your understanding

Formulating responses to prompts in psychology

In psychology, you will be asked to explain the relationship between theories of behaviour and the results of research in that area. This requires you to understand theories of behaviour and the research related to those theories. It is therefore important to have a rich understanding of the research methods explained in Chapter 1 on concepts in psychological research.

A well-developed response will have multiple sections: describing a theory, giving an example of research, and explaining the link between the research and the theory.

Example answer

Explain the theory of localization of function.		
Section	**Description**	**Example**
Theory	Describe the theory that explains the behaviour. You should be explicit here and link the behaviour to a cause or reason predicted by the theory. This should be more than a sentence; it is more likely to be a short paragraph.	Behaviour is partly determined by brain structure. The connection between patterns of behaviour and parts of the brain is a rich area of research. A strict version of the **theory of localization states that** every behaviour is associated with a certain brain region. Research into localization has found partial support for this theory. Generally speaking, behaviour is largely determined by particular structures in the brain. For example, declarative memory processing takes place in the hippocampus, breathing and balance are regulated in the cerebellum, and the amygdala processes fear and emotion. However, some functions such as memory storage are distributed throughout the brain.
Evidence	Describe the research that you are using to show the theory can explain behaviour accurately. Often this will include points based on APRC and is likely to be a paragraph.	**One study that supports localization is** Maguire (2000). **The aim** of this study was to investigate the role of the hippocampus in navigational and spatial memory. Maguire did this by examining whether there was a correlation between the amount of a taxi driver's experience and the amount of gray matter volume.

Section	Description	Example
Evidence (*continued*)		Maguire gathered 16 healthy, right-handed London taxi drivers. These drivers had all completed a multi-year training called "the Knowledge" that required them to memorize the thousands of streets in London—a very difficult task that requires excellent spatial memory skills. Maguire then measured this sample against a similar control group who were not taxi drivers and so had not spent years committing London's streets to memory. Maguire used a quasi-experimental method where the Independent Variable was the completion of "the Knowledge" and years of experience driving a taxi, the Dependent Variable was the volume of the hippocampus (as measured using MRI). All participants were scanned using MRI, which produces a 3-D brain image of each participant. **The results showed** that the taxi drivers had greater volume in their right posterior hippocampus than the control group. Additionally, Maguire found a positive correlation between the amount of time driving a taxi and the volume in the right posterior hippocampus.
Connection	Explain the connection between the results of the research and the theory you claim explains the behaviour. This section should always contain the words "**This study shows that** ..." or, "**This research illustrates that** ..." This is the most important part of your response because this is where you show that you understand how the research supports the theory. You have to link the results of the study explicitly to the prediction made by the theory.	**This study shows that** navigation and spatial memory is likely processed in the right posterior hippocampus. **This is shown in the results because** the taxi drivers had more volume in this location than the control group. Additionally, the correlational data showed a positive correlation between the amount of time driving and the volume of the right posterior hippocampus. **This supports the theory of localization because** the years spent memorizing and recalling the streets of London affected only one area of the brain—the right posterior hippocampus. The brains of the taxi drivers did not grow uniformly across their whole brain, only in the localized area associated with spatial memory. In addition, the right posterior hippocampus of the taxi drivers was larger than that of the non-taxi drivers suggesting it was the years spent studying and memorizing streets that produced the difference in the two groups. This suggests the function of processing spatial memories is localized in the right posterior hippocampus.

▲ **Table 6.5**

Taking it to the next level

Critical thinking

The IB encourages students to think critically. Students do this by:

- "asking questions and challenge assertions
- defining the problem
- examining evidence for and against a claim
- avoiding oversimplifying
- tolerating uncertainty
- employing gender evaluation
- employing methodological evaluation
- employing ethical evaluation
- evaluating by comparison".

Taken from: "Approaches to Teaching and Learning in Psychology" (https://ibpublishing.ibo.org)

Opportunities for critical thinking

It is often not enough just to show that research supports a theory. You need to think critically about the theory and the research. In other words, you have to challenge the connections that claim to link a theory to a particular study.

DP ready ATL **Thinking and self-management skills**

Critical thinking

Students often have no faith in their thinking and are reluctant to question the theories or practices of professional psychologists or researchers. They may think things like "Well, they are the experts, what do I know?"

Reflect on all the work you put into learning and the successes you have had in the past. Your ideas and criticisms are as valid as anyone else's as long as they are backed up with evidence. The tools you need in order to strengthen your critical thinking skills are in these pages. Never accept without question and never stop asking questions until you are satisfied with your understanding.

Thinking critically means to independently challenge ideas and beliefs. It is an ongoing practice of questioning why we should accept an idea as truth. There are many ways you can do this in psychology. The following table gives you some opportunities for critical thinking.

Opportunity for critical thinking	Question	Description
Alternative explanations	Are there any other explanations that could also explain the reasons for a specific behaviour?	Are there any explanations for the findings of a study other than the one given by the researchers? Some researchers specialize in one particular approach to behaviour, such as the biological approach. However, if they study behaviour from only the biological approach, they may ignore social or cognitive factors that can provide an alternative explanation.
Research method and design	Was the research well designed and appropriate?	Was the research method well designed and appropriate or were there problems in the design that you think might have affected the results? For example, research has shown that people often act differently if they know they are being observed. In a study that uses overt observation to study something embarrassing or socially awkward, for instance, participants may be acting unnaturally. This lowers the validity of the study.
Triangulation	Do different kinds of research or different researchers arrive at the same conclusions?	Researchers can choose to look at a single behaviour from different angles. For example, if you are studying stress and aggression you might choose to: **1.** observe behaviour **2.** measure cortisol levels in participants' blood **3.** interview participants about their feelings **4.** use fMRI to investigate which of the participants' brain regions are most active. If all of these different techniques give mutually supporting findings, this improves the trustworthiness of those findings.

Opportunity for critical thinking	Question	Description
Assumptions and biases	Did the researchers assume something they shouldn't have? Does the theory make an assumption that it shouldn't? Do the researchers have biases that affect their findings?	Sometimes researchers make assumptions about the things they are studying. For example, when studying empathy, researchers have assumed that the more similar you are to someone, the more empathy you share with that person. When creating a condition for high empathy, they therefore make the target person seem similar to the test subject. If this assumption is incorrect, it makes the findings invalid. More examples of bias can be found in Chapter 1 on concepts in psychological research.
Areas of uncertainty	Is anything left unexplained or vague? Are the terms well defined and the ideas well explained?	If a theory includes terms that are not well defined, the theory can lack construct validity. For example, there are many theories related to intelligence but we do not have a clear and commonly accepted definition of intelligence. If we cannot define intelligence, how can we measure it? If it cannot be measured, it cannot be studied. As we do not fully understand what intelligence is, there is some area of uncertainty around research about intelligence.

▲ **Table 6.6** Opportunities for critical thinking

Opportunities for critical thinking are often introduced with specific keywords or phrases that can help your reader understand what is coming. This is called **signposting**. It is when you use words or phrases as signals, like road signs, to help the reader predict and understand what you are about to say. Signposting can improve communication by making your arguments clearer in your writing. Try using the words in the box below when you are introducing critical thinking.

DP ready ATL **Communication skills**

Signposting

These words or phrases are useful when signposting opportunities for critical thinking.

- However ...
- On the other hand ...
- An alternative explanation for this might be ...
- Something that remains unclear is ...
- Yet, the findings of this study may be in question because ...
- The researchers seem to be assuming ...
- One question left unanswered is ...

The best critical thinking should be creative, spontaneous and unique. In other words, simply repeating someone else's criticism may show you studied a topic—but it does not show you understand a topic, it simply means you remembered someone else's critical thinking. Try to use your own understanding to question theories and ideas using the opportunities listed in this chapter. Effective critical thinking shows you understand something very well and that you have challenged its accuracy.

Short answer responses and essay responses

What's the difference?

In IB psychology there are only two main ways in which you will be asked to show your understanding—short answer responses and essays. You can find some of the main differences between them in the table below.

Short answer response	Essay
Its length is approximately 500 words.	Its length is approximately 1200 words.
It is focused on knowledge and understanding.	It must include critical thinking and show a deeper understanding.
Command terms for a short answer response are: explain, outline, describe.	Command terms for an essay are: evaluate, contrast, discuss, to what extent.
It normally focuses on one topic or behaviour.	It may focus on linking topics or behaviours

▲ **Table 6.7** Contrasts between the short answer response and the essay

Chapter conclusion

Writing in psychology should be scientific—clear and concise. Include only what is needed for your reader to understand your message. You should not be colourful or unnecessarily descriptive in your writing. Answer the prompt in the first sentence, explain your answer, give an example, then explain the connection—once you have done these things, stop writing. Psychology straddles the natural and human sciences and this should be reflected in your writing. You need to be only descriptive enough to be clear.

Reflection Activities

1. **Claim, support and question—practise writing a response.** Make a claim about one or more of the concepts you have learned in this book. Gather evidence to support your claim (or claims) and identify questions that are left unanswered by your claim. Ask a partner to evaluate your writing.
2. **Step into the mind of your teacher** to try to identify what it is your teacher is looking for in a strong response. Create two lists. One list is the things that you think your teacher wants to see in your responses. Beside each item, record why your teacher wants to see this. The second is a list of things that your teacher does not want to see in your responses. Similarly, beside each one, record why you think your teacher does not want to see this.

Big ideas

- Teachers give you tests to check for understanding. Show them you understand by explaining your claims.
- Try not to leave anything for your teacher to infer—avoid making statements without explanation; instead, make sure you are explicit and give reasons for what you write.
- Above all, strive to be clear and concise. Key vocabulary is helpful, but don't use a word if you're unsure of its exact meaning.

- Command terms tell you what you need to do in a response.
- Make sure you understand the command terms and tailor your writing to match what it's asking you to do.
- For example, you are required to explain yourself in all your responses, but an 'evaluate' prompt will ask you to do something very different from a 'contrast' or 'discuss' prompt.

- You must use research in your answers.
- Research studies are evidence for your claims.
- Using personal anecdotes or hypothetical stories is not appropriate.
- Evidence taken from published research must be included in your explanation.

- Critical thinking shows that you understand what you are writing about.
- There are many opportunities for critical thinking in psychology, involving, for example, examining alternative explanations, assumptions and areas of uncertainty.
- Effective critical thinking is creative, spontaneous and unique.

Bibliography

Bandura, A, Ross, D and Ross, SA. 1961. "Transmission of aggression through imitation of aggressive models". *The Journal of Abnormal and Social Psychology*. Vol 63, number 3. Pp 575–582.

Baron-Cohen, S, Leslie, AM and Frith, U. 1985. "Does the autistic child have a 'theory of mind'?" *Cognition*. Vol 21, number 1. Pp 37–46.

Bartlett, F. 1932. *Remembering: A Study in Experimental and Social Psychology*. Cambridge, UK. Cambridge University Press.

Berry, J and Katz, D. 1967. "Independence and conformity in subsistence-level societies". *Journal of Personality and Social Psychology*. Vol 7, number 4. Pp 415–418.

Bouchard, TJ, Lykken, DT, McGue, M, Segal, NL and Tellegen, A. 1990. "Sources of human psychological differences: the Minnesota study of twins reared apart". *Science*. Vol 250. Pp 223–228.

Broca, PP. 1861. "Loss of speech, chronic softening and partial destruction of the anterior left lobe of the brain". *Bulletin de la Sociétè Anthropologique*. Vol 2. Pp 235–238.

Caspi, A, Sugden, K, Moffitt, TE, Taylor, A, Craig, IW, Harrington, H, McCLay, J, Mill, J, Martin, J, Braithwaite, A, Poulton, R. 2003. "Influence of life stress on a depression: Moderation by polymorphism in the 5_HTT gene", *Science*. Vol 301. Pp 386–389.

Darley, JM and Gross, PH. 1983. "A hypothesis confirming bias in labeling effects". *Journal of Personality and Social Psychology*. Vol 44, number 1. Pp 20–33.

Dittrich L. 2017. *Patient HM: A Story of Memory, Madness, and Family Secrets*. New York, USA. Penguin Random House.

Festinger, L and Carlsmith, JM. 1959. "Cognitive consequences of forced compliance". *Journal of Abnormal and Social Psychology*. Vol 58. Pp 203–211.

Harlow, HF. 1958. "The nature of love". *American Psychologist*. Vol 13. Pp 673–685.

Harris, S. 2012. *Free Will*. New York, USA. Free Press.

Hofstede, G. 2011. "Culture's Consequences: Comparing values, behaviors, institutions, and organizations across nations". Thousand Oaks, California, USA. Sage.

Loftus, EF and Palmer, JC. 1974. "Reconstruction of automobile destruction: An example of the interaction between language and memory". *Journal of Verbal Learning and Verbal Behavior*. Vol 13. Pp 585–589.

Ludwig DS, Peterson KE and Gortmaker SL. 2001. "Relation between consumption of sugar-sweetened drinks and childhood obesity: a prospective, observational analysis". *The Lancet*. Vol 357. Pp 505–508.

Mandela, N. 1994. *Long Walk to Freedom*. New York, USA. Little, Brown and Company.

Martinez, JS and Kesner, RP. 1991. (eds.) *Learning and Memory: A Biological View*. New York, USA. Academic Press.

McDaniel, BT, and Coyne, SM. 2016. "'Technoference': The interference of technology in couple relationships and implications for women's personal and relational well-being". *Psychology of Popular Media Culture*. Vol 5. Pp 85–98.

Pichert, JW and Anderson, RC (1978). Taking different perspectives on a story". *Journal of Educational Psychology*. Vol 69. Pp 309–315.

Ritchhart, R, Church, M and Morrison, K. 2011. *Making Thinking Visible: How to Promote Engagement, Understanding and Independence for All Learners*. San Francisco, CA, USA. Jossey-Bass.

Rosen, LD, Lim, AF, Carrier, LM and Cheever, NA. 2011. "An examination of the educational impact of text message-induced task switching in the classroom: Educational implications and strategies to enhance learning". *Psicologia Educative (Spanish Journal of Educational Psychology)*. Vol 17, number 2. Pp 163–177.

Rosenhan, DL. 1973. "On being sane in unsane places". *Science*. Vol. 179. Pp 250–258.

Sapolsky, RM. 2017. *Behave: The Biology of Humans at our Best and Worst*. New York, USA. Penguin Random House.

Scoville, WB and Milner, B. 1957. "Loss of recent memory after bilateral hippocampal lesions". *Journal of Neurology, Neurosurgery and Psychiatry*. Vol 20, number 11. Pp 11–21.

Sharot, T, Martorella, EA, Delgado, MR and Phelps, EA. 2007. "How personal experience modulates the neural circuitry of memories of September 11". *Proceedings of the National Academy of Sciences*. Vol 104, number 1. Pp 389–394.

Spencer, SJ, Steele, CM and Quinn, DM. (1999). "Stereotype threat and women's math performance". *Journal of Experimental Social Psychology*, 35(1), 4–28. http://dx.doi.org/10.1006/jesp.1998.1373.

Tajfel, H, Flament, C, Billig, MG and Bundy, RF. 1971. "Social categorization and intergroup behaviour". *European Journal of Social Psychology*. Vol 1. Pp 149–177.

Thigpen, CH and Cleckley, H. 1954. "A case of multiple personality". *Journal of Abnormal and Social Psychology*. Vol 49. Pp 135–151.

Toi, M, Batson, C and Steiner, ID. 1982. "More evidence that empathy is a source of altruistic motivation". *Journal of Personality and Social Psychology*. Vol 43, number 2. Pp 281–292.

Van Ijzendoorn, MH and Kroonenberg, PM. 1988. "Cross-cultural patterns of attachment; A meta-analysis of the Strange Situation". *Child Development*. Vol 59. Pp 147–156.

Index

Headings in **bold** indicate key terms.

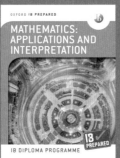

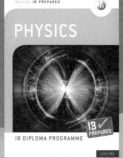

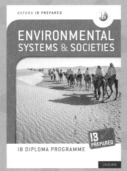

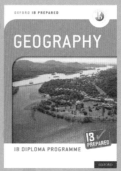

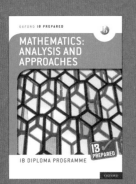

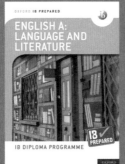

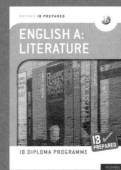

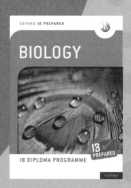

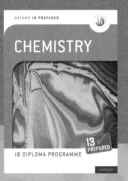

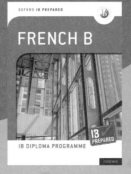

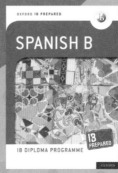

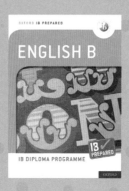

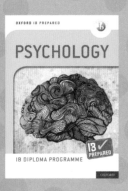

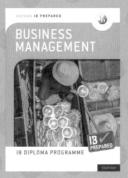

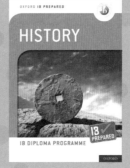